10|98

Racism

Other Books in the Current Controversies Series:

Racism

David Bender, *Publisher*
Bruno Leone, *Executive Editor*

Bonnie Szumski, *Editorial Director*
Brenda Stalcup, *Managing Editor*
Scott Barbour, *Senior Editor*

Jennifer A. Hurley, *Book Editor*

CURRENT CONTROVERSIES

No part of this book may be reproduced or used in any form or by any means, electrical, mechanical, or otherwise, including, but not limited to, photocopy, recording, or any information storage and retrieval system, without prior written permission from the publisher.

Cover Photo: © Chris Brown/Sipa Press

Library of Congress Cataloging-in-Publication Data

Racism / Jennifer A. Hurley, book editor.
    p. cm. — (Current controversies)
    Includes bibliographical references and index.
    ISBN 1-56510-809-4 (lib. bdg. : alk. paper). — ISBN 1-56510-808-6
(pbk. : alk. paper)
    1. Racism—United States. 2. United States—Race relations. I. Hurley,
Jennifer A., 1973–   . II. Series.
E185.615.R2144   1998
305.8'00973—dc21   97-52383
                                                                                      CIP

© 1998 by Greenhaven Press, Inc., PO Box 289009, San Diego, CA 92198-9009
Printed in the U.S.A.

Every effort has been made to trace the owners of copyrighted material.

Contents

esteem. Although white society can be blamed for causing these feelings, it cannot be blamed for their persistence. Instead of accepting some personal responsibility for their problems, many blacks use racism as a catch-all excuse. In order to succeed, blacks must cast off their victim status and take responsibility for their own progress.

Chapter 2: Is Racism Institutionalized in America?

Yes: Institutionalized Racism Is Prevalent

Chapter 3: Does Affirmative Action Remedy the Effects of Racism?

Yes: Affirmative Action Is Beneficial

Chapter 4: How Can Racial Problems Be Resolved?

that mandates equality but one that allows individuals the freedom to make their own choices. In order to attain this goal, affirmative action, antidiscrimination laws, and all forms of governmental aid should be eliminated.

The forces of institutionalized racism have created a system that is hostile and unfair to inner-city blacks. The only way to correct this inequality is to implement social and economic policies aimed at helping African Americans out of poverty. Most importantly, the government needs to appropriate money toward improving inner-city conditions and providing decent-paying jobs.

Foreword

By definition, controversies are "discussions of questions in which opposing opinions clash" (Webster's Twentieth Century Dictionary Unabridged). Few would deny that controversies are a pervasive part of the human condition and exist on virtually every level of human enterprise. Controversies transpire between individuals and among groups, within nations and between nations. Controversies supply the grist necessary for progress by providing challenges and challengers to the status quo. They also create atmospheres where strife and warfare can flourish. A world without controversies would be a peaceful world; but it also would be, by and large, static and prosaic.

The Series' Purpose

The purpose of the Current Controversies series is to explore many of the social, political, and economic controversies dominating the national and international scenes today. Titles selected for inclusion in the series are highly focused and specific. For example, from the larger category of criminal justice, Current Controversies deals with specific topics such as police brutality, gun control, white collar crime, and others. The debates in Current Controversies also are presented in a useful, timeless fashion. Articles and book excerpts included in each title are selected if they contribute valuable, long-range ideas to the overall debate. And wherever possible, current information is enhanced with historical documents and other relevant materials. Thus, while individual titles are current in focus, every effort is made to ensure that they will not become quickly outdated. Books in the Current Controversies series will remain important resources for librarians, teachers, and students for many years.

In addition to keeping the titles focused and specific, great care is taken in the editorial format of each book in the series. Book introductions and chapter prefaces are offered to provide background material for readers. Chapters are organized around several key questions that are answered with diverse opinions representing all points on the political spectrum. Materials in each chapter include opinions in which authors clearly disagree as well as alternative opinions in which authors may agree on a broader issue but disagree on the possible solutions. In this way, the content of each volume in Current Controversies mirrors the mosaic of opinions encountered in society. Readers will quickly realize that there are many viable answers to these complex issues. By questioning each author's conclusions, students and casual readers can begin to develop the critical thinking skills so important to evaluating opinionated material.

Current Controversies is also ideal for controlled research. Each anthology in the series is composed of primary sources taken from a wide gamut of informational categories including periodicals, newspapers, books, United States and foreign government documents, and the publications of private and public organizations. Readers will find factual support for reports, debates, and research papers covering all areas of important issues. In addition, an annotated table of contents, an index, a book and periodical bibliography, and a list of organizations to contact are included in each book to expedite further research.

Perhaps more than ever before in history, people are confronted with diverse and contradictory information. During the Persian Gulf War, for example, the public was not only treated to minute-to-minute coverage of the war, it was also inundated with critiques of the coverage and countless analyses of the factors motivating U.S. involvement. Being able to sort through the plethora of opinions accompanying today's major issues, and to draw one's own conclusions, can be a complicated and frustrating struggle. It is the editors' hope that Current Controversies will help readers with this struggle.

Greenhaven Press anthologies primarily consist of previously published material taken from a variety of sources, including periodicals, books, scholarly journals, newspapers, government documents, and position papers from private and public organizations. These original sources are often edited for length and to ensure their accessibility for a young adult audience. The anthology editors also change the original titles of these works in order to clearly present the main thesis of each viewpoint and to explicitly indicate the opinion presented in the viewpoint. These alterations are made in consideration of both the reading and comprehension levels of a young adult audience. Every effort is made to ensure that Greenhaven Press accurately reflects the original intent of the authors included in this anthology.

Introduction

Prior to the civil rights movement of the 1950s and 1960s, racism was easy to identify. No lengthy debates were needed to decipher the horrible specter of hooded Klansmen or the restaurant signs declaring "We don't serve coloreds." One writer describes this form of racism as "a type of madness, a pathological hatred and cruelty that took its most despicable form in outright murder." These open displays of hatred reflected a time when racism was not only prevalent, but proud.

Overt demonstrations of racism are, for the most part, no longer tolerated in the United States, and many Americans see this fact as evidence that racism is steadily declining. Those who believe racism is diminishing cite statistics indicating that African Americans and other minorities have made substantial progress since the days of the civil rights movement. According to the 1990 census, for example, "51 percent of Asians, 43 percent of Hispanics, and one-third of blacks" reside in suburban neighborhoods. Furthermore, contends Roderick Harrison of the U.S. Census Bureau's Racial Statistics, the poverty rate for black families is "about the lowest it's been in 25 years." Some social critics allege that these statistics reflect not only economic improvement, but also a shift in the attitudes of white Americans. In a study conducted to determine whether whites who professed racial tolerance truly were tolerant, Stanford University researchers found that "whites who said they thought well of blacks meant what they said; even when they had a socially acceptable excuse to think badly of blacks, they did not take advantage of it." Studies such as these encourage optimism among some commentators, who maintain that although racist attitudes linger in certain parts of the country, American society as a whole rejects racism.

Others, however, allege that the belief in the decline of racism amounts to denial of the true state of race relations in America. In fact, these critics maintain that today's racism is more dangerous than that of the past because such widespread disbelief in its existence prevents any change from occurring. In the words of author David K. Shipler, "A good deal of prejudice has gone underground since the civil rights movement and now produces insidious, coded behavior that impedes blacks but is hard to attack." Taboos that prohibit openly racist behavior, Shipler and others say, have caused racism to take on more subtle forms: workplace discrimination, institutional policies and procedures, and

13

deep-seated racist assumptions that range from doubts about minorities' intelligence to the belief that blacks are more prone to criminal behavior. Some social commentators believe that racial tensions cannot be resolved until white Americans admit to these racist assumptions and openly acknowledge the current prevalence of racism.

Critics of this view, on the other hand, contend that it is exactly this method of approaching race relations that reignites tension among the races. As columnist William Raspberry states, "People who might be moved to help remedy racial inequality are not inclined to do so if it means acknowledging that the inequality is their fault." Raspberry and others allege that the media inflate the scope of American racism, encouraging blacks and whites to view each other as enemies. In order for racism to be finally put to rest, these critics claim, reconciliation, not more debate, must take place.

Disagreement also prevails when addressing acts of racially motivated violence. Those who believe race relations are improving view hate crimes as the residue of a dying racist culture. The perpetrators of these acts, they claim, are usually social outcasts, teenagers, or the mentally ill; their actions are rash and unplanned—in no way resembling the stealthy, highly organized methods of groups like the Ku Klux Klan. In sum, those who allege racism is declining portray hate crimes as isolated perversions, not reflections of mainstream American values.

Others strongly disagree, maintaining that innovations in communications technology have allowed hate groups to spread their ideology to an unprecedented extent. Some suggest that this resurgence in hate groups—among them Neo-Nazi and white supremacy organizations—marks a return to the type of unfettered violence that was prevalent before the civil rights movement, a development that has dangerous implications for minorities. These critics charge some white Americans with naiveté about the hideous crimes currently perpetrated upon blacks and other minorities. They warn that the racial climate in the United States will never improve as long as the general public ignores or underplays such acts of racial violence.

As commentators struggle to define the scope of racism, Americans remain divided over how to view race relations in the United States. Some Americans display a sense of hopelessness. For instance, columnist Jonetta Rose Barras writes, "Blacks and whites . . . can't agree on anything, distrust each other immensely, and in general, continue to view the world from completely different vantage points." In contrast, other Americans emphasize the strides society has made toward ameliorating the problem of racism and express confidence that the situation will only continue to improve. *Racism: Current Controversies* offers a variety of perspectives on the status of race relations in America and provides different views on how to eradicate racism and its legacies.

Chapter 1

How Serious Is the Problem of Racism?

CURRENT CONTROVERSIES

Chapter Preface

In the fall of 1994, two security guards at an Eddie Bauer store in Washington, D.C., accused a black teenager of shoplifting the shirt he was wearing. Although a salesperson recalled selling the teenager a shirt the day before, the guards still insisted that he remove his shirt since he could not produce a receipt. The young man located the receipt at home and brought it to the store, which returned the shirt but did not offer an apology. Enraged by the incident, the National Association for the Advancement of Colored People (NAACP) led a lawsuit against Eddie Bauer, and in October 1997, $1 million in damages was awarded to the teenager and the two black friends who had accompanied him into the store. While this particular incident may have been resolved, civil rights leaders assert that the store's treatment of the black teenager is emblematic of a larger problem: the negative stereotypes that many whites have of blacks—especially of young black men.

Civil rights advocates, among others, contend that young black males are plagued by unsubstantiated suspicions that they are criminals. According to *New York Times* columnist David Shipler, this prejudice runs so deep that "some black parents warn their children never to run out of a store or a bank: Better to be late than to be dead."

Yet others maintain that these suspicions are a rational response to the high proportion of crimes committed by young African American men. In a *Washington Times* survey, urban cab drivers "all admitted that as a consequence of previous threats, robberies and assaults, they employ a kind of heightened scrutiny before they will stop for young black men," a scrutiny that some believe is an exercise in caution rather than a display of racism.

Still others argue that incidents such as the one at Eddie Bauer are isolated events and are not indicative of the overall state of race relations in America. Those who believe that racist stereotypes do not play a large role in the lives of young black males cite a November 1997 *Time*/CNN poll, which states that 89 percent of black teens considered the impact of racism in their lives "a small problem" or "not a problem at all."

Views on the prevalence of racism vary widely. The following chapter presents different perspectives on the volatile issue of whether racism remains a serious problem in America.

Racism Is Not Declining

by Joe R. Feagin and Hernan Vera

About the authors: *Joe R. Feagin and Hernan Vera are coauthors of the book* White Racism, *from which this viewpoint has been excerpted.*

Until civil rights laws were passed during the Lyndon Johnson administration in the 1960s, most African Americans faced blatant discrimination that was legally prescribed or permitted. Few had the resources to vigorously counter this racism, and the legal system offered little support. In the years following the civil rights revolution, as state-enforced segregation was demolished, many felt optimistic about the future. Black people began moving into many formerly forbidden areas of U.S. society, and whites began to encounter a greater black presence in historically white public facilities, workplaces, businesses, churches, schools, and neighborhoods.

However, the civil rights revolution came to a standstill in the 1980s, and many African Americans now believe that the country and its government are moving backward in the quest for racial justice. Presidential use of the White House as a "bully pulpit" for conservative political agendas during the Reagan and Bush years of the 1980s and early 1990s was particularly devastating to racial relations. Federal civil rights enforcement programs were weakened significantly in this period. The political denial of white racism made its way into intellectual circles and the mass media, where the concept of the "declining significance of race" became fashionable. Since the mid-1970s many influential commentators and authors have argued or implied that white racism is no longer a serious, entrenched national problem and that African Americans must take total responsibility for their own individual and community problems.

A majority of white Americans in all social classes, including jurists, scholars, and commentators, now appear to believe that serious racism is declining in the United States; that black Americans have made great civil rights progress in recent decades; and that blacks should be content with that progress. Whites see widespread discrimination in most institutional arenas as a thing of the past. In particular, many whites believe that the black middle class no longer faces significant discrimination and is thriving economically—indeed more so than the white middle class. Whites typically view problems of the black underclass as the central issue for black America and believe that that class's condition has little to do with discrimination. The white notion that any black person who works hard enough can succeed is even reflected in white reactions to the Bill Cosby show described by researchers Sut Jhally and Justin Lewis. Many whites felt the series, which portrayed a successful black upper-middle-class family and became the highest-rated sitcom on national television during the 1980s, showed a "world where race no longer matters." Jhally and Lewis noted that this view of the show enabled whites to "combine an impeccably liberal attitude toward race with a deep-rooted suspicion of black people."

One aspect of the contemporary denial of racism is the common white refusal to notice or comment on racial differences, especially regarding programs to eradicate racial discrimination. Nobel prize–winning author Toni Morrison has described this escapism eloquently: "Evasion has fostered another, substitute language in which the issues are encoded, foreclosing open debate. . . . It is further complicated by the fact that the habit of ignoring race is understood to be a graceful, even generous, liberal gesture. To notice is to recognize an already discredited difference. . . . According to this logic, every well bred instinct argues *against noticing* and forecloses adult discourse."

Hate Crimes

The substantial white consensus on the decline of racism is not based on empirical evidence. On the contrary, research shows that black men and women still face extensive racial discrimination in all arenas of daily life. Recent in-depth studies have documented continuing antiblack discrimination, ranging from blatant acts reminiscent of the legal segregation period to subtle and covert forms that have flourished under the conditions of desegregation. The belief in the declining significance of race cannot be reconciled with the empirical reality of racial discrimination. Great anger over white racism can be found today in every socioeconomic group of black Americans, from millionaires to day laborers.

White supremacy groups have been at the forefront of attackers of African Americans. Membership in the Ku Klux Klan, the largest white supremacy group for most of the twentieth century, reached five million in the 1920s. After a period of decline, Klan

> *"One aspect of the contemporary denial of racism is the common white refusal to notice or comment on racial differences."*

membership began to grow again in the 1970s, and in the early 1990s the number of white Americans in various Klan factions was estimated at about ten thousand. Newspaper reports have documented Klan violence against minorities and have described paramilitary training camps designed to prepare Klan members for a "race war." From the 1970s to the 1990s, the Klan and other white supremacy groups have been involved in hundreds of antiblack and anti-Jewish attacks; several members of such groups have been convicted of murdering or assaulting black people. Other white supremacy groups such as the White Aryan Resistance (WAR), headed by white supremacist Tom Metzger, have emerged in recent years. One nationwide count found more than three hundred hate groups active in 1992, ranging from skinheads to a variety of neo-Nazi and other white supremacy organizations. White supremacy groups in the United States have been estimated to have at least thirty thousand hard-core members, with perhaps another two hundred thousand active sympathizers.

> *"One nationwide count found more than three hundred hate groups active in 1992."*

During the 1980s and 1990s hundreds of acts of vandalism and intimidation were directed at black and other minority Americans. One of the most notorious incidents occurred in 1986 in the Howard Beach area of New York City, when three black men were beaten and chased by white youths. One of the men died when he was chased into the path of a car. A few days later five thousand people, black and white, marched through Howard Beach to protest the attack. In 1991 alone, twenty-five hate-motivated murders of minority Americans by white killers were recorded in the United States. Many other hate killings undoubtedly went unreported. In one recent incident, two white men went on a rampage in a Washington, D.C. suburb. They were looking for black pedestrians to attack. They ended their night by tearing the clothes off a black woman and calling her "nigger." In 1993 two white men were convicted in south Florida of the kidnapping, robbery, and attempted murder of a black stockbrokerage clerk who was vacationing in Tampa. The black man was set ablaze by the whites, who left a note saying, "One less nigger, more to go."

Discrimination

Hate crimes targeting African Americans represent only the tip of the racist iceberg. Black people also continue to face discrimination in the workplace, in business, in colleges, in public accommodations, and in historically white neighborhoods. Millions of cases of discrimination occur each year. More than half of the black respondents in a 1989 ABC News survey agreed that black workers generally faced discrimination when seeking skilled jobs; 61 percent gave a similar reply regarding managerial jobs. A 1991 Urban Institute report presented a study in which white and black applicants with similar qualifications were sent to the same employers to apply for jobs; a significant proportion of the black applicants suffered discrimination in the hiring process. Even if a black applicant is hired, discriminatory barriers are likely to impair career progress. Racial discrimination continues to handicap African Americans today in all major institutional arenas of our society.

The effects of employment and other economic discrimination have been documented by Andrew Hacker, who is one of very few white social scientists to examine declining-significance-of-race arguments, in a book published by a major commercial press. Hacker presents data showing persisting and major economic inequalities between black and white Americans: for example, black workers still make on the average much less than white workers and face discrimination in many areas of employment. Other data underscore Hacker's conclusions. Consider unemployment, a social plague

> *"Racial discrimination continues to handicap African Americans today in all major institutional arenas of our society."*

that few Americans today attribute solely to lack of individual effort. Unemployment robs people not only of income but also of self-respect and personal and family happiness. Since the 1940s the black unemployment rate has consistently been about twice the white unemployment rate. In recent recessions black workers have lost jobs at twice the rate of white workers. The black underemployment rate, which includes those working part time and those making poverty wages, is even higher than the unemployment rate. Some estimate that at least a fifth of all black workers are unemployed or underemployed.

Economic Inequality

Persisting racial inequality can also be seen in the wide gaps in black and white family income and wealth. Today the median income of black families is about 58 percent that of white families. Blacks are almost three times as likely to live in poverty as are whites, and the median net worth of black families is less than 10 percent that of white families. These data underscore the long-term advantages of being white in this society. Young white Americans sometimes argue that they have not personally held slaves or discriminated against black people and therefore should not have to pay the price of remedies for racial discrimination. However, this argument fails to take into account the many ways in which young whites have benefited from their forebears' access to land, decent-paying jobs, and wealth at a time when most African Americans were excluded from those things. Two decades of modest government remedial programs like affirmative action have not offset several hundred years of white advantage. Although the economic benefits of white privilege have gone in disproportionately large amounts to the employer class, all white groups derive at least some psychological benefit from having a group below them, from the feeling of superiority that is especially important for whites who are not doing well economically.

Sociologist Sidney Willhelm has pointed out that black and other minority workers, often concentrated in racially stratified low-wage jobs, have been abandoned as capitalists have turned to automation to restructure corporations and increase profits. In his view the U.S. economy no longer needs large numbers of black workers for full-time jobs, and this abandonment of much black labor has created major costs for both black and white communities. As black workers become less necessary "in an automated society, they turn to crime with greater frequency in order to obtain the material needs of life; they confront a white America increasingly determined to meet crime with state violence." Much of the crime committed by poor black men can be seen as individualized revolt against unemployment, substandard housing, and the other by-products of economic discrimination. Whites, especially those in the upper economic classes, have helped create the high cost of such crime by perpetuating the wasteful system of racial exploitation. This connection between crime and unemployment or underemployment is by no means limited to black Americans, for in recent decades increasing crime rates have affected most racial and ethnic communities in the United States. Moreover, U.S. history is replete with instances of members of racial and ethnic groups, including white immigrants such as the Irish and the Italians, turning to crime when racial-ethnic discrimination or the workings of the capitalist economy prevented them from securing decent-paying jobs. . . .

Defining Racial Discrimination

One active part of racism, discrimination, has rarely been defined in the social science literature. For example, in *An American Dilemma* Gunnar Myrdal noted widespread discrimination in U.S. society but never delimited it. Subsequent researchers of black-white relations have usually not provided a specific definition. Researchers who have ventured on more precise delineations in recent years have emphasized group power and institutionalized factors: for instance, Thomas Pettigrew has suggested that discrimination is "an institutional process of exclusion against an outgroup." Joe R. Feagin and Clairece B. Feagin have defined discrimination as "practices carried out by members of dominant groups which have a differential and negative impact on members of subordinate groups." The crucial point of these definitions is that the ability to carry out significant and repeated discriminatory acts flows from the power one group has over another. In addition, both individual and collective discrimination can occur in an array of locations—in public accommodations, schools and colleges, workplaces, and neighborhoods.

> *"The cognitive notions and stereotypes of contemporary racism ... make as little empirical sense as the hostile fictions that underlay the Nazi Holocaust."*

Discriminatory practices are supported by ideological constructions taken on faith. Racial myths are part of the mind-set that helps whites interpret their experience and that influences behavior, alters emotions, and shapes what whites see and do not see. The cognitive notions and stereotypes of contemporary racism, which include myths of the dangerous black man, the lazy black person, the black woman's fondness for welfare, and black inferiority and incompetence, make as little empirical sense as the hostile fictions that underlay the Nazi Holocaust. However, such antiblack fictions are sincerely held by many whites.

Racial Myths

The persistence of antiblack discrimination indicates how deeply myths of racial difference and inequality have become embedded in white thinking. Such myths often influence the important decisions that whites make, from selecting a spouse to choosing a residential neighborhood. Yet white views of blacks are often not based on significant personal experience with African Americans. In contrast, black views of whites are much more likely to be grounded in personal experience because most blacks have had substantial experience with whites by the time they are a few years old. In her classic analysis, *Killers of the Dream,* Lillian Smith noted that prejudiced thinking and antiblack practices become "ceremonial," that they "slip from the conscious mind deep into the muscles." These attitudes and propensities are learned at such an early point in a white child's development that they become routinized and unconscious. Smith also pointed out the insidiousness of racial learning in early childhood: "The mother who taught me tenderness . . . taught me the bleak rituals of keeping Negroes in their place."

The stereotyped portrayals of African Americans and the unrealistically sanguine views of contemporary racial relations often presented

> *"The powerful may hide or deny their racist attitudes out of fear of disgrace, but racist acts have not ceased."*

in the mainstream media help perpetuate the racist myths held by ordinary white Americans. Leonard Berkowitz, among many others, has argued that the mass media play an important role in reinforcing antisocial images and behavior. The U.S. media are overwhelmingly white-oriented and white-controlled. White control of powerful institutions—from the mass media to corporate workplaces to universities to police departments—signals white dominance to all members of the society.

At the individual level, much antiblack discrimination is perpetrated by whites who are not overtly aware of their ingrained prejudices and negative emotions. A white supervisor in the workplace may refuse to hire a black applicant because of the belief that white workers or customers are uncomfortable with people unlike themselves. Even in predominantly white colleges and universities, black students and faculty members are frequently victims of white prejudices, many of which seem buried deep in white consciousness. Whites do not need to be aware of their racial motivations to inflict harm on blacks.

The paradoxical phenomenon of whites who claim not to be racist perpetrating racially harmful acts can be explained in part by the fact that "racism" has come to be held in such opprobrium that few whites are willing to accept "racist" as a personal trait. This marks a change from the past. At an earlier time in U.S. history, even white power-holders paraded their racism as a sign of honor. Employers and politicians publicly joined the Klan in the 1920s and 1930s. Today the powerful may hide or deny their racist attitudes out of fear of disgrace, but racist acts have not ceased. The layers of euphemisms and code words that often cover racist acts today can make it difficult to demonstrate that such acts are in fact intentionally discriminatory.

White Racism

Racism is a fundamental part of U.S. culture and is spread throughout the social fabric. Because virtually all whites participate in the racist culture, most harbor some racist images or views. At the extreme end of the spectrum are white perpetrators of physically violent racist acts: these whites share with other whites some common antiblack attitudes, but one distinguishing feature is their fixation on blacks. Obsessive racists may use their racial prejudices to resolve deep psychological problems. Many white supremacists seem to fit into this category. At the opposite end of the spectrum, the least obsessive racists may hold traditional antiblack prejudices simply to conform to their social environments.

Racism, however, encompasses more than the way whites view the black "others." It also involves the way whites view themselves as a result of participating in a culturally and structurally racist society. Prejudice, a term that ordinarily refers to negative views of others, can also apply to positive views of oneself or one's own group. Prejudices and related discriminatory practices reflect an internal representation of oneself as well as of the hated other. In the process of developing this self-definition, whites have created a set of "sincere fictions"— personal mythologies that reproduce societal mythologies at the individual level. Whites generally use these fictions to define themselves as "not racist," as "good people," even as they think and act in antiblack ways. It is common for a white person to say, "I am not a racist," often, and ironically, in conjunction with negative comments about people of color. The sincere fictions embedded in white personalities and white society are about both the black other *and* the white self. Long ago Frederick Douglass termed the white fictions about the black other "an old dodge," "for wherever men oppress their fellows, wherever they enslave them, they will endeavor to find the needed apology for such enslavement and oppression in the character of the people oppressed and enslaved."

Racist Hate Groups Are Thriving on the Internet

by Nathaniel Sheppard Jr.

About the author: *Nathaniel Sheppard Jr. is a Washington correspondent for the* Chicago Tribune.

The Ku Klux Klan used to terrorize people in the dead of night with ropes, torches and burning crosses. Now it sneaks in quietly through home computers to deliver its pictures of horror and high-tech messages of hate. In no time at all, it seems, the global web of computer networks known as the Internet has become the new frontier for neo-Nazis, the Klan and other White supremacist groups. And amid a new generation of angry White males and a growing climate of intolerance in the United States and abroad, the Internet, with its 24 million users, has become fertile ground for recruitment.

Almost unnoticed by old-line civil rights organizations, these so-called Net Nazis and other White nationalist groups have set up an impressive cyberspace network, with extensive links to European counterparts. There are scores of colorful "home pages" (points of entry on the Internet's World Wide Web of computers) and several White nationalist "newsgroups" (organized around topics of interest) on the highly popular USENET network, a system of bulletin boards on which to post messages, pictures and sound files. As of March 1996, these newsgroups included: *alt.politics.white-power; alt.revisionism; alt.politics. nationalism.white* and a skinhead newsgroup, *alt.skinheads.*

Transcending Time and Distance

The Internet's lightning speed and disregard for national borders has eliminated constraints of time and distance. And though they can often be starting points, on-line service providers, such as CompuServe and America Online, are not necessary to reach some bulletin boards. Computer users with a modem can tap directly into these areas if they have the right "address." And frequently, access to one area links users to others of similar themes. In short, spreading hate has become easy, inexpensive—and unrestricted.

Reprinted from Nathaniel Sheppard Jr., "Hate in Cyberspace," *Emerge*, August 1996, by permission of the author.

The approach can be as direct as the use of the "N" word in an on-line conversation or as grotesque as the picture of a prone Black man being kicked by a booted White person. This image was disseminated on the Internet in April 1996 by Skinheads USA.

"White racist groups no longer have to rely on putting fliers on windshields, passing out pamphlets on corners or using the U.S. mail," says Angie Lowry, an analyst for the Southern Poverty Law Center's Klanwatch Project in Montgomery, Ala. "With a reasonably good computer and a fast modem, they can instantly reach people worldwide."

> *"Spreading hate has become easy, inexpensive—and unrestricted."*

No one seems more aware of that power and potential than the groups themselves. White nationalists are moving deftly to fine-tune their cyberspace techniques.

"USENET offers enormous opportunity for the Aryan Resistance to disseminate our message to the unaware and the ignorant," says Milton John Kleim Jr., a White power strategist, in his essay, "On Tactics and Strategy for USENET."

He continues, "The State cannot yet stop us from 'advertising' our ideas and organizations on USENET. . . . NOW is the time to grasp the WEAPON which is the Net, and wield it skillfully and wisely while you may still do so freely. . . . Each USENET 'cyber guerrilla' must obtain a listing of all Net NEWS groups that are available on their system, and search through the list for groups suitable for our posts."

Klanwatch has monitored hate groups on the Net since 1995, a period in which the number of groups it observed grew from 50 to more than 100, Lowry says.

"Their Web pages are amazingly sophisticated. They are very readable and have good graphics," she says. "The Net makes it easier for those who share their views to reach them than in the old days, when you had to send $20 to a post office box and wait for a brochure."

Says Klanwatch Project director Brian Levin: "There are racist, horrific, godless messages on the Net that encourage people to violence. They can say that every Black in the United States should be killed, that there should be another Holocaust. But the people posting these messages can't be prosecuted because they can't be specifically linked to subsequent actions."

A "Rising Climate of Hate"

Unapologetic White supremacists on the Internet illustrate the brazen nature of racism in this post-Reagan-Bush climate of neo-conservatism. They are part of what Richard W. Roberts, chief of the criminal section of the Justice Department's civil rights division, calls "a rising climate of hate in this country that accounts for the 66 defendants in 43 hate crime cases we prosecuted in fiscal year 1995, the highest number [of cases] ever."

H.T. Smith, a past president of the National Bar Association (NBA), put it this way at a spring 1996 NBA symposium called "The Resurgence of Hate Crimes and Other Anti-Civil Rights Violations": "Hate groups are using the Net to push people who already are on the edge, people who have lost jobs. Groups like Christian Identity are trying to create a race war in the quest to make America a place for Whites only."

Challenging Hate on the Net

Civil rights and human rights organizations haven't been as quick to exploit the Internet in their fight against bigotry. The NAACP has been consumed with its own reorganization in the aftermath of leadership and fiscal scandals. Rev. Joseph Lowery says resources at his Southern Christian Leadership Conference already are stretched thin by other anti-discrimination and anti-violence efforts.

"If it appears to be something that is major, we will certainly deal with it," says Lowery. "But right now, we have to choose our battlegrounds. We don't have the staff, energy or resources to fight every battle on every front."

Aside from the Klanwatch Project, the Los Angeles–based Simon Wiesenthal Center and the Anti-Defamation League of B'nai B'rith in New York have been the highest profile human rights organizations challenging hate on the Net. But law enforcement officials cannot investigate groups unless they make threats against specific individuals or organizations or can be documented to have harassed individuals.

> *"There are racist, horrific, godless messages on the Net that encourage people to violence."*

Part of the Telecommunications Act of 1996, which was passed in February 1996 and is designed to clean up speech on the Internet, is being challenged in U.S. District Court in Philadelphia. So far, 15 states have passed laws regulating speech on the Net, but what may be illegal in one state may be legal in another.

Most lawsuits have focused on copyright violations and libel. However, separate suits brought against Prodigy, Netcom On-Line Communication Services Inc. and America Online in 1995 did not address whether the services could be held responsible as gatekeepers for information posted by thousands of users of chat rooms, forums and home pages.

Prodigy settled out of court with a company whose officials sued over allegedly defamatory comments posted by a subscriber using a bulletin board. New York State Judge Stuart Ain ruled that Prodigy was more than a distributor of messages because it screened its postings. Prodigy now uses an editorial staff to monitor postings and censor inappropriate notes. Additionally, in January 1996, a federal court in Virginia ruled in favor of the Church of Scientology after it objected to material posted on the Internet.

Reining in hatemongers seems an almost insurmountable task. The First

Amendment so far has shielded hate groups. The Wiesenthal Center urges that there be no speech censorship, despite the stridently anti-Semitic tone of the groups. Meanwhile, the American Civil Liberties Union (ACLU) said it would defend free speech for everyone on the Internet, including Net Nazis.

"At issue here is when is hate speech simply an expression of unpopular views and when does it rise to the level of harassment," says Don Haines, an ACLU legislative counsel who handles issues of privacy and cyberspace.

"The tricky part is that when confronted with offensive material on-line, a person can simply shut off the computer and it is gone. The answer then is not less speech but more speech to counter that which is offensive," he says.

Some hate postings on the Net come from college students on campuses where administrators are unable or unwilling to intervene, according to the Wiesenthal Center. Through a section on its Web site, "Perspective on Hate on the Internet," the center identifies universities where hate postings have originated, such as Georgia State, Northeastern, Rutgers, Idaho State, South Florida and the universities of California at Santa Barbara, Texas at Austin and Pittsburgh.

In the fall of 1995, then–Georgia State University student Joe Bunkley used campus-based computers to maintain a contact list of White nationalist and Nazi organizations. Reid Christenberry, Georgia State's associate provost for information systems and technology, says the school's policy is not to regulate speech unless it violates state or federal law.

"The university received about 100 complaints on Bunkley's posting," Christenberry says. "Most of the notes say they realize there may not be anything we can do because of the First Amendment but express their disdain over the content of his messages and that something ought to be done about them. We have responded that we can't as long as he does not violate the law, [even though] part of students' registrations and tuition fees cover Internet access."

Spreading a Racist Vision

The selection of offensive material is broad and plentiful. The Internet has helped White nationalists spread their vision for a battle they believe is a prelude to a race war.

The White-Power FAQ (frequency asked questions), a Net text file, describes White power as "an empowering philosophy of White racial nationalism and ethnicity. It refers to a diverse range of philosophies, from leftist National Socialism, to White Pride, to rightist White Supremacy.

> *"Civil rights . . . organizations haven't been as quick to exploit the Internet in their fight against bigotry."*

"Perhaps the simplest imperative about what White power stands for," according to the FAQ, exists in the so-called "14 words" that have become a rallying cry of White separatists worldwide: "We must secure the existence of our people and a future for White children."

One on-line group targeting cyberspace is CNG. The group's founder, Jeff Vos, cannot decide what CNG should stand for. Its Web page says he was torn between Cyber Nazi Group, Cyber Nationalist Group or Computer Nationalist Group. What he is clear about, though, is its Internet mission: developing and distributing propaganda and gathering information on enemies.

> *"The Internet has helped White nationalists spread their vision."*

The CNG, which is anti–ethnic minority, anti-Jewish and anti-homosexual, advocates White-only immigration to the United States. It also believes that "all non-Whites must be either exported or segregated to prevent further bastardization of our people, domination of our land, jobs and positions of education and employment."

Hate Group Tactics

The organization encourages members to use a variety of tactics to manipulate the Internet, such as "impersonat[ing] the enemy in posting" material, "embarrassing the Left and infuriating the public" with numerous indiscretions, such as pretending to be a homosexual supporting the legalization of pedophilia.

Vos offers other tips to cyberguerrillas, telling them, "By maintaining an offensive attitude, your opponent will be forced into a defensive [losing] role in order to deal with you. . . . Winning is exposing the most people to your ideas, without losing your ability to keep doing so.

"Use humor. Politically incorrect points can be advanced through jokes instead of regular discourse.

"Utilize conservative research: *National Review* and *American Spectator* [magazines] as well as conservative books often contain articles advocating similar policies to the ones we want. Use their research to promote our policies."

Culture and religion also are tools. There are two White power record companies on-line. The most prominent, Resistance Records, features heavy-metal White nationalist bands, such as RAHOWA (Racial Holy War), Berserkr and Aryan. Visitors to the company's home page can hear excerpts or entire songs and buy materials by credit card. And the Church of Jesus Christ Christian-Aryan Nations and Christian Identity Online provide religious guidance. Members of both believe that God created Blacks and other non-Whites along with animals to be beasts of burden. Whites, on the other hand, were created separately, as they see it, and divinely imbued with the right and duty to rule over non-Whites.

Both "churches" ask also that people take an equally great leap of faith and accept their postulation that Jesus was a Gentile and that Anglo-Saxon, Celtic, Germanic, Scandinavian and kindred White people—not Jews—are the true Israelites.

"White supremacist organizations are doing a much better job on the Net than anti-hate groups," notes Noah Chandler, a research associate at Democratic Renewal, an Atlanta-based organization that functions as a clearinghouse on hate groups and hate crimes. "Technologically, they have done a good job. Some groups are credit card ready and you can order materials on-line."

Chandler says his organization is working with groups such as the Seattle-based Coalition for Human Dignity to build what he hopes will become a network of organizations that will counter cyberhate.

Individuals also have joined the battle. "These pages shocked and angered me so, I started my own page, called 'The Hate Page of the Week,'" says Frank Xavier Placencia, a political science student at Rice University in Houston. "I started this page in order to remind us that there is still a great deal of hatred in this world, that racism and anti-Semitism remain great threats to our society."

Andrew Mathis, a college student in New York City, has set up a Web page to press for a boycott of Internet service providers that give access to hate groups. "I realize there is nothing I can do to destroy these groups by any legal means. . . . I suggest a boycott . . . money talks," he wrote on his Web page.

In response to public pressure, some Internet service providers have pulled the plug on hate groups, but their numbers are small. Still, this action has only served to drive hate groups closer together, many under the umbrella of the newsgroup *natall.com.*

Dangerous Links

Despite such efforts, cyberhaters still have the upper hand. To wit: Stormfront, a staunch White nationalist organization in the forefront of the Aryan assault on the Net, maintains a Web page with extensive links to articles on domestic and international racial issues, militias, a disputable history of the White race, essays on government violence at Waco and Ruby Ridge, text and graphics libraries, German and Spanish language sections, and links to cyberhate groups in Canada, Germany, France, Great Britain and the Netherlands.

The Stormfront Web site also provides electronic links to White nationalist newsgroups on the USENET network, an Internet mailing list, a White nationalist news service and the names and addresses of other separatist groups. The site even provides a link to download a free version of Netscape Navigator, a popular software program used to explore Web sites.

"[Some on-line hate groups] believe that God created Blacks and other non-Whites along with animals to be beasts of burden."

The Aryan Crusader's Library is a repository for resource material on alleged White supremacy and is used by revisionist historians. It, too, offers links to more White supremacist groups than you could wave a swastika at and is linked to a map of the "Web Pages of Greater White Amerikkka." This map identifies the locations of racist groups in Hillsboro, W.Va.; Newport

Beach, Calif.; Atlanta; Maumee, Ohio; West Palm Beach, Fla.; Detroit; and Austin, Texas. It also shows the site of a neo-Nazi organization in Toronto. On Mexico, it notes, "To Hell with Mexico." In April 1996, the library also included links to groups in 14 European countries.

Carolinian Lords of the Caucasus

The up-and-coming Carolinian Lords of the Caucasus (CLOC) did not get a spot on the map but is gaining attention with a Web page emblazoned with a burning cross. As part of its contribution to "keeping Amerika White," the organization initiates Internet flame wars, or the exchange of angry messages between hate groups and their detractors.

CLOC boasts that "with over 3,500 complaints to our various [systems administrators] and over two hundred posts slandering us in [the newsgroup] *news.admin.net-abuse.misc,* it is clearly on the forefront of the great war for Aryan domination of the Internet." It takes credit for the demise of seven new groups by overwhelming them with White Nationalist material.

CLOC member R.C. Richards wasn't disappointed about the verdict for O.J. Simpson in October 1995. "It was a good week for the white race because oj simpson was found innocent," reads his quote on Placencia's "Hate Page of the Week." "Even libs on this newsgroup, who are real crackpots, are embarrassed by the verdict and are making excuses . . . what they're saying is that the black jury had IQ's

> *"[One] Web site also has electronic links to . . . [groups] which give details for making bombs, poisons and weapons."*

as low as *The Bell Curve* [which promotes the theory that non-Whites are intellectually limited] says they do and they got hoodwinked by the high priced jewish lawyers. . . . They're saying that oj got off because blacks are dumb.

"It won't be long before the nigras see what a fiasco this whole thing has been," Richards continues, "and they'll turn on the jewry and blame the jewry. but it'll just be one more case of the nigras doing what they do best: blame somebody else for their condition."

Skinheads USA

Also among cyberhate Web pages with extensive links to other separatist groups abroad is Skinheads USA. After the warning, "If you are not interested in the survival of the White race piss off," visitors are taken from a page that depicts a punching fist and a crossed-out emblem of the United Nations to another that features a "write a caption" contest for a photograph, this time of a Black woman being set upon by Whites.

The Skinheads' page also lists "Communist dirtbags and other WANKERS (those closely associated with liberals and minorities)," including anti-racism and anti-fascist organizations, Placencia's "Hate Page of the Week" (described as "kind of kewl"), and the Wiesenthal Center's "Hate on the Net" (described as "an extension of Kosher Net . . . dedicated to all us naughty Net Nazis").

The Web site also has electronic links to anarchist newsgroups, including several which give details for making bombs, poisons and weapons.

The Ku Klux Klan

The veteran hate groups won't be outdone by their younger counterparts. There is a Web page for the Knights of the Ku Klux Klan, which the Skinheads revere as "the world's oldest, largest, and most professional Whites' civil rights organization," and the John Birch Society, which once served as a lightning rod for Right-wing extremists. The John Birch Society's home page boasts of its political effectiveness over the years. A Klan Web page heading states, "Things the media told you that just aren't true," and lists as lies of "the liberal media" the notions that Klan members hate Black people, oppose Catholics and must "break the law and commit crimes against Black people."

It defines its agenda on the Internet as one in which "America [is] First," meaning the government should protect jobs in the United States, "not those in Mexico, Vietnam, Somalia, Haiti, or some other third world country." The Klan also advocates drug testing for welfare recipients, ending affirmative action and race-based college scholarships, closing the American border and outlawing homosexuality and interracial marriages, both of which the organization blames for the spread of AIDS.

In some ways, it appears that White power strategist Milton John Kleim Jr. is on to something when he revels in the fact that "the state cannot yet stop us. . . ."

Whether that always will be the case, however, remains to be seen. In the meantime, Lowry, of Klanwatch, says the White nationalist presence on the Net has one salutary aspect: "It allows us to know what they are doing and thinking, and that is helpful."

Ironically, a quote from the cyberhate group CNG's manifesto—taken from 18th-century British statesman Edmund Burke—offers all of us a prescription and a warning: "In order for the forces of darkness to triumph, it is sufficient that good men do nothing; positive and militant steps are required to check the spread of evil in the land."

Church Arsons Are Evidence of Widespread Racism

by Kevin Alexander Gray

About the author: *Kevin Alexander Gray is a graduate fellow in the School of Public Affairs at American University in Washington, D.C., and serves as the South Carolina representative to the National Board of the American Civil Liberties Union.*

Three Black men were walking down a lone country road in the South when a tourist from the North, who happened to be white, drove speedily around a blind curve and struck the three men, killing them all. When the white sheriff arrived on the scene, seeing the bodies strewn across the roadway, he comforted the distraught tourist by saying, "We'll charge the one in the middle of the road with obstructing traffic. We'll charge the dismembered one with littering." And, as for the victim whose body was thrown 50 feet from the point of impact, the sheriff said, "We'll charge him with leaving the scene of an accident."

When I informed a neighbor of my impressions of the recent House Judiciary Committee Hearing on church arson, he responded by recalling this sardonic, southern tale. His meaning was unmistakable: in the wake of the current epidemic of Black church arsons, the victims run the risk of being blamed by law enforcement.

There is good reason for his cynicism. It was at the House hearing that the Reverend Earl Jackson, representing the Christian Coalition, testified that on the night of February 1, 1996, after four Black churches in Baton Rouge had been torched, one of the local ministers was told by agents of the U.S. Bureau of Alcohol, Tobacco and Firearms (BATF) that "race was not a factor." Adding insult to injury, agents then gave church members lie detector tests, thereby implying that they were suspected of having conspired to burn down their own churches for the insurance money.

Reprinted from Kevin Alexander Gray, "Politics Lit the Fires: Behind the Blazes, a Cultural Conspiracy," *Southern Christian Leadership Conference National Magazine*, January/February 1997, by permission of the publisher.

Chapter 1

Accusing the Victims

Green Bay Packer football player Reggie White, associate pastor of the Inner City Church in Knoxville, Tennessee, which was torched in January of 1996, has also accused BATF investigators of trying to pin the fire on church members.

"The system has said our own people burned that church down," White declared at a service held at a local high school. White's pastor, the Reverend David Upton, was questioned at least 10 times in connection with the fire. On one occasion, Upton was strapped to a lie detector in a windowless room. Cooperative at first, Upton now says, "I will not talk with them unless our attorney is present."

In response, Jerry Dennis, agent-in-charge of the Baton Rouge BATF office, stated that the questioning was "one of the things you have to do. We are out to solve these fires, and we're not going to back down from talking to anybody."

While it is common practice in arson investigations to interrogate the alleged victims as suspects, such intimidating questioning in the case of Black churches, many of which were either uninsured or underinsured, was insensitive, if not unjustifiable. Furthermore, prior to the church fire in Charlotte, North Carolina, on June 6, 1996, all 30 people arrested and prosecuted in connection with the arsons have been white males whose ages ranged from the early teens to the middle forties.

A Racial Conspiracy?

Is there an organized conspiracy to create terror in the Black community? And, if so, who's responsible, and what's their motive? Those who proffer answers fall into three groups—those who reject the notion of any racial conspiracy, those who point to an explicit racial conspiracy, and those who point to an implicit racial conspiracy.

Those in the first group, like the BATF, dismiss racial motivation by practicing an artificial color blindness that permits them to consider the arsons as unrelated, coincidental acts of vandalism with little or no political or racial significance. Jerry Dennis of the BATF told the *Baton Rouge Advocate* that his investigators had found no link between the East Baton Rouge fires and church fires in other states "except that they were churches and they had a fire." Such rhetoric stokes the fires of conspiratorial theories grounded in the infiltration of the BATF by white supremacists who organize and participate in the "Good Ol' Boys Roundups."

> *"Victims [of church arson] run the risk of being blamed by law enforcement."*

For those in the second group, acts of intimidation against church buildings—symbolic spiritual and political centers—constitute an organized campaign stemming from an explicit conspiracy to politically destabilize the African-American community. They note that many of those charged in connection with

33

the fires have been members of the various state "Realms" within the Invisible Empire of the Ku Klux Klan, or members of the Aryan Faction, and the Skinheads for White Justice. To them, the fires are acts of war by an invisible enemy. But there is little evidence of communication or planning among those who have been arrested and convicted for the various church fires around the country whose persistence creates an illusion of a conscious conspiracy.

Cultural Conspiracy

For those in the third group, the fires represent random, widespread expressions of deeply-rooted racial hatred, bubbling to the surface in a cauldron of social unrest scorched by the flames of ill-conceived social policies—policies which target economic and political effects (poverty and disenfranchisement) on African-Americans, rather than the root cause (dispossession) of those effects—policies that help to perpetuate widespread racial hatred and fear in the minds of poor and lower-middle-class whites who are scapegoating their own lack of economic success. This subtle but more plausible explanation calls for a more complex solution than the simple suppression of organized hate groups.

What we face, in the words of the Reverend Jesse L. Jackson, Sr., is a "cultural conspiracy." "Cultural conspiracy" is the product of respectable leaders of mainstream political and cultural institutions responsible for the ill-conceived social policies which inadvertently foster widespread societal attacks on racial, ethnic, or religious minorities on a variety of fronts.

> *"The fires represent random, widespread expressions of deeply rooted racial hatred."*

Those who subscribe to this theory of implicit, "cultural" conspiracy reject theories of explicit, conscious conspiracies, but they hold that what others regard as independent, coincidental events as the effects of a common cause. They reject the theory of widespread, random, coincidental occurrence, holding instead that most similar occurrences are causally connected.

The "cultural conspiracy" is embodied by a laundry list of policies—from Proposition 187 [a California state measure denying public benefits to illegal immigrants] and curfews in predominantly Black neighborhoods to affirmative action and welfare programs. Stereotyping and scapegoating are key ingredients in fostering a hostile climate.

Racist Myths

Talk of neighborhood-enforced curfews invokes the impression of a lawless community placed under house arrest to keep Black criminals from invading white neighborhoods. The myth of a Black-on-white crime wave persists despite the reality that most crimes are not interracial. For racists, private acts of violence and intimidation are validated by the perception of state and institutional suppression of a particular racial group.

When asked why he thought his fellow Klan members, arrested in connection with two South Carolina fires, might burn down a Black church, a Klansman replied, "That's where they learn it [to get on welfare]. Have you ever noticed that, when there's free cheese or milk and stuff, we don't know nothing about it, but they're the first in line?" The myth persists, exploited by politicians of both parties, that welfare rolls are filled with lazy Blacks who refuse to work when the reality is that whites comprise the majority on public assistance.

> *"The myth persists . . . that welfare rolls are filled with lazy Blacks who refuse to work."*

Bill Clinton's former political consultant, Dick Morris, produced both former President George Bush's Willie Horton ads (in which a Black felon is released to prey on a white victim) and Senator Jesse Helms' "Hands" TV commercial (in which a pair of white hands crumple a job rejection letter as a disappointed voice blames affirmative action). These ads are examples of the manipulation of racial cues which promote the notions of Black winners at the expense of white losers and white victims at the hands of Black criminals.

On the pseudointellectual front, the "cultural conspiracy" is exemplified by *The Bell Curve* and proposals for racial genetic testing to determine predisposition to criminal behavior or other innate inferiority. Such unscientific notions imply that Black virtue and success are abnormal and that Blacks must be controlled and subsidized at the expense of whites.

On the legal front, the "cultural conspiracy" sanctions racially disparate drug sentencing, which bloats the Black prison population, and law-enforcement "profiles" which transform Black drivers of expensive cars into criminal suspects.

Widespread racial fear of Blacks is perpetuated by policies which criminalize the sort of activity (traffic in illegal substances) that naturally abounds in an economically suppressed subculture and which escalates the level of violence normally associated with such activity.

Central to the "cultural conspiracy" are plantation-style welfare and affirmative action policies which, whatever their intent, far more effectively than the Helms' "Hands" commercials or Bush's Willie Horton ads, foster the notion of Black winners at the expense of white losers, thereby perpetuating racism in our society. These policies are misdirected at the twin decoys of poverty and disenfranchisement rather than at the appropriate target of dispossession. Poverty (substandard consumption) and disenfranchisement (substandard political power) are merely the lingering effects of dispossession (substandard ownership of capital).

Dispossession

For those who rank the protection of vested interests above the realization of justice, perpetual treatment of the symptoms of poverty and disenfranchisement seems less problematic than finding a cure for the disease of dispossession. After all, dispossession is deeply rooted in a national legacy of government-sanctioned slavery, Jim Crow, and segregation. Even the civil-rights movement of the 1960s balked at addressing the problem of dispossession, settling instead for socialistically inclined, bureaucratically administered, welfare and affirmative-action policies which effectively repudiated the abolitionists' goal of "forty acres and a mule" for the freedmen. "Forty acres and a mule" means the right to full participation in and profit from the individual private ownership of capital, the means of production in a capitalist society.

Consequently, the descendants of those once "legally" possessed on private plantations where they were "guaranteed" employment, housing, and medical care by their slavemasters have become dispossessed second-class citizens on a national plantation system where white, "liberal" politicians offer them false promises of "equal opportunity" education and employment, of "affordable" housing, and of "access" to medical care, where white "conservative" politicians exhort them to "pick themselves up by the bootstraps" of their non-existent boots, and where the government continues to renege on its promise of "forty acres and a mule" as scant restitution for the institution of slavery which left them dispossessed. No, there is not an organized conspiracy to commit senseless acts of racial violence against Blacks and Black institutions in America, but there is a highly organized conspiracy behind the persistence of racial fear and hatred that fuels those acts of violence.

Liberals and conservatives, as the leadership of the Republican and Democratic parties, are the co-conspirators. Both have conspired to deny the descendants of slavery their rightful inheritance of the capital owed their ancestors as restitution for the institution of slavery. They have conspired instead to "ease the

> *"[Governmental] policies . . . have fostered the illusion that Black gains must come at the cost of white losses."*

pain" of dispossession by instituting government policies which have trapped all but the most courageous, enterprising, and fortunate African-Americans in conditions of dependence on one big national plantation system. These policies, in turn, have fostered the illusion that Black gains must come at the cost of white losses and have thus enabled certain whites to scapegoat their own economic failures, thereby ensuring the persistence of racism in America.

Racism May Ultimately Lead to Black Genocide

by Tony Brown

About the author: *Tony Brown is a PBS television commentator, syndicated radio talk show host, author, and entrepreneur.*

When I began writing this viewpoint, I was tentative about bringing up the subject of genocide and its more subtle form, *triage,* out of fear of being labeled paranoid or alarmist by those not familiar with the history of conspiracies against the Black community. No more. Not after the mass media made my case for me with its rush to hail the publication of *The Bell Curve,* which the *New York Times* editorialists called "a flame-throwing treatise on race, class and intelligence." The *Times* noted that the book has "a grisly thesis: IQ, largely inherited and intractable, dictates an individual's success an economic death knell for much of America's black population."

While Americans in general blame their pessimism on the fear of economic and social decline, a growing number of Blacks share the belief that there is a plot to promote racial warfare in order to keep their race marginalized, or, most frightening of all, to exterminate Blacks altogether. In this viewpoint, I will examine the inflammatory but persistent issue of racial genocide in this country. And I will explore the deep-seated, if not openly expressed, fear among Blacks that the ultimate goal of White Americans is to wipe out the entire African-American community. As one man said on my television program, "The logical conclusion of racism is genocide." The thought of this may be so repulsive to some people that they deny that it is even a possibility, but to do that is to deny history. Bosnia and Rwanda are the latest reminders that the world has not abandoned "ethnic cleansing" as a geopolitical solution or weapon.

Triage

Let me note that I think a campaign of genocide against Black Americans is a highly unlikely scenario, for political as well as other reasons, unless there is some radical shift in this country to an authoritarian government. On the other hand, I believe that a more insidious threat exists to Blacks in America. As a historically marginalized people, this sociological minority is more vulnerable than any other group to a more subtle campaign of extinction, a form of selective elimination known as triage.

The term *triage* first came into common use in this country in reference to a system of emergency medical treatment developed by the French and implemented by American medical units during the Vietnam War. It is defined as the sorting of and allocation of treatment to patients and especially battle and disaster victims according to a system of priorities designed to maximize the number of survivors.

On the battlefield, the priority is to save those who can be saved, and not to waste precious resources on either those who are not in danger of dying or those who are already too far gone. In a societal sense, triage takes on more malevolent tones. You might think of it as the "rational" approach to genocide, culling those who are the least productive, or beyond redemption. . . .

The Bell Curve

In *The Bell Curve*, Charles Murray and coauthor Richard Herrnstein, a Harvard psychologist who died just before the book was published, infer that welfare programs, affirmative action, Head Start, and any other efforts to help elevate the lives of the American underclass have been a waste of time because Blacks are genetically flawed. In fact, the unstated implication is that Blacks in general are a waste of time. And that, of course, officially marginalizes an entire race of people. This makes Blacks candidates for eventual extermination, at least to anyone who has studied the history of genocide or triage.

There is nothing new in Herrnstein and Murray's book. And there is nothing unusual about the news it delivers. There is also nothing valid about it. Studies of the Black African immigrant population in Great Britain have shown that they have higher educational achievement than any other population segment in that country—a fact that Herrnstein and Murray seemed to have overlooked.

FINDS TOUCH OF AFRICA IN 28 MILLION WHITES read the headline in the *Sunday News* of June 15, 1958. Historian J.A. Rogers dug up an Associated Press story in the *Sunday News* that reported on an article in the *Ohio Journal of Science*. It claimed that 21 percent of, or approximately forty million, White Americans today have African ancestors. Without racial purity, how do we measure racial intelligence?

> "A growing number of Blacks share the belief that there is a plot . . . to exterminate Blacks altogether."

What really troubles me more than anything else about *The Bell Curve* is its timing. White people are under stress, and Black people don't need to have them aggravated. Because of the runaway national debt, Whites' standard of living is threatened, and they only have to look across the office or down the street to find someone to blame. We all know what happens when the people with the strength and the numbers come under stress. The laws of survival kick in. The strong go looking to bash the weak. And the weak had better go looking for a good place to hide.

The Bell Curve's authors recognize this, even as they encourage it. In the book, they predict that "racism will re-emerge in a new and more virulent form." The authors offer that "instead of the candor and realism about race that is so urgently needed, the nation will be faced with racial divisiveness and hostility that is as great as, or greater than, America experienced before the civil rights movement. . . . If it were to happen, all the scenarios for the custodial state would be more unpleasant—more vicious—than anyone can now imagine." It isn't difficult to imagine what the authors are suggesting.

> **"Any Black . . . who is not highly suspicious is crazy."**

By "custodial state," *The Bell Curve*'s authors say they mean "a high-tech and more lavish version of the Indian reservation for some substantial minority of the nation's population, while the rest of America tries to go about its business." In its harshest forms, they write, "the solutions will become more and more totalitarian.". . .

Fear of Genocide

There is every reason to believe that Black people are still easy targets for genocide. Black people know that, and they often talk about it among themselves. Generally, however, we are duplicitous when we discuss the subject around Whites. With good reason. We don't want to feed the flames.

A Black physician whom I know well was quoted in the *New York Times* as telling a reporter that when Blacks spread rumors about genocide, they victimize their own people by making them feel powerless and thereby provide poor Blacks with another excuse for not helping themselves. That same Black man told me later in a private discussion with several other Blacks present that the CIA was flooding the streets of the inner cities with drugs to kill Blacks.

When out of White earshot, this prominent doctor freely offered his belief that racism and government conspiracy are at the core of the social crisis among Blacks. He is not a hypocrite, though he may seem one. He is merely exhibiting the duality reflected in the lives of most Blacks living in a world dominated by Whites.

Fears of genocide run deep among Blacks even today. Another Black intellectual drove this lesson home to me once after I informed him that his own particular conspiracy theory had no basis in fact. "Just because you don't think ain't nobody standin' behind you don't mean they ain't," said this very well educated, articulate scholar. He intentionally affected a Black rural dialect to emphasize that this suspicion is deeply rooted in our culture.

He was reminding me that any Black, especially a Black man, who is not highly suspicious is crazy, especially given our experience in this country. While it is imperative to remain in touch with reality, it's important that we know and understand history. . . .

Could Genocide Happen?

Many Blacks fear that genocide is a real possibility because they recognize, on some level, just how hopeless their condition has become. And they recognize, perhaps intuitively, that it will only get worse. They see the poor quality and lack of focus in their elitist Black leadership. They see the counterproductive behavior of a growing "gangsta" subculture among Black youths. They see the emergence of media-conscious Black hate-mongers. They see White denial of the fact that our problems—Black and White—are intertwined with the nation's own destiny. Most of all, they see a knowledge sector and a new world of high technology being built without them in cyberspace.

Black anxieties are heightened when they hear demands for an end to the very problems that have become euphemisms for Blacks—crime, illegitimacy, poor values, poor schools, and, most of all, violence. At best, Blacks feel ambivalent about most proposed solutions to societal problems because they realize that their racial community is recognized as America's socioeconomic Achilles' heel. Eventually, Blacks fear, conditions in this country will reach a breaking point, and the ax will come down—on them.

I believe that if Blacks found and brought about solutions to their own problems, it would not only give a boost to the lives of Blacks, it might also jumpstart the entire nation and move our United States back into its leadership role in the world. Blacks and Whites alike understand that if America is to remain a viable nation, we must solve these problems.

If our national economy goes bankrupt, we all know which racial group would be judged too far gone to be saved. Already, Black Americans have been systematically cut off from economic activity and economically and socially marginalized by racism. When high rates of unemployment, a lack of productivity, and an assortment of societal ills—crime, drugs, disease—are blamed on Black "racial traits," it naturally follows that the majority group would increasingly see Blacks as a drain overall on society. . . .

> *"If our national economy goes bankrupt, we all know which racial group would be judged too far gone to be saved."*

In a study by Lou Harris and Associates for the National Commission on the Causes and Prevention of Violence, it was determined that if a fringe group of White extremists, or some rogue unit of "rationalists" within government, succeeded in drawing Blacks and Whites into a race war, the outcome would be particularly catastrophic for Blacks. One question included in the survey offered this scenario: "Imagine that the government has just arrested and imprisoned many of the Negroes in your community even though there had been no trouble."

The responses to that scenario, published in a November 1970 *Psychology Today* article, were revealing. The overwhelming majority of White Americans would apparently be good Germans if the government turned to massive racial repression; 18 percent would protest nonviolently and only 9 percent would turn to violence—for a total of 27 percent who would resist. Blacks understandably would be more willing to act; 43 percent would use civil disobedience and one-fourth would attempt counterviolence. This may reflect a pragmatic judgment that if such things came to pass, Blacks would be wiped out if they rebelled.

It's my guess that, with a worsening racial climate since that poll was conducted in 1968, fewer than 27 percent of Whites would offer assistance to Blacks today. Even assuming that the numbers still hold, it means that 73 percent of Whites would offer no assistance to a "massive racial repression" of Blacks. Moreover, the survey question contained a big "if." It assumed "there had been no trouble." I interpret that to mean, for example, that no Black zealot had sounded the call to kill Whites, and that Blacks had not initiated violence against authorities. If Black-on-White violence had occurred, White support would undoubtedly be less than the 27 percent.

> *"73 percent of Whites would offer [Blacks] no assistance [in] a 'massive racial repression' of Blacks."*

To make matters worse, for Blacks at least, Blacks themselves would offer minimal resistance. As mentioned, less than half, 43 percent, would offer nonviolent resistance, and only 24 percent would resist violently. Another 33 percent would offer no resistance of any type.

It is anyone's guess just how far Whites would allow government repression of Blacks to go, or how much violence against Blacks would be tolerated. Only 14 percent of Whites "would fight to defend Blacks from unlawful and unjustified mass imprisonment," according to the Harris poll. Whatever the outcome, Americans generally regard violence and war as inevitable, the survey revealed.

With triage or genocide offered as solutions to national problems, it would only be a matter of time before they became the "final solutions" for other perceived group problems and value conflicts. After all, America clings to a history of racial animosity, as does the rest of the world. . . .

The Danger of Hate Talk

Everything has gone to hell for poor Blacks, a totally dispirited group that has been abandoned by all. They are helpless and broken, and a belief in a conspiracy to wipe them out could be a death wish, or perhaps even a cry for help.

My overriding concern, and I cannot overstate it, is the incendiary nature of the hateful rhetoric spewing from fringe groups of the Black community, whose venom threatens the entire Black population. Ignorant of history or perhaps inspired by history's darkest aspect—mass extermination—these zealots play with fire at our collective expense. The great majority of thoughtful Blacks find this racial intolerance among their own people repugnant. I predict that to exacerbate this dilemma, as economic conditions worsen for the lower stratum of Blacks, the belief in a White conspiracy of Black genocide will spread further and deeper.

> *"The great majority of thoughtful Blacks find . . . racial intolerance among their own people repugnant."*

Unfortunately, the most desperate increasingly will demand new fanatical leaders who sound like this: "I want to be one of the flamethrowers of God, break White folks' backs. I want to give you hell all the way to your [Whites'] graves. I ain't scared to die and I'm ready to kill."

Those are the words of Khalid Muhammad, the former chief spokesman for Minister Louis Farrakhan. Muhammad was speaking to an enthusiastic Black audience in Brooklyn. It was not his first verbal dare to White America. He told a Washington, D.C., rally in April 1986 that if any attempt to imprison or harm Farrakhan took place, "the people will burn this country to the ground."

Muhammad's hyperbole is greatly exaggerated and his influence substantially less than popularly imagined. But the number of Blacks who think, and, more important, feel, as Muhammad does is growing. If they are incited to violence, Blacks at large would be massacred, of course. But logic and facts do not get in the way of poor judgment or zealots who are "flamethrowers of God."

"It's as though White America is sleepwalking on the edge of a volcano of ethnic and racial differences," said Sanford Cloud, Jr., president of the National Conference of Christians and Jews, in a *Washington Post* interview. The biggest threat is that White America will suddenly awaken and respond to these increased tensions spawned by Black "gangsta" entertainers and fanatics who miscalculate the danger that an aroused majority historically poses to a despised racial minority.

Genocide expert Barbara Harff concludes that all of the genocide cases she has studied "were preceded by challenges to the dominant power strata" and accelerated by "polarization." In that historic context, think about the emergence of in-your-face Black threats, such as a rapper's call to kill "one White a week." There is an increasingly large audience attracted to this theater of the absurd. For example, after identifying the devil as the White race, Muhammad asked his Black audience in Brooklyn to support the Long Island Railroad mass murderer Colin Ferguson, who aimed only at Whites with his 9mm weapon. "I thank God for Colin Ferguson," said Muhammad, adding, "Colin Ferguson was commanded by God. God sends earthquakes. God sends hurricanes."

Some might argue that God sends genocide to eliminate Black people who are considered "redundant" and a threat to the majority.

I believe that America is a powder keg. Armies of White "survivalists" and militias are polishing up their rifles in anticipation of a violent showdown with Blacks. But they are not alone. Many mainstream Whites are increasingly resentful of Blacks. They see underclass Blacks as drug-pushing, car-jacking, gang-banging wild beasts. And they view middle-class Blacks as threats in the workplace and in their neighborhoods.

To the Black "gangstas" and "flamethrowers" and their would-be recruits, I offer this advice: "You are playing with fire." And the militias are poised to throw gasoline upon the flames.

Blacks Exaggerate the Problem of Racism

by James L. Robinson

About the author: *James L. Robinson is the author of* Racism or Attitude? The Ongoing Struggle for Black Liberation and Self-Esteem, *from which this viewpoint is excerpted.*

The famous black writer James Baldwin once wrote that the worst thing about his father was not that white people called him (the father) a nigger, but that he believed it. Despite the very serious recent recession, 1990 census tract data show that many blacks are better off today than ever before. Yet, when one listens to black leadership, it would appear that things are worse for all blacks. I believe the reason for this pessimism is twofold: One reason is political and the other is guilt. The political reason that black leadership seldom speaks about the progress many blacks have made is their fear that they might lose federal programs if whites believe blacks are not so badly off after all. These leaders are still caught up in the belief that somehow the federal government will spend large amounts of money on race-specific programs. The second reason we never hear anything good about black progress is guilt. I believe many middle-class blacks feel guilty about being better off. They feel that somehow their living a better life contradicts the suffering of less-well-off African Americans. Every time I hear middle-class black spokespeople say that things have not improved for blacks, what they mean is others, not themselves.

The 1980 and 1990 census data show clearly that black income gains are most prevalent among those who already had higher incomes to start. [Data presented by] Thomas and Mary Edsalls show that from 1973 to 1987 blacks in the lowest income brackets became 18 percent poorer, yet during the same period blacks in the highest income brackets became 33 percent richer. While these data show a definite need for improvement among the lower-income blacks, there is no reason for black leadership to say there is no improvement for any blacks. But when asked why one-third of blacks are doing so poorly, black leaders say the reason is continuing white racism in America. They tend to ignore other reasons like destructive ghetto lifestyles or changes in the global economy. Why this obsession with racism? Is racism a myth, as William Raspberry called it? I agree with Raspberry that racism has taken on mythological qualities for many black people, but the belief in racism also has certain functional attributes which Raspberry does not discuss. I think that functionally, the belief in "racism" as the main obstacle to black progress binds all African Americans together in a way that socioeconomic status does not. The belief in "racism" as a major source of black woes has come to define blackness in a way that allows all black people, from Oprah Winfrey to the lowest black person on the totem pole, to feel a sense of unity. "No matter how successful I become," says the middle-class black, "I can still say to my lower-class black brother, 'Hey, I'm not doing so good; I am still suffering because I am black.'" But the idea that being black means that all blacks suffer equally is to deny some of the real struggles and challenges facing inner-city poor blacks. It is not true that the blacks in the suburbs, making $50,000 a year, with two cars in the garage, are suffering as are their ghetto counterparts in the cities. . . .

Racism as a Scapegoat

Racism has become a term that all African Americans can use to explain whatever problems they confront because it absolves them of personal responsibility. If a black man deserts his family, it's due to racism. If a black college student has poor grades, it is because his white professors are racists. All problems are seen as coming from outside the self. During the 1960s black prison inmates called themselves political prisoners. They accepted no personal responsibility for their actions.

The real issues behind a black man's leaving his family or the college student's failures might require a very different explanation from racism. One possible reason black men leave their families may be that they feel they can't provide their families with the things they need. Unemployment is one contributing reason why poor families break apart, both white and black. As was stated earlier, if racism is the only culprit in creating fatherless black families, then why are there more of these families today than during the 1950s, when racism was worse?

The black family has been under siege for over thirty years, and its decline appears to be due, in part, to cultural and social dynamics that occurred when blacks left rural farm life for city life. In fact Nicholas Lemann argues in *The Promised Land: The Great Black Migration and How It Changed America* that what are called lower-class lifestyles are really rural lifestyles blacks brought with them when they left the rural South. Take the case of the

> *"The belief in 'racism' as the main obstacle to black progress binds all African Americans together."*

45

black college student who thinks racism explains why he or she receives poor grades. I worked with many black students when I taught at Rutgers University, and I found many to have a severe lack of confidence in themselves. Too many of my black students believed they were less intelligent than their white counterparts and consequently did not put forth the kind of effort that was needed. I understood this problem and tried to instill that sense of confidence, because I was once a black college student and I too had suffered these same feelings. I would dare say a number of African Americans in all walks of life share similar feelings of inadequacy. But rather than confront the feeling itself (which, after, all is a common feeling among all peoples), too many blacks chalk it up to "racism."

Feelings of Inferiority

African Americans can correctly blame white racism for helping create these feelings of inadequacy, but not for the continuation of these feelings. Continuing to feel inadequate, continuing to feel inferior is self-perpetuating. How I feel about myself depends not on what white people may think of me, but on what I think of myself. Feelings of low self-esteem and inferiority appear to be part of a larger problem in America. Many white people suffer from these feelings. In fact, the entire self-help phenomenon today is predicated on helping people overcome their low self-esteem and feelings of inadequacy (which create a number of addictions, aberrations in behavior, and dysfunctional families). For many blacks, these normal feel-

> *"Racism has become a term that all African Americans can use to explain whatever problems they confront."*

ings (in today's society) get intermingled with race. Instead of dealing with low self-esteem and feelings of inadequacy as part of the human condition in twentieth-century America, African Americans allow them to take on a more ominous social, political, and racial significance. The benefit African Americans obtain from holding racism to blame for most of life's problems is a moral superiority over white people.

The price African Americans pay for holding onto this vision of racism is a heavy one. As Glenn Loury, a black professor at Harvard, points out, even successful African Americans are not really happy: "The vicissitudes of life, the slights, the failure to get a job or a rude word from a supervisor, all are due to race." Loury goes on to talk about African Americans having a mild form of paranoia, which goes hand in hand with believing oneself to be a victim. If the evils of racism have done one thing, it is to create this cult of victims.

Victimization

What is the moral benefit of being a victim? Joseph Epstein wrote in a 1989 *New York Times Magazine* article that some segments of our society are becoming professional victims: "One senses that victims enjoy the moral vantage their victimhood gives them to overstate their case, to absolve themselves from all responsibility, to ask for the impossible and then to show outrage when it isn't delivered." Also, and most important, victims are not responsible for their plight or actions. If you ask a victim, "Why do you smoke crack?" he will answer in terms of victimization, for example, society, being poor, or having no job. Victims rarely take responsibility for their own actions. Yet only when they do take responsibility will they stop being victims and take control of their lives. It is a healthy sign that there is a debate about victimization currently going on among blacks. New voices, such as those of William Raspberry and Shelby Steele, say it is time to drop or mute the victim claims against whites and stress individual effort and the values needed to get ahead. The tragedy of black power in America, writes Steele, is that "it is primarily a victim's power. . . . Whatever gains this power brings in the short run through political action, it undermines in the long run. Social victims may be collectively entitled, but they are all too often individually demoralized."

> *"The permanent role of the victim is a trap."*

But what fuels the notion that blacks should stress their victim role? Is it black politics or the strategic idea, by black leadership, that there is power in grievance politics? And why shouldn't these leaders believe in this approach? After all, grievance politics or the redress of grievances was what brought about the successes of the civil rights movement. In the 1960s, during the movement, America underwent a radical change. Rather than being entitled to rights as individual citizens, people were entitled collectively—blacks, women, Hispanics—in the name of redressing their grievances. According to Steele and others, this has led to separate facilities on campuses, separate study programs, and affirmative action policies. Today there is an entrenched view that group entitlement, not individual effort, is the most appropriate vehicle of black advancement.

Conspiracy Theories

Once grievance politics, particularly under the leadership of Martin Luther King, Jr., held the moral high ground, but today it has degenerated into racial polarization, and the victim stance has mutated into an array of conspiracy theories. One example of such a theory is the notion that some black officials are going to jail not just because they are crooked, but because of racist prosecutions, says Benjamin Hooks of the NAACP. Another theory asks: Why are one-quarter of young black males behind bars, on probation, or dead by age thirty? Hooks answers his own question: "It's not the high rate of black crime and black-on-black homicide but because whites have made black males a hunted and endangered species." Vivian Gordon, a black-studies professor, asks a similar rhetorical question: Why are drugs so prevalent in the ghetto? Because whites are using substance abuse as "an instrument of genocide." None of these theories speaks in the least about the responsibility of those who are in jail or using drugs. But other conspiracy theories do manage to blame the alleged hostility of Jews and the success of Korean grocers as reasons for black degradation in the ghetto. One black writer seriously argued recently that the naming of the fourth black Miss America was an attempt to keep black males down by raising up black females. Unfortunately these arguments are coming not from the margins of the black community, but mainly from activists and academics, which could be a bad omen for the future. As Shelby Steele has argued, the permanent role of the victim is a trap, particularly as it is passed on to black children. It can function as a blanket excuse to explain any negative outcome as an excuse not to try. The rhetoric of victimization reinforces the view that the poor and the demoralized are little more than observers of their own lives. It teaches the young that they cannot be expected to succeed, except perhaps as part of a complaining victim group. It mocks the connection between striving and success. It makes black-white alliances unlikely, and it subtly depicts black success as a kind of commodity that whites control and refuse to dole out to the masses of blacks. . . .

Legitimizing Rage

My view is that most blacks have become so obsessed with race and have such sensitivity to it that they do "exhibit a mild form of paranoia," as Glenn Loury, the black Harvard sociologist, stated. I also believe that black anger, by both the middle and the underclass, is not only expected but encouraged by the larger white liberal academic and political establishment. For example, take the 1992 Los Angeles riots and the white liberal reactions to it. Most of the liberal intellectual response to the riots emphasized the need to "understand the rage" of the rioters.

For most reporters, academics, politicians, and the civil rights establishment, blacks who burned and rioted were not criminals, but people enraged by injustice. One prominent black liberal, Representative John Conyers, Jr., a Democrat from Michigan, announced, "Those weren't criminals, those were outraged citizens." One has to wonder if there is any crime a black could have committed during the riots that Congressman Conyers would have condemned as criminal. Senator Bill Bradley of New Jersey, often identified as a moderate liberal, described the riots as "desperation and anger that boiled over into sickening violence." And for five consecutive days after the riots ended, the *Los Angeles Times* published special supplements on "the roots of the riots."

> *"On college campuses [middle-class blacks] are taught that America is racist."*

One day, the entire supplement was entitled "Witness to Rage." The cover of an issue of *U.S. News & World Report* featured only two words: "Race and Rage." Professor Andrew Hacker, a chief liberal spokesman on race, lends legitimacy to black rage in *Two Nations Black and White: Separate, Hostile and Unequal.*

Right after the riots, the *Los Angeles Times* published long excerpts from his book on its opinion page. Hacker stated, "At times, the conclusion seems all but self-evident that white America has no desire for your presence or any need for your people. Can this nation have an unstated strategy for annihilating your people? How else, you ask yourself, can one explain the incidence of death and debilitation from drugs and disease; the incarceration of a whole generation of your men; the consignment of millions of women and children to half-lives of poverty and dependence? . . . Just as your people were once made to serve silently as slaves, could it be that if white America begins to conclude that you are becoming too much trouble, it will find itself contemplating more lasting solutions?" When the leading white liberal "expert" on race relations in America tells blacks that America wishes to exterminate them and the newspaper of the city in which the riots occurred publishes this a week after the riots, one can understand the legitimizing of black rage.

> *"The media . . . are patronizing and reluctant to criticize blacks."*

Less than a week after the riots the *Los Angeles Times* published on its opinion page the following statement of black liberal author Walter Mosley: "America is a brutal land. Its language is violence and bloodshed. That is why [Rodney] King was beaten; that is why another King was assassinated." On the same opinion page, the same day, the *Times* published a piece by Leon Litwack, Morrison Professor of American History at the University of California at Berkeley. He says, "The lawlessness began with the clubbing of black America, the conscious and criminal neglect and fashionable racism characteristic of the Age of Greed, over which Ronald Reagan and George Bush have presided." Leonard Fein, another prominent liberal writer, stated after the riots, "We have, as a nation, decided to bequeath to our children the rotten fruit of racism and bigotry, decided that it will be for them to choke on it. . . . We must stop now the persistent looting of human life, end the stealing of hope and the torching of health." Adding fuel to the fires was another angry black liberal spokesman, the Reverend James Lawson of Los Angeles, who said after the riot, "The rioters and looters were doing exactly what the United States had done to the men, women and children of Central American countries and in the Persian Gulf War."

Black Paranoia

Given the above statements by both white and black liberal scholars, it is a wonder that all blacks in Los Angeles did not riot. But the liberal intellectual community has been preaching this sermon for years. And in the face of this litany, how could any self-respecting black person not be angry? Yet as Glenn Loury stated, this anger also leads to unhappiness and a "mild form of paranoia." Middle-class blacks are overwhelmingly college graduates, and on college campuses they are taught that America is racist. A few years ago, Harvard sponsored a week-long program against racism called AWARE ("Actively Working against Racism and Ethnocentrism"), at which students learned from the keynote speaker, Professor John Dovidio of Colgate, that 85 percent of white Americans harbor some form of racism and the other 15 percent are outright racists. They also heard a Dartmouth dean say that major American universities are "genocidal in nature." And the president of Occidental College in Los Angeles said not long ago that blacks on predominantly white campuses "face a level of hatred, prejudice and ignorance comparable to that of the days of Bull Connor, Lester Maddox and Orval Faubus."

> *"Racism is not black America's worst enemy."*

I can remember being on college campuses during the 1960s, 1970s, and 1980s and don't remember this virulent level of racism. In fact, what I do remember is a number of white liberal professors and students being, if anything, overly solicitous toward black students. It is from academia, after all, that we get the strongest affirmative action programs. The complaint by many of my black colleagues during the 1960s and 1970s was about being patronized by whites who were overly sympathetic about our supposed ghetto sufferings. They (whites) expected us (blacks) to be angry at them and, as Shelby Steele described in *The Content of Our Character,* blacks could easily put them down using collective guilt. I think it is these former college students who have become politicians, professors, and members of the American media who say to rioters and arsonists, "We understand your rage." That was certainly the message black U.S. Representative Maxine Waters wanted the rioters to hear when she screamed at a Washington, D.C., rally following the riots, "No justice, no peace." Indeed, as a reward for her fiery speech, ABC News named Maxine Waters its "Person of the Week." The media, in particular, are patronizing and reluctant to criticize blacks. One incident during the riot shows just how ludicrous this reluctance can be. In an article entitled "Blacks and Liberals: The Los Angeles Riots," Dennis Prager describes a local Los Angeles reporter saying, "I see five black gentlemen throwing stones at cars." According to Prager, "Liberalism has so stifled moral honesty in relation to blacks that a reporter instinctively felt it necessary to call black thugs 'gentlemen.'"...

Black America must believe that racism is even more invidious and pernicious than ever before. If it isn't, then why aren't black people doing better? If it isn't because of racism, then how does one explain that one in four black youths between eighteen and twenty-nine are in state or local prison and that blacks commit 45 percent of violent crimes in America (1991 FBI crime statistics). The black psyche is reluctant to allow racism, as the cause of all its problems, to diminish in America. Racism is an easy answer which does not require much introspection. Without racism, other issues must be explored, and some of these issues have to do with what Glenn Loury calls "moral character."

African Americans have traditionally rejected discussions regarding black morality and particularly the morality of the lower classes. So we (blacks) scramble to find reasons for the unkind statistics which show a disproportionate number of our people on welfare, in jails, and having babies out of wedlock, and we quietly worry about why things have not improved more quickly for our people. The belief that racism is a sufficient explanation for the condition of many blacks in America relieves self-doubt and fear that something inherently negative about being black may be the real cause of our problems. To the extent actual racism becomes harder to use as an explanation, black voices become even more shrill in screaming racism.

Actual unambiguous racists like ex-Klan member David Duke become almost a relief because finally we can see a real one. After listening to Duke (who denies he's racist any longer), one will hear many African Americans give a satisfied sigh and say, "Well, at least he's honest." Jesse Jackson interviewed David Duke on his cable television program and treated him the way one would treat a worthy adversary. Last, real racism is not dead in America. It will probably always be with us. However, racism is not black America's worst enemy. Our worst enemy is the excuse racism provides many of us not to be the best we can be.

White Racism Is Subsiding

by Samuel Francis

About the author: *Samuel Francis is a syndicated columnist for Tribune Media Services, Inc.*

In the first week of December 1995, three white soldiers, soaked with booze and stoked with racial hatreds, cruised Fayetteville, N.C., looking for some blacks to harass. Allegedly, they wound up murdering two, a man and a woman whom they had never seen before.

The next evening in New York City, a gentleman named Roland James Smith, not so permeated by drinks as the white GIs in North Carolina but just as riddled with his own infection of hate, walked into a white-owned clothing store in Harlem, ordered blacks to get out, opened fire point-blank on the white people he saw, set the store on fire and then shot himself. He took a total of seven people with him.

White Racism Earns Media Attention

Both crimes, equally horrific, won national attention in the days that followed, but which do you think earned the attention of the federal government and continues to bubble on front pages across the nation, while the other seems to recede down the memory hole the mainstream media reserve for events that never happened?

The white killing of two blacks, of course, is the one that splattered itself across the front page of the *Washington Post* the day after it happened, while the *Post* relegated to its interior regions the mass murder committed by a black in New York. The *New York Times* has carried front page stories about the Harlem massacre, but then the killings took place in New York, and the *Times* quickly jumps the stories to the Metro section.

And it's the white killing that wins the concern of the fearless routers of "racism" in the federal government. The two suspects held in North Carolina apparently possessed Nazi paraphernalia and literature, but they stoutly deny they are part of any organized brand of "extremists" within the armed forces. Nevertheless, the watchdogs of the Pentagon have announced they're launching a full-scale "investigation" of the penetration of the armed forces by "skin-heads," "white supremacists" and "hate."

Black Racism Is Ignored

So far, no one in New York seems inclined to launch any investigation of the anti-white and anti-Jewish hatred that demonstrators outside Freddies' Fashion Mart have screamed for weeks. The late Mr. Smith, who took part in the demonstrations, had borne a racial chip on his shoulder for years, and the whole purpose of the protests against the store was to bludgeon its owners for expanding into the adjacent commercial space occupied by a black music shop.

Will the city government of New York launch "investigations" of the anti-white black racism that led to Mr. Smith's act of mass murder? Mayor Rudolph Giuliani immediately recommended that it be placed on the back burner. "I urge everyone to suspend judgment," he announced. "Everyone should wait and let the police do their job."

Today, after the O.J. Simpson verdict and dozens of similar racially inspired miscarriages of justice, after the Million Man March and millions of words spewed from the lips of Louis Farrakhan, Al Sharpton and the marchers of Afro-racism throughout the country, and after countless "hate crimes" aimed at whites by blacks steeped in Afro-racist ideologies and mytholo-gies, today the ruling class in govern-ment and the press still believes that white racial hatred is worse than black racial hatred.

> *"The most virulent and most physically dangerous expressions of racial hatred [come] not from whites but from blacks."*

It is quite true that there still are white racial extremists, like the Aryan Na-tions and assorted skinheads, and it's still true that occasionally, as with a band of neo-Nazi terrorists in the 1980s and perhaps the two suspects in the North Carolina killings today, these characters do their best to emulate the church bombers of the '60s.

A Decline in White Racism

But the larger truth today is that white racism, at least of that ilk, is dying. Even most of its own leaders no longer preach "white supremacy" but rather "white separatism," and, like the Aryan Nations, they retreat to remote rural lo-cations to build their Nordic utopias. And the even larger truth today is that the real racism, the most virulent and most physically dangerous expressions of racial hatred, comes not from whites but from blacks.

What is dangerous about Afro-racism is not just that it occasionally (more of-ten than many realize) leads to the kinds of murders committed by Roland Smith but that the establishment, white and black, that governs public discus-sion accepts black racism as somehow legitimate. That means that black animosities against whites are free to bubble and brew aboveground and gain acceptance and, eventually, power in the courts, the schools, the media and national politics.

There is no good reason for the racial pathologies of either race to win acceptance, but until whites and blacks not ridden by the demons of hatred demand that the pathologies of both races merit the same exile, we can expect more racial volcanoes like the ones that erupted in New York and North Carolina.

Most Church Arsons Are Not Racially Motivated

by Joe Holley

About the author: *Joe Holley is a freelance writer who lives in Austin, Texas.*

On Tuesday, January 2, 1996, the Memphis *Commercial Appeal* reported that a fire that destroyed a rural church in the area the previous Saturday appeared to have been set intentionally. Further, the newspaper reported, the burning might be related to fires that had destroyed three other black Baptist churches in western Tennessee in early 1995, nearly a year earlier. Two of the previous fires had been ruled arson; the third was of undetermined origin but remained under investigation.

"We reported it as spot news," the *Commercial Appeal*'s city editor, Jesse Bunn, recalls. Other papers throughout the South had also covered church fires as spot news, if they covered them at all.

Less than a week later, on January 8, 1996, fire broke out in Knoxville, across the state from Memphis, at the 400-member Inner City Church. According to the Nashville *Tennessean*, the Knoxville fire was the fifth fire set intentionally over the past year at Tennessee churches with black memberships. "Investigators don't believe the fires are linked, but the FBI is trying to determine if there is any evidence of civil rights violations," the Nashville paper reported.

In retrospect, the Knoxville fire appears to have been the catalyst—the incendiary element, if you will—that transformed spot news in various papers across the South into big news across the nation. Within a matter of days, the burnings at black churches became one of those soaring stories that occasionally burst onto the national radar screen, seemingly out of nowhere. Like child sex abuse at day-care centers and recovered memory, to name two, they quickly command national attention, acquire immense symbolic significance, and inspire a spate of national soul-searching. Weeks, months, sometimes years later, they fade, leaving questions in their wake: Was the problem solved or did the media merely lose interest? Had the media at last discovered a phenomenon that had been going on for years, unnoticed and unreported? Or were the media so alert that, in this case, the fires attracted attention as soon as they began flaming up? Or was the whole thing a product of media hyperbole?

Stages of Media Coverage

The story of the fires at black churches in the Southeast commanded headlines for seven months and evolved through three distinct stages. First was the trend stage, lasting less than a month, in which reporters began to see a pattern. Second was the major-story stage, in which the national media began connecting dots, raising the possibility that the phenomenon was fueled by an atmosphere of surging racial animosity, or even by a nationwide conspiracy concocted by white racist organizations, or by some awful combination of the two. This fevered second stage lasted approximately five months. The third stage, set in motion by a newspaper not known for its investigative prowess and a wire service whose raison d'être is spot news, was a time of sorting out and assessment.

The black-church-burning story is a textbook example of what can happen, both good and bad, when journalists are tempted to connect the dots. It's an example of how the media can be distracted, even misled for a while, but, given time, are able to right themselves, regain their balance, and tease out the complex truth.

The National Media Get Involved

Reggie White is an all-pro defensive end for the Green Bay Packers. He is also the associate pastor of the Knoxville church that burned in January 1996 and the man who, more than perhaps anyone, helped boost the church-burning story to the second stage. When his multiracial church went up in flames, White was preparing for the biggest game of his eleven-year NFL career, a conference championship game against the Dallas Cowboys. Articulate and outspoken, he had the ear of news organizations around the nation, and he wasn't reluctant to see larger and sinister forces at work.

"Until this country starts dealing with organizations that do things like this," White told sportswriter Michael Madden of *The Boston Globe*, "then we're still going to have problems. I think it's time for the country to take this stuff seriously. It's time to stop sweeping this stuff under the rug because progress in race relations hasn't been made."

> *"When flames consumed three small black churches [in Alabama] . . . the national media were ready to run with the ball."*

"When is America going to stop tolerating these groups?" White asked in a January 12, 1996, column by another sportswriter, Thomas George of *The New York Times*. "It is time for us to come together and to fight it. One of the problems is that the people financing and providing the resources for this type of activity are popular people with money who are hiding under the rug. Some of them may be policemen, doctors, lawyers, prominent people who speak out of both sides of their mouths. That makes it difficult to stop but not impossible. Not when we come together as one force against hate."

When flames consumed three small black churches in the small town of Boligee in rural Alabama, the football player–pastor seemed prophetic, and the national media were ready to run with the ball. "The destruction of the three churches in Greene County, long recognized as one of the poorest counties in America, follows a series of attacks on black churches both in adjoining Sumter County and in nearby Tennessee," Sue Anne Pressley of *The Washington Post* reported. It raises anew the disturbing specter of a time when the civil rights movement was at its most heated."

Pressley, based in Austin, Texas, was covering Barbara Jordan's funeral in Houston when she was dispatched to Alabama. She noted that church burnings in Alabama "have a particularly dark historical resonance. In a pivotal tragedy in the civil rights movement, four black girls were killed during Sunday School on September 15, 1963, when whites firebombed the 16th Street Baptist Church in Birmingham, about 100 miles east of Boligee."

The Boligee fires also attracted the attention of the *Los Angeles Times*'s Eric Harrison, based in Atlanta. "Church fires are lighting up the night in this isolated corner of the state," Harrison wrote. "The echoes of civil rights–era violence they evoke have been just as shocking as they are painful to the targeted African-American congregations." Harrison quoted Jim Cavanaugh, special agent in charge of the U.S. Bureau of Alcohol, Tobacco and Firearms, Birmingham office: "None of us wants to go back in history. Let's hope it's not that."

> *"No one has evidence of any national or regional conspiracy."*

But what else could it be?" Harrison asked rhetorically.

The Civil Rights Angle

Suddenly, black-church arson was one of those stories that cause the back of a reporter's neck to prickle. It was an important story with national implications; it offered clear-cut issues of good and evil, heroes and villains, and the intriguing, unanswered questions of a criminal investigation; it resonated with the heroic tones of civil rights history, particularly when the dateline was Alabama.

Reporters covering the South know that when a story involves civil rights, poverty issues, or criminal justice, one of the most useful clearinghouses of information is the Southern Poverty Law Center, based in Montgomery, Alabama. A nonprofit agency that tracks hate groups and promotes racial harmony, the center is inevitably quoted in stories that range from black-church burnings to skinhead activities to a bomb at the Olympics. It has earned a reputation for reliability and well-researched information.

Who Was Responsible?

Spokespeople for the Southern Poverty Law Center were reluctant to ascribe widespread church burnings to any kind of organized, wide-ranging effort on the part of white racist groups (even though in one church arson in South Carolina the organization would later file suit against the Ku Klux Klan). On January 19, 1996, for example, the center's well-known founder and head, Morris Dees, talked about the Boligee fires to Ronald Smothers of *The New York Times*'s Atlanta bureau. Dees noted that Greene and Sumter counties,

> *"[One arson suspect] was emotionally disturbed and thirteen years old."*

both overwhelmingly black, were not areas where white supremacist groups would thrive. He told Smothers that the incidents might be more the result of casual racism than organized racist attacks. "This is deer-hunting season, and you have a lot of hunting clubs up there and a lot of drunk white boys who might be angry at not getting a deer," Dees said. "It's still bigoted, insensitive, and intimidating," he added, "but it's not organized."

But spokespeople for another, lesser-known clearinghouse of information, the Atlanta-based Center for Democratic Renewal, were not so circumspect. The CDR, originally called the National Anti-Klan Network, held a press conference in March 1996 to release a preliminary report showing a drastic increase in black-church burnings beginning in 1990. "You're talking about a well-organized white-supremacist movement," the Rev. Mac Charles Jones, a CDR board member, told *The Christian Science Monitor*. On CNN, he called it "domestic terrorism."

Other church leaders and civil-rights spokespeople did not raise the CDR notion of an organized conspiracy by racist organizations, but some of them did view the church fires as fueled by a rising and pervasive atmosphere of racism, an atmosphere nurtured by right-wing politicians.

In its June 3, 1996, issue, *Newsweek* ran a story quoting the Rev. Jesse Jackson, who blamed a "'cultural conspiracy'—a seeping intolerance fed by white politicians' attacks on affirmative action and immigration." In its July 1 issue, *Time* alluded to "the national epidemic of violence against black churches" and quoted the National Urban League president, Hugh Price: "The flames of bigotry and intolerance are soaring higher than they have in a generation." In a column that ran in the March 18 issue of *Time*, national correspondent Jack E. White wrote that the church fires were most likely incited by the resentful, fear-driven rhetoric of Pat Buchanan and other conservative politicians. . . .

In some of the coverage, these two levels of conspiracy—rising hatreds fueled by right-wingers, and organized terrorism—seemed to fuse somehow, as sources, politicians, and journalists labored to explain what seemed to be a widespread epidemic of church burnings.

Newsweek noted in an article headlined "Fires in the Night" (June 24, 1996) that "many of these cases remain unsolved, and no one has evidence of any national or regional conspiracy. But the sheer number of black church arsons, which now equals the worst years of white racist terror in the 1950s and '60s, suggests a spreading virus of copycat malice."

"The fires just keep coming, one after the other, mostly in southern states. . . ." *U.S. News & World Report* observed on June 24, 1996.

An epidemic of church-burnings is a compelling issue for politicians, particularly in an election year, and in the House Judiciary Committee's hearings on the fires, which began on May 21, 1996, lawmakers heard testimony from officials with the Federal Bureau of Investigation, the Bureau of Alcohol, Tobacco and Firearms, the Southern Baptist Convention, the Christian Coalition, the Southern Christian Leadership Conference (SCLC), and the National Association for the Advancement of Colored People (NAACP).

Black lawmakers and church leaders criticized the government for not taking the fires seriously enough. *The New York Times* quoted Representative Sheila Jackson Lee, a Texas Democrat: "I'm concerned at the politeness of this hearing. You've got burned churches and burned history. You have intimidated communities."

The *Times* also quoted Dr. Joseph E. Lowery, president of the SCLC, and a well-known civil-rights veteran: "We're not surprised by the feeble response to the church burnings. It just represents the fifty-first state in this nation: the state of denial."

Lowery added: "We are witnessing a serious and frightening assault on African-Americans in this country. We must hold accountable the racist groups that fan the flames of intolerance."

The Story Reaches a Crescendo

Stage two of the church-burning story reached its crescendo in early June 1996, as President Clinton invited a group of southern black ministers and other church officials to the White House, and then used his weekly Saturday radio address to discuss "a recent and disturbing rash of crimes that hearkens back to a dark era in our nation's history." The president mentioned the Matthews Murkland Presbyterian Church, in Charlotte, North Carolina, which had burned to the ground two days earlier; according to the president, it was the thirtieth African-American church damaged by suspicious fire in the South over the previous eighteen months.

> *"Of the sixty-four black-church fires examined, only four can conclusively be shown to be racially motivated."*

59

We do not now have evidence of a national conspiracy, but it is clear that racial hostility is the driving force behind a number of these incidents," Clinton said.

It was a reasonable assumption and possibly true, but there were complicating factors in this particular case. Two days later, the authorities in Charlotte arrested and charged a suspect. Although the suspect was white and, according to *USA Today*, held anti-black attitudes, she was also emotionally disturbed and thirteen years old. There was apparently no connection between the fire she allegedly set and other fires.

The Charlotte incident was one of several telling indications that the church-fire story was more complicated than much of the coverage would suggest. . . .

USA Today's Analysis

By April 1996, *USA Today* had run some twenty stories related to the black-church fires. At that point, reporter Gary Fields recalls, "the editors called in the cavalry." Fields and a dozen additional reporters fanned out across the South. They conducted more than 500 interviews, examined fire records in every southern state, and visited the sites of forty-five church arsons. The paper published the results of its investigation in its June 28–30, 1996, weekend edition.

That initial four-page report, perhaps the longest and most comprehensive story *USA Today* has ever published, included a half-page chart listing arson or "suspicious" fires at black churches since January 1, 1995, with the number of members at each church, when it was founded, the time and date of the fire, damage, insurance, arrests, if any, and other facts. The chart included eighteen fires previously unreported by federal authorities.

> *"Churches of every color are a traditional favorite of arsonists."*

WHY ARE THE CHURCHES BURNING?, the paper's lead headline asked, and its story, by Fields and fellow reporter Richard Price, demonstrated that the answer was far from simple.

No Single Answer

In analyzing what it found to be a "surge" in black-church burnings over the last eighteen months, *USA Today* ruled out "any possibility of a national or even regional conspiracy," and went on: "The evidence, in fact, suggests the opposite: there is no one answer to the frightening collection of torched churches across the South, black and white. The crimes stem from teenage vandalism, public drunkenness, derangement, revenge, insurance or other frauds and, to be sure, open or latent racial hatred. But no single thread runs through the black church arsons."

Yet secondly, the paper's investigation did isolate "two well-defined geographic clusters or 'arson zones' where black church arsons are up sharply" and the "patterns suggest racial motives." One was a two-hundred-mile oval in the mid-South that encompasses western Tennessee and northwestern Alabama, and the other "stretches across the Carolinas, where the rate of black church arson has tripled since 1993."

Outside those two clusters, which along with possible "copycat" burnings accounted for the recent upsurge of fires, the paper said its investigation "dispels the notion that an epidemic of racially driven arsons has swept the South during the mid-1990s. Of the sixty-four black-church fires examined, only four can conclusively be shown to be racially motivated. Fifteen others—most of them in the arson clusters—are consistent in some respects with racist burnings. Ten arsons clearly were not racist and evidence is strong that another seventeen had nothing to do with race." Of the remaining eighteen, *USA Today* found that four appeared to have been listed erroneously and the other fourteen offered no real clues.

USA Today also presented profiles of some church arsonists. They appeared to have acted from a variety of motives, the paper reported on July 1, 1996, and most of them were poor, white, uneducated, and often drunk.

In a phone interview some weeks after the investigative report, Fields was justifiably proud of the enterprise reporting he did on the church-burning story. He strongly believes that churches have been burning for a long time and that journalists never smelled the smoke. Yet he and Price uncovered another factor that complicates any racial calculations.

"The recent concern has risen in part," the two wrote, "because the nation stumbled upon a phenomenon that's gone on for decades and mistook it for something new. The phenomenon: churches of every color are a traditional favorite of arsonists. Although the pace has been declining in recent years, arsonists still torch an average of 520 churches and church-owned buildings a year, a rate of ten a week."

No Evidence of Conspiracy

Another national news organization, The Associated Press, followed a week later with an equally useful and thorough piece of public-service journalism. Based on a review of six years of federal, state, and local data, AP's report also questioned what had evolved in the preceding three months or so into the conventional wisdom about black-church burnings.

"Amid all the frightening images of churches aflame," the wire service reported on July 5, 1996, "amid all the fears of raging racism, a surprising truth emerges: There's little hard evidence of a sudden wave of racially motivated arsons against black churches in the South. . . . There is no evidence that most of the seventy-three black church fires recorded since 1995 can be blamed on a conspiracy or a general climate of racial hatred. Racism is the clear motivation in fewer than twenty cases.". . .

The Associated Press spelled out its findings:

• Largely because of a few nights' work by serial arsonists, there had been an eighteen-month jump in the number of church burnings. Such fires are relatively rare in most states, so arson sprees quickly alter the statistical picture. Louisiana, for example, had seven cases of black-church arsons all year; four of them occurred in one night in the Baton Rouge area.

• The number of white-church fires also has increased. Florida, Georgia, Tennessee, Oklahoma, and Virginia have seen more fires at white churches than at black churches since 1995.

• Evidence points to racially motivated arson in twelve to eighteen of the seventy-three fires the wire service counted since 1995, while racism is unlikely in fifteen of those black-church fires. (Black suspects were named in nine of those fifteen; another six of the fifteen churches were burned as part of arson sprees that included both white and black property.)

• In the remaining dozen cases where there have been arrests, the question of racism is more subtle. The gallery of suspects includes drunken teen-agers, devil worshippers, burglars, and three separate cases where firefighters are accused of setting blazes they then helped put out. . . .

A Complicated Truth

The truth we are left with about arson at black churches seems to be this: there has been an increase in the reported number of black-church burnings in the South. In some of those fires, racist hatred was the motive. But other causes also came into play, including vandalism and pyromania. White churches also burn. The Associated Press, in fact, counted seventy-five white-church fires and seventy-three black-church fires since 1995. If there are, as presumed, more white churches than black churches in the nation, the wire service pointed out, those numbers "suggest a bias." Yet there does not seem to be a widespread organized racist conspiracy, despite the efforts of some to portray one.

Comprehending the more complex truth, as *USA Today*'s Gary Fields points out, required healthy skepticism in the face of large claims, and good old-fashioned reporting. And it took hurry-up journalism's missing ingredient: time.

Claudia Smith Brinson, an editorial writer and columnist with *The State* in Columbia, South Carolina, points out another requirement for parsing out the facts: knowing the community. Brinson, who has closely followed the vandalism and fire at St. John Baptist and at other churches in the Columbia area, says that journalists, whether working on church fires or domestic violence or any other complex story, "should keep working backwards until they get to deep beginnings.". . .

In August 1996, it happened that a black teenager in Greenville, Texas, site of a cluster of fires in June, including two black-church fires, confessed to setting them. He did it, he told the police, because he was angry at his mother for not letting him stay with her, and because he claimed she used drugs.

The fires in Greenville had "deep beginnings," to use Brinson's phrase, in the experiences of a troubled youngster, experiences not unrelated to racism, perhaps, but not nearly so visible and obvious as the fires he confessed to lighting.

Blacks Have Made Significant Progress in Society

by Abigail Thernstrom and Stephan Thernstrom

About the authors: *Abigail and Stephan Thernstrom are coauthors of* America in Black and White: One Nation, Indivisible.

An American Dilemma, Gunnar Myrdal called the problem of race in his classic 1944 book. He saw a painful choice between American ideals and American racial practices.

But in 1944, 10 years before *Brown v. Board of Education*, most white Americans were not in much pain on the matter of race. Indeed, when asked in a survey that same year whether "Negroes should have as good a chance as white people to get any kind of job," the majority of whites said that "white people should have the first chance at any kind of job." Blacks belonged at the back of the employment bus, most whites firmly believed.

Much has changed since then. In the half century since Myrdal wrote *An American Dilemma,* there's been dramatic, heartening progress. An obvious historical point? Fighting words, it turns out. Or at best, astonishing.

Denying Progress

Historical allusions denying progress are a staple of racial discourse. Thus, best-selling author Andrew Hacker (as well as others) have referred to the "new slavery" in discussing welfare reform. In 1992, as speaker of the California assembly, Willie Brown saw the ghost of the Klan-supported poll tax lurking behind the movement for term limits. The end of Reconstruction is repeating itself, the Rev. Jesse Jackson lamented in response to the Republican congressional victories in 1994.

Yesterday and today, one and the same. Slavery, the Klan, the end of Reconstruction: an ongoing story. Decades of extraordinary change denied.

Reprinted from Abigail and Stephan Thernstrom, "Black Progress," *San Diego Union-Tribune,* September 21, 1997, p. G-1, by permission of the authors.

Such denial and doubts are a sure recipe for dangerous, racially-divisive despair—suggesting, as it does, that all the hard work of both blacks and whites has been for naught.

Black Status Has Improved

And yet, despite the rhetorical continuity, evidence that the status of blacks has been radically transformed is overwhelming. Just a half century ago it was a major violation of the southern social order for whites to address a black man as "Mr. Washington"—no less shake hands with him. Only a third of the nation's whites had no objection to a black with the same education and income moving into their block. In 1942 in the North, half of all whites believed blacks were not as intelligent as whites.

American apartheid in the South (little different from the South African version), a sharp color line in the North: one result was a black poverty rate in 1940 of 87 percent.

An accurate picture of the changing status of blacks from 1940 to 1970 reminds us of how far we have come in a relatively short period of time; how much there is to celebrate, even though the road ahead is still long. Racial problems today, however grave, are not the same as those of yesterday, and we need to understand the difference if we are to talk about them with a clear head.

> *"Evidence that the status of blacks has been radically transformed is overwhelming."*

In addition, the historical record has profound implications for today's debate about racial preferences. Too often it's assumed that the significant advances blacks have made in modern times all occurred in the 1960s and after, and that they were the result of civil rights protest, federal legislation, and affirmative action policies.

That assumption is wrong, we believe.

In fact, by numerous measures, black progress was greater in the pre-affirmative action decades than it has been in the years since. Black family income doubled in the two decades from 1940 to 1960. And while the fraction of black families with middle class incomes rose almost 40 points between 1940 and 1970, it has subsequently inched up only another 10 points.

At a slower pace, however, black advancement did continue. The conventional view both minimizes that ongoing progress and depicts slippage as an ever-present danger.

How can there be such a disconnect between reality and that perceived by so many others?

Progress Is Not a Handout

In part, we suspect, the much greater pessimism of our critics is closely related to their misunderstanding of the historical record. Those who view themselves as part of the civil rights community (and we include much of the media) see progress as the consequence of presidential action (President Harry Truman's desegregation of the armed forces, for instance), judicial decisions and federal civil rights legislation.

Given that perspective, no wonder that African Americans see their gains as exceedingly fragile. Convinced that progress has been almost entirely a handout by whites with political and judicial power, they fear that all will be lost without the strong and protective arm of the federal government, which, they believe, can no longer be counted on.

> *"Black progress was greater in the pre-affirmative action decades."*

But the real lesson of history, as we read it, is quite the opposite. The record of the decades from 1940 to 1970 suggests there is no reason to believe that blacks will sink without extraordinary protection against white and Asian competition in the form of racial double standards. There is no reason to think that the black middle class will shrink, or that the black poverty rate will climb.

Before the 1970s, blacks advanced without preferences. Since then, the impact of those preferences appears to have been marginal, much of the economic research suggests. Black progress, then, has not been a white handout, although changing white racial attitudes and the great civil rights legislation of the 1960s, as well as *Brown v. Board of Education* and its progeny certainly played a part.

But even in 1943, southern blacks were displaying a new assertiveness. One author depicted whites as shocked to find blacks suddenly expecting to be waited on in stores just as quickly as they were. Myrdal's *An American Dilemma* thus got one point terribly wrong. He depicted blacks as so beaten down by white racism, so stripped of all autonomy, individuality, and communal life, as to leave as a mystery how black advancement could have begun in the 1940s. Indeed, he left as an even greater puzzle how a disciplined and powerful mass movement for civil rights could have emerged in the 1950s and 1960s.

Myrdal's picture of black progress as entirely dependent on white goodwill was wrong, but his faith in the capacity of whites to change—a faith shared by Dr. Martin Luther King, the National Association for the Advancement of Colored People (NAACP) and other civil rights leaders and organizations—was right.

Change in White Attitudes

The transformation of white racial attitudes is part of the unrecognized story that begins in the early 1940s. By 1956, the number of northern whites skeptical about the level of black intelligence had dropped from approximately 50 percent to 17 percent. Ten years later, 71 percent of whites said they had no objection to a black "with the same income and education" moving into their block.

In the South, too, the signs of early change are startling. From 1940 to 1960 acceptance of school integration by white southerners jumped from 2 percent to

31 percent, and of integrated transportation from 4 percent to 52 percent. Black progress was thus the work of blacks and whites together. In fact, to lose that confidence in the moral capacity of whites, as so many in the civil rights community have now sadly done, is to give up on the possibility of continuing racial change. If racism is truly permanent, as Derrick Bell and others persist in arguing, then racial equality is a hopeless project, an unattainable ideal.

Actually, white racial attitudes have so radically changed that today 87 percent of blacks say they have a white friend, while 86 percent of whites report having a black friend. It has become not the least bit unusual for blacks and whites to have brought someone of the other race home to dine, and most blacks and whites say their neighborhood is racially mixed.

The racial divide has certainly not disappeared; the O.J. Simpson trial was a sobering reminder of that fact. But the ground gained should not be ignored. Even in the most intimate of relations, there has been substantial change. By 1993, 12 percent of all marriages contracted by African Americans were to a white.

Two Nations: Black and White, Separate, Hostile, and Unequal, Andrew Hacker called his best-selling book of a few years back. Gloom and doom on the racial front evidently sells, but our argument is quite different. We see one nation, much less unequal than it used to be, and by many measures, less hostile.

Political Attitudes

Our quarrel is with Hacker and others on the left, and with their going-nowhere picture of black America and white racial attitudes. But we also disagree with many on the right and their see-no-evil view.

It seems extraordinarily hard for liberals to say we have come a long way from the days of the Jim Crow South and an appallingly racist North. But it often seems hard for conservatives to say, yes, there has been a terrible history of racism in this country, and indeed that racism has not disappeared.

Conservatives seem to think that they concede too much if they acknowledge the ugliness of our racial history and the persistence of racism. They appear to fear that they will be forced to buy the whole system of racial preferences and indeed the whole argument for reparations if they admit the ugliness of the past.

And liberals, from their different perspective, are also blind to history. To admit dramatic progress, they seem to believe, is to invite white indifference. It's as if everything blacks

> *"Black progress ... has not been a white handout."*

now have rests on the fragile foundation of white guilt and an unwavering commitment to race-conscious policies.

We differ from most other writers on race in another respect. We are data devotees. We're not much interested in the anecdotes, the "telling" stories, that litter so much writing on race. We want reliable facts that answer such questions as: How many blacks work in professional jobs? How many black families have middle class incomes? How many now live in suburbia? How many black students are graduating from high school and attending college? Are whites voting for black politicians?

In a far-flung search for data on, for instance, demographic change, white racial attitudes, black and white life expectancy, homeownership, schooling, employment and earnings, inevitably we found good news and bad news.

> *"If racism is truly permanent, [as some believe,] . . . then racial equality is a hopeless project."*

The bad news is well known. The poverty rate for black Americans has been basically stagnant since the 1970s, for instance. In 1995, half of all murder victims in the United States were African Americans, although blacks are just one-eighth of the population. And so forth.

It is the good news that is insufficiently familiar. More than 40 percent of African Americans today consider themselves members of the middle class. Forty-two percent own their own homes, a figure that rises to 75 percent if we look just at black married couples. Black two-parent families earn only 13 percent less than those who are white. Almost a third of the black population lives in suburbia. And so on.

We have let the underclass define our notion of black America, and that image is very misleading.

Racial Preferences Must Be Eliminated

Discussions of race inevitably are inextricably intertwined with the question of racial preferences, a subject on which we have strong views. Racial preferences, we believe, have been bad for America; bad for blacks and bad for whites.

In fact, we are so opposed to racial classifications that we come close to arguing for their elimination from the U.S. Census, even though in our research we have heavily relied on census data ourselves. The census does not ask questions about religion. Why should it ask about race?

Indeed, we think ending racial preferences will be in itself a positive move, helping to bring blacks and whites together, reducing race-consciousness, which is already perniciously high.

"We cannot walk alone," Dr. King said in his wonderful 1963 "I Have a Dream" speech. The destiny of whites and blacks is inextricably entwined. But how to walk together? That question has lost none of its urgency in the 50 years since Myrdal wrote *An American Dilemma,* race remains our most important domestic issue.

Myrdal's work was full of hope; he believed fervently that racial equality was an attainable ideal. We, too, are unreconstructed optimists in the great tradition of Dr. King and his movement for racial justice.

Chapter 2

Is Racism Institutionalized in America?

Chapter Preface

In 1995, Jonny Gammage, a thirty-one-year-old black businessman, was stopped in Pittsburgh by five white police officers for "driving erratically." According to reports, Patrolman John Vojtas struck Gammage, inciting a confrontation that left Gammage dead from suffocation. As Gammage lay on the ground following the assault, Vojtas purportedly stated, "I hope he dies." In October 1996, an all-white jury acquitted Vojtas of involuntary manslaughter.

Incidents such as this have fueled charges that police aggressively pursue, brutalize, and even kill black men. Adversarial relations between the police and African Americans can be traced back to the 1800s, when slave patrols—the first organized police forces in the United States—were used to keep slaves in check. Almost two centuries later, the police's reputation is still tarnished in the eyes of blacks. Many African Americans attest that they are frequently pulled over for "routine checks," during which officers often make racial threats or instigate violence. Police critics contend that the practice of "profiling" blacks as criminals is an integral part of police force ideology, as is racist jargon. For example, one police officer in Torrance, California, testified to the department's use of the epithet "NIT—Nigger in Torrance."

Responding to accusations of racism, some police officers admit to using "aggressive tactics," but they claim that these tactics are necessary in light of the prevalence of violent crime. "Simple traffic stops often result in crimes being solved and wanted criminals apprehended," says one officer. Other officers point to a movement away from military-style policing and its racist connotations. They allege that many departments vigorously enforce an antiracist philosophy within the ranks and require officers to participate in sensitivity training. The new policies, claim police supporters, do not tolerate racial targeting of any kind. Some departments maintain, however, that police reform, no matter how stringent, cannot always modify the covert racist attitudes held by individual officers.

The police force is perhaps the most prominent group under attack for institutionalized racism (an institution's widespread acceptance of racist beliefs). The following chapter provides diverse perspectives on whether the police force and other American institutions are racist.

Blacks Face Economic Discrimination

by Marc Breslow

About the author: *Marc Breslow is an editor at* Dollars and Sense, *a bi-monthly magazine that examines economic issues from a liberal perspective.*

During the 1960s and early 1970s the standard of living for blacks improved greatly. But since the mid-1970s, years in which Republicans have dominated the U.S. presidency, real wages for blacks have fallen sharply, both in absolute terms and relative to whites. Unemployment for blacks has risen, while remaining at more than twice white levels. Among male teenage African Americans the trend has been disastrous—the jobless having risen from 28% in 1973 to 40% in 1993.

Racists claim that such trends can be explained by genetics, or by the moral failure of black families. Conservatives blame the government for interfering with free markets, arguing that policies such as the minimum wage and welfare have reduced the available jobs and destroyed work incentives. And there are explanations that say whites have more "human capital"—education and experience—than blacks, so they are worth more on the job market.

But the truth is that African Americans have faced both racial discrimination and class oppression. As the American economy and the federal government have favored those with property income and high educational levels, those with neither, regardless of their race, have suffered. Since African Americans began with less wealth and education than whites twenty years ago, they have been hurt disproportionately by the recent trends.

The Decline of Equal Opportunity

Equal educational opportunity, never a fact, has receded as a goal under the pressure of federal and state budget deficits. With funding for public education still largely a function of local property taxes, residential segregation means that access to quality education is based on the class status and race of one's

Reprinted from Marc Breslow, "The Racial Divide Widens: Why African-American Workers Have Lost Ground," *Dollars and Sense*, January/February 1995, by permission of *Dollars and Sense*, a progressive economics magazine published six times a year. First-year subscriptions cost $18.95 and may be ordered by writing to *Dollars and Sense*, One Summer St., Somerville, MA 02143.

parents. And while colleges have become much more expensive, financial assistance is far scarcer.

Meanwhile, racism has persisted and sharpened. For a brief period during the late 1960s and early 1970s equal employment opportunity, affirmative action, and equal housing laws helped the job opportunities and living standards of blacks to rise greatly. But since then, as enforcement of these statutes has weakened, African Americans have faced renewed discrimination in applying for jobs, in gaining promotions, in finding housing, and in applying for mortgages.

As unemployment has risen for all U.S. workers, blacks, who have always been at the end of the employment line, have been the last hired and the first fired. When the American economy provided close to full employment, making all workers more desirable, white employers hired blacks even when they might have preferred not to. But when there are many applicants for every available job, it is far easier for employers to discriminate—and to indulge the racist preferences of their white employees and customers.

Flawed Explanations

The blatantly racist explanation for racial inequality has been around since the slave trade—blacks are stupid. It's not anyone's fault, you see, it's just in their genes. This is the premise of *The Bell Curve*, by Charles Murray and the late Richard Herrnstein. Their thesis rests on the well-known fact that African Americans score lower, on average, than whites on IQ tests. Never mind that the tests are biased to begin with, or that how one does on any test is largely a result of environmental factors rather than genes—such as the quality of schools one attended, the level of prenatal and pediatric health care received, and the safety of one's neighborhood.

But many economists, few of whom would buy Murray's genetic fantasies, still assert that inequality is a valid result of differences in "human capital" between races—the levels of education, training, and experience that employers value and pay for. It is true that African Americans have, on average, less education than whites. As of 1992, 22% of white Americans had graduated from college, while 12% of blacks had done so. Similarly, 81% of whites and 68% of blacks were high school graduates. Such statistics tend to shift the burden from employers, who hire the most qualified workers, to other forces in society that, for example, deny blacks equal access to education.

> *"Blacks, who have always been at the end of the employment line, have been the last hired and the first fired."*

These differences in graduation rates, however, can explain only the *continuation* of historic inequality in wages and unemployment levels. They cannot explain *increases* in the gap between white and black wage levels that have taken place in recent decades. In fact, the gap should be decreasing, because the "human capital" of African Americans, as shown by formal education, has been getting closer to that of whites. Black high school graduation rates more than doubled from 1970 to 1992, while for whites the increase was about 50%. And among blacks between the ages of 25 and 29, who are among those young people most susceptible to unemployment, the graduation rate in 1992 was almost equal to that for all Americans of those ages.

Moreover, standardized test scores have risen for blacks compared to whites during the past two decades. The National Assessment of Educational Progress, for example, reported that the gap between reading scores for 17-year-old whites and blacks fell from 50 points in 1979–80 to 30 points in 1989–90 (when whites averaged 297 and blacks 267). In mathematics, the gap fell from 38 to 21 points.

Is the Economy to Blame?

How to explain increasing inequality if diverging levels of education and skills are not the reason? Some economists pin the blame on the overall worsening of the U.S. economy during the past 20 years. Historically, African-American earnings and employment have risen during economic booms and fallen during recessions.

For example, male black teenagers had an unemployment rate of 41.0% in 1985. This fell dramatically to

> *"In 1989 [young black college graduates] earned 17% less than [white graduates]."*

32.1% during the hot economy of 1990, but rose again to 40.1% in 1993. Is there any reason to believe that the educational qualifications, work habits, or prison records of African-American youth improved from 1985 to 1990, and then fell again? No. Employers simply hire according to the demand for their products and services, with blacks at the end of the line during both booms and recessions.

Several analyses comparing dozens of metropolitan areas with differing levels of unemployment have found that the relative position of blacks improves with a strong local economy. One such study, by economist Richard Freeman of Harvard University, found that when overall unemployment declines by one percentage point, the employment rate increases by 1.9 percentage points for all youth, but by 4.3 points for black youth.

But while U.S. economic performance does have a strong impact on African Americans, it is less clear that the deterioration of their status compared to whites can be blamed solely on recent macroeconomic trends. The ratios of black to white earnings and unemployment have not varied consistently with the business cycle.

Explaining Inequality

In order to test the "human capital" theories, several researchers have compared whites and blacks who have the same levels of education and experience.

Freeman and John Bound, of the University of Michigan, conducted one influential study, finding that even while "controlling" for education and experience among men, large white-black earnings differentials have increased over time. They argue that the fault for the worsening situation of African Americans lies with "the economic decline of inner cities, loss of manufacturing jobs, fall in the real minimum wage, and drop in union density.". . .

What does this mean? First, African Americans were stuck in industries whose employment and real wages were in decline during the past two decades. This was particularly true for manufacturing, which provided a large fraction of those well-paying jobs held by black males. Blacks have lost their jobs, and failed to find new ones, at far greater rates than whites—due to being at the bottom of seniority rankings and at the end of hiring lines.

> *"Discrimination against blacks appears to be highest in the types of jobs offering the highest wages and future income potential."*

As a result, black high school graduates and dropouts in the Midwest, where such industries as auto and steel manufacturing were in crisis, fared particularly badly. The wages of black males in the Midwest fell 23% relative to whites from 1973 to 1989. Blacks began the period with proportionately more workers employed in durable goods manufacturing than whites, but by 1988 had far lower employment than whites.

Second, even within the same industry, *and with the same educational levels and years of experience,* the occupational status of African Americans fell relative to whites. Bound and Freeman state that "In the 1970s young black college graduates were as likely to be managers or professionals as were young white college graduates; in 1988–89 black graduates were thirteen percentage points less likely to be in those occupations than whites." From 1974 through 1977 young black college graduates actually earned slightly more, on average, than white graduates, but in 1989 they earned 17% less than whites. This was a far sharper drop than for high school graduates and dropouts—belying the notion that it is only those with little education who have faced problems in the modern U.S. economy.

Third, as the proportion of workers represented by unions has fallen, wages have dropped, with severe consequences for black workers, who were overrepresented in unions. From 1983 to 1992, the proportion of white workers represented by unions fell from 22% to 17%, while the rate for blacks fell from 32% to 24%. And finally, the fall in the real value of the minimum wage has hurt African Americans, who are more concentrated in occupations paying the minimum than are whites.

These results make it difficult to claim, as do some conservative economists, that unions and the minimum wage cause black unemployment by forcing employers to pay more than they believe workers are worth. Since the real minimum wage fell sharply in the 1980s (from $5.28 per hour in 1980 to $4.25 in 1992, in 1992 dollars), and the number of union jobs did also, employment opportunities for low-paid workers should have expanded, not declined.

Racism Renewed

The question remains *why* black men have been stuck in declining industries and in lower-paid occupations. A reactionary could answer that they are all on drugs, in prison, or have poor work habits. But a more convincing answer is that racism remains strong in America. As economic opportunities have declined, blacks have returned to the end of the queue. When there are several or many well-qualified applicants for any decent job, all of whom have the requisite educational backgrounds, employers can easily discriminate. Bound and Freeman argue that enforcement of equal employment opportunity and affirmative action laws in the late 1960s and early 1970s helped African Americans to make large gains. When enforcement of these laws became lax in more recent years, discrimination surged.

Some jobs, such as in the skilled trades, are still allocated by formal apprenticeship systems that largely exclude blacks. Many other positions, particularly professional ones, are filled through networking among friends and colleagues (the "old boys network"), rather than through broad-based advertisements—sometimes with discriminatory intent, but with discriminatory results in any case.

A study published by the Urban Institute in 1991 provides the "smoking gun" to document the continued prevalence of racism by employers. The Institute used a "hiring audit" methodology to directly test for discrimination in hiring. Pairs of testers, one black and one white, were carefully matched in terms of age, physical size, education, experience, and "such intangibles as openness, apparent energy level, and articulateness." Each pair of auditors then applied for the same entry-level jobs, as identified in newspaper classified advertisements. Discrimination was evaluated by comparing the experiences of each pair.

The Institute conducted 476 individual audits in Chicago and Washington, D.C., using ten pairs of testers, during the summer of 1990. The method identified three stages to a hiring process—obtaining an application, getting an interview, and being hired. The study found that in 20% of the cases the white member advanced further in the hiring process, while the black member of an audit pair did so only 7% of the time. In 15% of the cases only the white member received a job offer, while in 5% of the cases only the black member got an offer. These differences might not appear dramatic, but they could be large enough to explain most of the difference in unemployment rates between blacks and whites.

> *"American society continues to provide overwhelming advantages to . . . whites, the privileged race."*

The Institute also concluded that "minorities are more likely to encounter discrimination in entry-level clerical jobs and in jobs involving client sales and service than in blue collar positions . . . discrimination against blacks appears to be highest in the types of jobs offering the highest wages and future income potential."

Such discrimination may not be solely a function of racism by employers. Businesses also respond to racist attitudes by existing (white) employees—as shown by several surveys documenting such discriminatory preferences—and by their customers. As the Urban Institute noted, discrimination was greater for jobs where there would be interaction with customers.

"Soft" Skills

Evidence for more complex forms of racism comes from other surveys, in which employers indicate that even though African Americans may have improved their "hard" skills through education, they still lack "soft" skills that are important to businesses. Philip Moss and Chris Tilly, both economists at the University of Massachusetts-Lowell, interviewed employers in the auto parts manufacturing, retail clothing, insurance, and public sector industries in Los Angeles and Detroit. They found that almost as many employers were concerned about soft skills, such as ability to interact with customers and co-workers (friendliness, speaking skills, appearance) and motivation (enthusiasm, commitment, dependability), as they were with "hard" skills. Many of those interviewed saw black men as deficient in such skills.

"When blacks and whites were equally creditworthy . . . , blacks were 56% more likely to be turned down for mortgages than were whites."

Ability to make co-workers and customers feel comfortable is important to any firm. But as Moss and Tilly note, "Soft skills are related to culture, so that one part of the perception [of black men] appears to be due to an inappropriate reading of cultural differences as ability differences. Decisions to hire whites instead of blacks are the likely result when employers make decisions on this basis, at least when equal opportunity statutes are not aggressively enforced.

Equal Opportunity?

The Bound/Freeman and Urban Institute analyses take as a given that, on average, African Americans have less education and experience than whites. So these analysts examined wage and hiring losses that blacks suffer even when compared to equally qualified whites. But it is just as important to ask why differences in "human capital" persist, despite decades of supposed commitment to providing equal opportunity to all members of American society.

The truth is that American society continues to provide overwhelming advantages to the children of privileged classes, and to whites, the privileged race. Not only in applying for jobs, but in every other area of life, including education, housing, and health care, blacks begin with severe disadvantages. By the time a young black worker reaches the job market he or she is, on average, far less likely to have the skills and attitudes demanded by employers. This is not due to genetics, nor to an inferior culture, but to the drawbacks of being low-income and of the "wrong" race in America.

Equal opportunity in education is far from a reality. With public school funding dependent primarily on local taxes, usually property taxes, throughout the United States, support for schools closely correlates with the income levels in a community. While many have argued that spending does not equal educational quality, one would be hard-pressed to find parents who would voluntarily send their children to lower-spending school districts.

In recent years several state supreme courts have ruled that the financing systems for public schools unconstitutionally deprive low-income children of equal educational opportunity. In response, state governments have made attempts to "share the wealth," yet these have been fought tooth and nail by the more affluent school districts.

Additional Barriers

The success of young adults in the job market is also influenced by other environmental factors, such as the proximity of one's neighborhood to available jobs. Many researchers argue that there is a "spatial mismatch" between job locations, which are increasingly in the suburbs, and the residences of African Americans, who are largely in the central cities and lack cars to get to the jobs.

Such residential segregation is enforced both by overt discrimination in the housing market and by class-based housing restrictions. Zoning laws legally prevent moderate-income housing from being built in the suburbs. Landlords and realtors regularly refuse to rent to black tenants. Even in recent years, blacks moving into working-class white neighborhoods have often been harassed into leaving, at times under threats of violence.

It is now undeniable that banks and mortgage companies discriminate against blacks applying for home mortgages. A study by the Federal Reserve Bank of Boston showed that, even when blacks and whites were equally creditworthy (in terms of credit history, income, and size of loan applied for), blacks were 56% more likely to be turned down for mortgages than were whites.

Employment, schools, and housing are all elements of the economic crisis facing African Americans. The dominant white society can deal with this crisis by the racist methods which are now omnipresent in political platforms—denying welfare benefits, reducing funding for social programs, and building more prisons. Such a course can only lead to further racial polarization, in which blacks take the brunt of an inequitable and unstable capitalist economy. Or America can stop blaming the victims, and provide the jobs, educational funding, and anti-discrimination enforcement needed to make equal opportunity a reality.

The Criminal Justice System Is Racist

by Nkechi Taifa

About the author: *Nkechi Taifa serves as a clinical instructor and director of the Public Service Program at Howard University School of Law in Washington, D.C. She is also cochair of the Criminal Justice Section of the National Conference of Black Lawyers.*

The issue of race as a key influence in the manner in which the criminal justice system in this country is administered must be honestly acknowledged. Invariably, people of color are subjected to unwarranted disparate treatment at every stage of the criminal justice process—from the selective deployment of law enforcement personnel to communities of color to police misconduct and brutality; from stops and arrests premised on racially based profiles to prosecutorial discretion in decisions of charging and pretrial detention; from the lack of diversity in jury pools to the improper use of peremptory challenges to remove Blacks from juries; and from the racial disparity in mandatory minimum sentences to the racial application of the death penalty. Such disparate treatment is a direct reflection of the institutionalization of racism in the criminal justice system.

Defining the Justice System

A special summit of the American Bar Association, although not expressly utilizing the term "institutionalized racism," defines racial and ethnic bias in the justice system as "measured by statutes, rules, policies, procedures, practices, events, conduct and other factors, operating alone or together, that have a disproportionate impact upon one or more persons/people of color." In elucidating this concept, the ABA Summit found it essential to define comprehensively the parameters of "the justice system" to illustrate better how the "contaminating" effect of racism permeates the system as a whole. In "Achieving Justice in a Diverse America: A Summit on Racial and Ethnic Bias in the Justice System," the ABA stated:

Reprinted from Nkechi Taifa, "Racism in the Criminal Justice System," *Christian Social Action*, June 1996, by permission of the author and of *Christian Social Action*.

"The justice system includes the courts and the interrelated components that take part in the administration of justice, including law enforcement agencies, prosecution and defense agencies, correctional departments, law firms that provide representation in courts, and the law schools that produce lawyers.

"This broad definition is required because individuals and various policies and practices of those components of the system continuously intersect. To the extent that race and ethnic factors come into play, those encounters will be negatively viewed by racial and ethnic minorities whom we describe as people of color. Bias in any of the components of the system reaches into and actually, or perceptually, contaminates the system as a whole. Thus, the contaminating effort of bias in any component of the system, if unremedied, can have a profound and deleterious effect, not only on people of color, but also an effect on the integrity of the entire justice system.

> *"Bias in any of the components of the [criminal justice] system . . . contaminates the system as a whole."*

"Our definition, therefore, rejects the limitations of 'active' bias to discrete and provable instances of intentional bigotry that may be remedied by making the specific victim whole and imposes sanctions on the wrongdoer. We view our challenge as extending also to passive bias where it has a systemic effect on the administration of justice."

Explosion in Incarceration

One product of this systemic racism can be found in this country's unprecedented explosion in incarceration. The United States has the dubious distinction of having surpassed the one million mark in its prison population. Over half (55 percent) of that population is Black, although African Americans comprise only 12 percent of the United States population. Black men in the United States are incarcerated at a rate five times higher than Blacks in former *apartheid* South Africa, with one out of every three young Black men either imprisoned, on probation or parole at any given moment. Alarmingly, there are more young Black men in prison and jail than in college.

One can only wonder how many of those one in three African American youth were victims of the Mark Fuhrmans of the country? [Mark Fuhrman was one of the Los Angeles Police Department officers who investigated the O.J. Simpson case.] How many of the "one in three" were the subjects of racial profiles or the result of racially selective prosecution? How many were victims of police brutality? How many were subjected to exorbitant bail or preventively detained pretrial? How many were not tried by a jury of their peers? How many were denied the right to higher education or [rehabilitative] treatment in prison?

Disturbingly, the Supreme Court has been unwilling to tackle the issue of racism in the criminal justice system head-on. When presented with a golden opportunity in the 1987 case of *McClesky v. Kemp,* where the double standard of justice in death penalty decisions was conclusively demonstrated, the Court, although not disputing the evidence that race more likely than not influenced sentencing decisions in capital cases in Georgia, ruled that Warren McClesky was not entitled to relief. Ostensibly, the High Court realized if it sought to remedy racism in the application of the death penalty, it might be constrained likewise to remedy racism at other key stages of the criminal justice process as well. Warren McClesky was executed.

> *"Black men in the United States are incarcerated at a rate five times higher than Blacks in former* apartheid *South Africa."*

The Supreme Court [has had] the opportunity to consider once again an issue involving institutionalized racism in the criminal justice system in *US v. Armstrong.* There charges involving crack cocaine offenses were dismissed against five Black defendants who alleged that the Los Angeles US Attorney's office selectively prosecuted them based on their race. [On May 13, 1996, the Supreme Court ruled that the black defendants had not proven that they were prosecuted on the basis of race.]

Current federal penalties for the possession and distribution of crack cocaine are 100 times more severe than sentences for the exact same amount of powder cocaine. The weight of the evidence, however, has not found crack to be *more* addictive or dangerous than the powdered form of cocaine, and has found no medical or scientific distinction between the two. Indeed, although the greatest number of documented crack users are White, national drug enforcement and prosecutorial practices have resulted in the "war on drugs" being fought almost exclusively in inner-city Black communities. In Fiscal Year 1994, this resulted in the 96.5 percent of those sentenced federally for crack cocaine offenses being people of color. . . .

Using the wildly differing penalties between crack and powder cocaine as an example, US Sentencing Commissioner Michael Gelacak recently predicted:

". . . (We) are creating what I perceive to be a sort of a time bomb in our penitentiary system. We are creating a class of individuals who are going to jail for 10/15/20/30 years at a time and who, when they get there, are asking themselves the question and knowing the answer, and the answer is that they are there for an unjust reason; that they have been singled out and haven't done anything different than the cocaine abuser. Those people are not going to be happy campers when they come out of jail. We have created a societal problem that hasn't hit yet, but it is going to at some point down the road."

Long-Range Implications

The long-range implications of what is increasingly becoming the "criminalization of a race" are shuddering. Increased incarceration will not only result in more Blacks having stigmatizing felony records insuring negative consequences for future employment, it will mean virtual disenfranchisement for large segments of African Americans. Such long-term impact on voting rights—coupled with the concomitant disruption and disintegration of families, obliteration of vital reproductive years, termination of parental rights and diminished life prospects—results in incalculable damages to African American people.

It is not too strong to characterize the infliction of these conditions of life upon diasporic Africans in America as genocidal. Although not as visually evident as the wholesale annihilation of a people, or the kidnapping and enslavement of a race, these consequences nevertheless conform to the internationally accepted definition of genocide, which includes not only "killing members of a group" and "causing serious bodily or mental harm to members of a group," but also "deliberately inflicting on the group conditions of life calculated to bring about their physical destruction in whole or in part."

Indeed, resort to the international arena to attempt to bring focus to egregious US policies and practices is increasing. In a letter to former Secretary of State Warren Christopher, three human rights organizations cautioned that continuation of the disparity in cocaine sentences and other issues of race discrimination in the US criminal justice system constitute possible violations of the International Convention on the Elimination of All Forms of Racial Discrimination (CERD), which condemns laws and practices with an invidious racially discriminatory effect, regardless of intent.

"Call to Action" Issued

Numerous groups have outlined recommendations to combat the unequal administration of justice in America. The National Commission on Crime and Justice has issued a "Call to Action" that advocated several areas for change. In addition to massive public education, that body called for the implementation of cultural sensitivity training programs for persons at all levels of the criminal justice system, the establishment of independent monitoring programs and civilian complaint review boards to oversee allegations of police brutality and misconduct, an increased implementation of community-based alternatives to incarceration and well-funded, viable treatment programs.

The commission's "Call to Action" also stressed the importance of family impact studies, which review the potential impact of incarceration on the family of the convicted person. The commission also cautioned that

> *"[The] consequences [of racism in the criminal justice system] . . . conform to the internationally accepted definition of genocide."*

increased prison construction must be halted and resources channeled in directions of crime prevention. It demanded that prisoners have access to programs that combine education, life survival skills, vocational training and stress management. Furthermore, it said that when they are released, they must not be discriminated against in employment, housing, education or access to services on the basis of their prior imprisonment. . . .

However, while policies and programs such as those discussed above are critical to initiating change in the criminal justice system, until the infection of racism is removed from society's institutions as a whole, equal justice under the law will remain an elusive ideal.

It is tragic that the 100th anniversary of *Plessy v. Ferguson* finds this country still committed to the imposition of discriminatory laws and the continuation of unjust policies and practices. Creation of a criminal justice system truly worthy of the title "justice" requires the elimination of systemic racism and a national resolve to confront honestly the issue of crime in society.

Environmental Racism Threatens Minorities

by Dorceta E. Taylor

About the author: *Dorceta E. Taylor teaches environmental sociology at Washington State University.*

Hazel Johnson lives in Altgeld Gardens, a predominantly black housing project on Chicago's Far South Side. She refers to the neighborhood of 10,000 residents as a "Toxic Doughnut" because the homes are encircled by landfills, factories and other industrial sites that emit toxic and/or noxious fumes. West of the Doughnut, the coke ovens of Acme Steel discharge benzene into the air, to the south is Dolton's municipal landfill, to the east is Waste Management's landfill, and to the north lie beds of city sewage sludge. There are 50 abandoned hazardous dump sites within a six-mile radius of the neighborhood. The toxic stew around the Doughnut is so potent that Illinois inspectors aborted an expedition in one of the dumping lagoons when their boat began to disintegrate.

Illness was common in the area, but it wasn't until her husband died of lung cancer and other family and friends became ill that Hazel wondered if the death and illnesses were linked to the environment. She surveyed 1,000 of her neighbors and was astounded at the number of cancers, birth deformities, premature deaths, skin rashes, eye irritation, and respiratory illnesses that they reported. Hazel and the group she founded, People for Community Recovery (PCR), contacted the City of Chicago about the findings and urged it to investigate the illnesses. The City conducted a controversial study that found high rates of cancer among African Americans on Chicago's South Side, but did not investigate whether the rate was higher than that for African Americans elsewhere, or whether the health effects were related to the toxins in the area.

Dissatisfied with the findings, PCR commissioned its own study, and persuaded the federal Agency for Toxic Disease Registry to do a health study. Meanwhile, because the neighborhood was not connected to Chicago's water supply system, residents suspected that some of the health problems were

Reprinted from Dorceta E. Taylor, "Environmental Justice: The Birth of a Movement," *Dollars and Sense*, March/April 1996, by permission of *Dollars and Sense*, a progressive economics magazine published six times a year. First-year subscriptions cost $18.95 and may be ordered by writing to *Dollars and Sense*, One Summer St., Somerville, MA 02143.

caused by contamination of their well water. PCR lobbied for and obtained a hookup to municipal water pipes. Then, after discovering that Waste Management wanted to expand its landfill, PCR staged a series of protests (with the help of Greenpeace) that blocked the expansion.

The Toxic Doughnut is but one of many environmentally hazardous areas where poor and working-class people make their homes. Community activists in the burgeoning "environmental justice" movement have given names like "Street of Death," "Cancer Alley," and "Death Valley" to similar areas.

Organizations such as the Sierra Club, Audubon Society, Wilderness Society, and Nature Conservancy focus much of their attention on wildlife and wilderness preservation, and attract a mostly white, upper-middle class following. In contrast, environmental justice groups recruit a broad coalition of working- and middle-class activists from various racial backgrounds. Such organizations focus on toxic contamination, occupational safety, and the siting of noxious and hazardous facilities.

Groups whose members are people of color, on which this viewpoint focuses, are a vital component of the environmental justice movement. They have brought national attention to environmental racism (when people of color suffer disproportionately from health hazards) and environmental blackmail (when communities are forced to choose between protecting their health or losing their jobs). Until people of color made these terms commonplace in environmental circles, more traditional environmental activists paid little attention to policies that led to grave impacts on minority communities.

Environmental Racism

There is ample evidence that the operations of the Environmental Protection Agency (EPA) and other federal and state agencies have had discriminatory impacts on communities of color. A 1992 *National Law Journal* study, for example, found that fines for hazardous waste violations under the Resource Conservation and Recovery Act varied greatly between white and minority areas. On average, companies were charged $336,000 for violations in white neighborhoods, but only $55,000 in minority neighborhoods. Similar imbalances held for violations of other environmental laws.

> *"Illinois inspectors aborted an expedition in one of the dumping lagoons when their boat began to disintegrate."*

The study also showed that the EPA waited longer to evaluate whether dangers in minority areas should be placed on the National Priorities List of "Superfund" sites, and once evaluated, the agency was less likely to place such sites on the list. One reason is that EPA's "Hazard Ranking System" scores sites individually, so that it fails to take into account the cumulative effects of having several hazardous sites near a poor community. And even for those designated, it took less than 10 years to clean up sites in white neighborhoods, but between 12 and 14 years for sites in minority areas.

The courts have also responded badly to environmental justice cases. Even when communities have shown that there is a discriminatory pattern of siting facilities, the courts contend that simply proving discriminatory impact is not enough. To win a suit, communities must prove that the offending corporation or agency *intended* to discriminate when they made siting decisions.

Examples abound. In Houston, six out of eight municipal incinerators were placed in predominantly African American communities. During a 20-year period in King and Queen County, Virginia, all the landfills were placed within one mile of communities that were at least 95% African American. But in both cases, the courts ruled against the communities which brought lawsuits over these issues.

A Viable Movement

This failure of government to protect people of color in the face of increasing environmental threats, along with the dismissive attitude of corporate decision-makers, led to the growth of the environmental justice movement. Also important has been dissatisfaction by grassroots activists with the agenda of mainstream environmental organizations. Some of these are direct-action-oriented groups like Greenpeace and Earth First! that focused their attention primarily on whales, nuclear disarmament and forest preservation.

> *"On average, companies were charged $336,000 for violations in white neighborhoods, but only $55,000 in minority neighborhoods."*

Others are legal, technocratic, and lobbyist-oriented associations like the Natural Resources Defense Council and the Environmental Defense Fund.

Although many organizations formed during the 1960s and 1970s began as grassroots groups critical of the reform agenda of the pre-1960s environmental organizations, most eventually adopted similar agendas and lost their close ties to the grass roots. Like their predecessors, these associations lacked racial and social class diversity and failed to adopt an environmental justice agenda.

Filling the vacuum, people of color environmental justice organizations have grown rapidly in recent years—despite the failure of the mainstream to recognize them. As late as 1994 only five people of color groups were listed in the Conservation Directory, and none were listed in the Gale Environmental Sourcebook. Yet in the same year, the People of Color Environmental Groups Directory contained over 300 such organizations.

Roots of Struggle

Organizations devoted to combatting environmental racism emerged out of struggles for social, political, and economic justice. Native American groups, for example, contending with the erosion of cultural values and treaty rights, have used these issues to call attention to the environmental hazards on their reservations. In one case, the Navajos living near Rio Puerco, New Mexico, face increased health risks from the numerous uranium mines around them, which contaminate their drinking water and animals. As a result, the Navajos have developed a strong environmental justice agenda.

> *"[Black communities in 'Cancer Alley'] have high rates of cancer, birth defects, spontaneous abortions, infant mortality, and respiratory illnesses."*

Many African American associations and leaders have their roots in the Civil Rights movement. Some, like the Gulf Coast Tenants Association (GCTA), which was founded to improve housing conditions for Blacks, have taken on environmental justice agendas. Working in and around "Cancer Alley," the 90-mile stretch running along the Mississippi River from Baton Rouge to New Orleans, and home to about one-fourth of the chemical manufacturing plants in the United States, the GCTA constantly communicates with communities in which chemical spills and "accidental" releases of toxins are routine. These communities have high rates of cancers, birth defects, spontaneous abortions, infant mortality, and respiratory illnesses.

Latinos in the farmworker movement have made the link between labor and environmental justice struggles into a key organizing tool. Farmworkers in California and other parts of the South and West, through their participation in the United Farm Workers union, have launched successful grape boycotts and focused the nation's attention on the harmful effects of pesticides. They have documented illnesses from pesticide poisoning, including death, infertility, birth defects and miscarriages, and respiratory infections.

Similarly, Asian Americans concerned about immigrant rights and hazardous working conditions in the computer and garment industries have formed environmental justice groups. These include the Asian Women's Advocates and the Santa Clara Center for Occupational Safety and Health, both in California.

Throughout the United States, environmental justice groups are now able to mobilize many people and to raise questions about environmental racism in corporate decision making, government policies, and within the environmental movement itself. They are increasingly effective at disrupting the status quo on the siting of dangerous facilities. As a result, many are taking notice of these organizations and are either incorporating them into the environmental dialogue, or attempting to discredit their claims and destroy their credibility. We can expect continued struggle in the years ahead.

The Media Disregard Black Crime Victims

by **Peter Downs**

About the author: *Peter Downs is a freelance writer based in St. Louis, Missouri.*

In late 1995, Eddie Burton faced the cameras to send out a plea for information on the abduction and murder of young LaChrisha "C.J." Jones. To his right, C.J.'s mother placed a black and yellow ribbon on the site where the body of the 17-year-old African American was found 10 months before. Once the cameras stopped rolling, Burton, a spokesman for Families Advocating Safe Streets (FASS), an organization of clergy, concerned citizens and African American support groups, gave the assembled press corps a piece of his mind. He angrily contrasted the lack of attention from the St. Louis media at the time of Jones' murder with the week of headlines that followed the abduction and murder of a 22-year-old white woman eight months later.

"Black victims don't get the attention," Burton vented, so their families "feel the press and the police don't care." The press conference's organizer, Jeanette Culpepper, who founded FASS after her own son was murdered, agreed. "When a black kills a white, all hell breaks loose," she said. "But when it's black on black, it's all right."

The *St. Louis Post-Dispatch*'s index bears out Burton's and Culpepper's claims. In the three weeks following the disappearance of 9-year-old Kimbre Young in 1993, for example, the newspaper ran only two stories on the African American girl's case. Five months later Cassidy Senter, a 10-year-old Caucasian girl, was the second to disappear from a suburban neighborhood. In the four weeks following her disappearance the newspaper ran more than 23 stories about her.

White Victims Receive More Attention

It appears there has been little research on the issue of racial imbalances in reporting on crime victims. But the data that are available indicate a real disparity

Reprinted from Peter Downs, "Paying More Attention to White Crime Victims," *American Journalism Review*, December 1995, by permission of the *American Journalism Review*.

that is pervasive in many American cities.

A 1994 Chicago study on violence in television news and "reality" programming (shows such as "COPS" and "Rescue 911") by Robert Entman, then an associate professor of communications at Northwestern University, found that, on average, stories about white victims of violent crimes lasted 74 percent longer than stories about black victims. The total time given to white victims was 2.8 times more than the total time devoted to both black and Hispanic victims.

"In comparable cases, you will find a greater number of column inches or seconds on TV for white victims than for black victims anywhere in the Midwest," says Sonia R. Jarvis, professor of communications at Washington, D.C.'s George Washington University.

Dr. Alvin Poussaint, a Harvard University psychiatrist, says anti-black bias in reporting on murder victims "isn't arguable." No newspaper he's seen "isn't guilty of giving more attention and sympathy to white murder victims than to black murder victims," he says, "giving even more sympathy to the white victim if the perpetrator is black."

Tim Larson, news director at KSDK-TV in St. Louis, admits that the critics are right. But he says the media are caught in a double bind. If a news organization emphasizes reports on black victims, he says, "we get criticized for only covering crimes in the black community."

Not so, counters Jarvis. "We're not suggesting that the media report more crime or that whites get less coverage," she says. "We're suggesting that black deaths also get treated [with a] sense of loss."

Racist Assumptions

Many argue that prejudice and stereotyping inevitably play a role in the media's coverage of black crime. Marsha Houston, professor of communications at Tulane University, says the "killing of a white person is always treated as a significant loss," while the killing of a black person is usually dismissed with an "assumption that that person was involved in the drug scene" and is not worth reporting.

Jarvis adds that this assumption holds true across the country. The only exception she's seen was in the East Coast media, she says, when it reported the death of Len Bias, who had just been drafted by the Boston Celtics. In general, she says, the news media depict African Americans as "throwaway people who can be ignored."

> *"When a black kills a white, all hell breaks loose. . . . But when it's black on black, it's all right."*

Jim Amoss, editor of the *New Orleans Times-Picayune*, argues that any such bias is probably inadvertent. "Most metropolitan dailies are essentially white-run organizations," he says, "and still, in 1995, white readers and editors gravitate to whites as their own kind. Their hearts go out more to white crime victims than to black victims."

Arthur Silverblatt, professor of communications at St. Louis' Webster University, says that economics, not prejudice, is at the heart of decisions to play up homicide stories with white victims. He says that such decisions derive from competition for viewers with money. "As the white community is the community with more income," he says, "they are the people whose viewership matters more."

Is Coverage Improving?

Mike Ward, news director at WMAQ Channel 5 in Chicago, says that with newsrooms becoming increasingly diversified, there is a good chance that coverage of crimes against blacks is improving, even though the sheer number of black homicide victims in urban areas complicates efforts to provide in-depth analysis. "There is no way," he says, "that we or anyone else can cover the totality of crime in the city and suburbs of Chicago, where there are over 900 murders a year."

Ward says that in his newsroom, staffers try to concentrate on the objective facts of the story. "Whether reporting on a drive-by shooting or whatever," he says, "we look at what is the crime rate, is it going up or down, and are people forming [neighborhood crime watch] units or do they already have them?"

"On average, [television news] stories about white victims of violent crimes lasted 74 percent longer than stories about black victims."

But Jarvis says that providing context for the news involves more than simply reporting whether or not the crime rate is up or down. The problem, she says, is that "we're not seeing the issue framed in a way that would encourage a positive public policy response. . . . If the kinds of killings we see going on daily in urban centers were instead being committed by foreign terrorists, would the American people stand for it?"

Racism in the Criminal Justice System Is Exaggerated

by William Raspberry

About the author: *William Raspberry is a syndicated columnist.*

There are not more college-age black men in jail than in college. I suspect that old canard was launched when someone said (presumably accurately) that more college-age black men are in jail cells than in college *dormitories*—a statistic that would leave out off-campus students and almost all technical school and community college enrollees.

So what's the truth? The Justice Department's Bureau of Justice Statistics says that in 1993 approximately 157,000 black males aged 18 to 24 were in local jails and state and federal prisons.

During the same period, according to the education branch of the Census Bureau, 379,000 black males in the same age group were in post-secondary education—better than 2-to-1 in favor of college.

A Useless Statistic

The number of incarcerated black men has increased since that period, and I wouldn't be shocked to learn that the number of black college students has gone down. Still, we're not close to having more in jail than in college.

But it isn't just the inaccuracy of that much-cited statistic that bothers me; it's the *uselessness* of it.

Even when it's accurately put. The current issue of *Postsecondary Education Opportunity* puts it accurately enough. In 1994, it observes, 678,300 black men were behind bars and only 549,600 were enrolled in higher education.

You will note that those numbers, from the Bureau of Justice Statistics and the National Center for Education Statistics, include men of *all ages*. Removing the 24-year-old upper limit obviously adds more inmates than college students.

But again: What's the point? The more-in-jail claim almost always is cited not as a sign of criminal behavior but of bad policy choices or of societal neglect. It's in the same category as "you could send a young man to Harvard for what it costs to keep him in jail."

Postsecondary Education Opportunity makes the policy-choice implication plain when it notes that some states (Alabama, New Mexico and Mississippi among them) have *more* black college students than prisoners, while others (including Georgia, Maryland and Virginia) have fewer black collegians than inmates. As the editors put it: "Some states appear to be committed more to the higher education of their young black male residents. Other states appear to have written off young black males, their futures,

> *"The jail vs. college statistics . . . invite us to view young black men essentially as victims without the power to make sound choices."*

their families, and the contributions that could have been made to the prosperity and welfare of the state. Instead, these states put more young black men behind bars than they enroll in their higher education systems."

You see: No mention of incidence or seriousness of crime. No comparison of high school completion rates. No indication even of statewide unemployment rates—or of any number of factors that might affect college attendance.

The picture you get is of some faceless panel of white officials—like graders at a slave auction—inspecting a line of hopeful young blacks and, on little more than racist whim, assigning this one to college, the next two to jail.

I don't want for a moment to underplay the awfulness of the college/incarceration statistics (the accurate ones) or the importance of social policy in producing those statistics.

Bad schools, limited opportunity, poverty, discrimination, deliberate and otherwise—all play a role. So does the fact that black men are more likely than whites to serve time for the same or similar offenses. Even the disparity in the mandatory sentences for crack cocaine (preferred by black drug abusers) and powder cocaine (the choice of whites) plays a role.

Personal Responsibility

But so do the attitudes, efforts and choices of the individuals. Possession of crack cocaine may be unfairly punished relative to possession of cocaine in its powder form, but possession is a choice. To a greater extent than we are willing to acknowledge, jail is a choice.

The jail vs. college statistics—undeniably dismaying—invite us to view young black men essentially as victims without the power to make sound choices in their own interest. But are they only victims? Here's what W.E.B. Du Bois wrote of this same group in the years immediately following Emancipation:

"They were consumed with desire for schools. The uprising of the black man, and the pouring of himself into organized effort for education . . . was one of the marvelous occurrences of the modern world, almost without parallel in the history of civilization." These newly free men displayed what Du Bois called "a frenzy for schools."

Instead of looking for someone to blame, shouldn't we be asking ourselves what happened to that "frenzy" for education—and how we might begin to get it back?

Current Drug Laws Are Not Racist

by Ed Bryant

About the author: *Representative Ed Bryant is a Tennessee Republican.*

Imagine what it would be like if the penalties for traffic laws were treated the same. One hundred mph in a 45 mph zone would draw the same penalty as 50 mph in that same zone. Driving under the influence would land you the same fine for driving under the minimum speed limit. Sound compatible or consistent? In a roundabout way, this same sentencing structure has been advocated concerning crack and powder cocaine penalties.

There has been much misunderstanding about Congress' rejection of the United States Sentencing Commission's recommendation to lessen the sentencing guidelines for crack possession and trafficking in order to bring them in line with powder cocaine offenses. Regrettably, equal treatment under the law has been shoved aside in this debate and instead supplanted by the issue of race. With an overwhelming bipartisan show of support, Congress was right to reject the Sentencing Commission's advice of loosening crack penalties. . . .

In order to better understand the disparity between the penalties for crack and powder cocaine offenses, crack's effects on its users and society in general must be taken into account.

Effects of Crack

Crack cocaine is one of the most highly addictive of any illegal drugs sold within the American drug culture, more so than powder cocaine. Not surprisingly, although crack experienced its initial popularity among abusers in urban America in such cities as Los Angeles and New York during the mid-1980s, it continues to gain popularity and is moving beyond inner-city urban America and into smaller cities and communities as well. Talk to rural or suburban sheriffs, and many will say that crack has become a significant problem in their communities.

In numerous instances, violent crime and crack go hand in hand. According to the U.S. Sentencing Commission, from the period of Oct. 1, 1992, through Sept. 30, 1993, an alarming 28 percent of all crack cocaine defendants in federal court cases possessed a dangerous weapon when they were arrested, as compared to just 15 percent of powder cocaine defendants. And consider this: A 1988 study by the University of Illinois-Chicago found that 60 percent of the drug-related murders in New York City that year were associated with crack.

Again, according to the Sentencing Commission, of all drug-related defendants in federal courts from October 1992 to October 1993, crack defendants by far have the worst histories of criminal activity and behavior—15 percent of them having previously committed a crime and committed their crack offense within two years of being released from a prior sentence, compared to just under 7 percent of powder cocaine offenders under the same circumstances.

Serving as a United States attorney for the Western District of Tennessee, which is a representative cross-section of urban, suburban and rural America, I witnessed firsthand the demise of family, of personal responsibility and of basic moral values that crack inflicts upon its victims.

My experience as a prosecutor showed me that crack is easily concealed and sold very cheaply, by and large on city street corners and within crack houses.

Crack Versus Powder Cocaine

Much of the powder cocaine in this country comes through primary source cities such as Miami, New Orleans, Houston and Los Angeles, for example, with relatively few hands having touched it. From these cities the cocaine spreads to Detroit, Birmingham, Indianapolis and many other cities and communities as well, where much of it is cooked into crack and distributed into the many hands of organized dealers, gangs and loose-knit pushers.

It should come as no surprise that such an addictive, cheap drug is highly profitable. Consider a 1990 study of crack's profitability for dealers in Washington, D.C. From 1985 to 1987, crack was the most lucrative source of income for pushers on the streets of D.C., yet there were more street dealers who were selling powder cocaine than crack.

As the cocaine moves from city to city, the distribution pyramid expands to include more people, many of whom happen to be black. The greatest number of arrests and convictions against crack dealers and users occurs at the larger end of the distribution pyramid (on the streets and in the "crack houses"), but the high-volume dealers at the smaller end of the pyramid are also caught and convicted—there just aren't as many of them to prosecute in the first place.

> *"Violent crime and crack go hand in hand."*

If true fairness concerning punishment is to be realized, then race absolutely must not be a factor in determining the level of that punishment. Because blacks may happen to choose to deal crack in their neighborhoods, does that mean we should ease our penalties and thus allow more crack dealers to promptly resume their cold-hearted, cash-thirsty, addiction-ridden trade? I am of the belief that we must not get into the business of determining punishment purely based upon race or prosecuting by quota. The law should know no race, it should see no color. It must only render justice.

Indeed, while the Sentencing Commission may have recommended lessening the penalties for crack cocaine offenses, it nonetheless did

> *"Race absolutely must not be a factor in determining the level of . . . punishment."*

note that "neither the decisions of the courts nor the research conducted by the Commission support a finding that racial bias or animus undergirded the initiation of this federal sentencing law." Lest it be forgotten, the courts have consistently issued rulings against charges of racial discrimination pertaining to penalty guidelines for crack. These are the most important points to keep in mind. For these reasons, we don't need to take the commission's advice to lower crack punishment guidelines.

And what about the victims of crack? Do the law-abiding citizens of all races who live among the crack dealers and the users, who are forced to witness and live in the crossfire of the violent crime and the thoughtless disregard for human kindness and decency in their neighborhoods—do they deserve to see crack viewed by law enforcement as a problem that should be treated less severely? Would it not be grossly unfair to these people to debilitate the current message of strong deterrence to crack traffickers and users by not keeping in place strict punishment guidelines? I certainly think it would be a grave injustice to society to weaken our stand against crack.

We may well need to give serious consideration to closing the gap between powder and crack cocaine penalties if it is determined that there is in fact a need to do so. That's something I plan to examine closely in the near future, because thus far no solid evidence has been offered that would warrant such a shift in policy. In the meantime, the current penalties must stand. America must begin to fully realize the magnitude of the numerous cultural, social and economic ills crack has wickedly inflicted and continues to inflict upon our nation.

Charges of Environmental Racism Are Unfounded

by Christopher Boerner and Thomas Lambert

About the authors: *Christopher Boerner is an Ansehl Fellow and Thomas Lambert is a Hardin Fellow at the Center for the Study of American Business at Washington University in St. Louis, Missouri.*

Eliminating "environmental racism" has fast become one of the premier civil rights and environmental issues of the 1990s. Over the past 15 years, what began as a modest grassroots social movement has expanded to become a national issue, combining environmentalism's sense of urgency with the ethical concerns of the civil rights movement. According to "environmental justice" advocates, discrimination in the siting and permitting of industrial and waste facilities has forced minorities and the poor to bear disproportionately the ill-effects of pollution compared to more affluent whites. What's more, advocates contend, the discriminatory application of environmental regulations and remediation procedures has essentially let polluters in minority communities "off the hook.". . .

The first major attempt to provide empirical support for environmental justice claims was conducted by Robert D. Bullard, a sociologist at the University of California, Riverside, in the late 1970s. Examining population data for communities hosting landfills and incinerators in Houston, Texas, Professor Bullard found that while African Americans made up only 28 percent of the city's population, six of its eight incinerators and fifteen of its seventeen landfills were located in predominantly African-American neighborhoods. The presence of these facilities, he suggests, not only makes black Houston the "dumping grounds for the city's household garbage," but also compounds the myriad of social ills (e.g., crime, poverty, drugs, unemployment, etc.) that already plague poor, inner-city communities.

While limited in scope, Professor Bullard's research has helped shape the policy debate surrounding environmental justice. His Houston study played a central role in one of the first, though unsuccessful, legal cases involving environmental

Reprinted from Christopher Boerner and Thomas Lambert, "Environmental Injustice," *Public Interest*, no. 118, Winter 1995, pp. 61–82, by permission of the authors and the *Public Interest;* ©1995 by National Affairs, Inc.

discrimination, *Bean v. Southwestern Waste Management Corp.*, and forms the basis for two often-cited books, *Invisible Houston* and *Dumping in Dixie.*

Community Demographics Near Waste Facilities

The second widely discussed study examining community demographics near commercial waste Treatment, Storage, and Disposal Facilities (TSDFs) was conducted by the U.S. General Accounting Office (GAO) in 1983. The purpose of the study was to "determine the correlation between the location of hazardous waste landfills and the racial and economic status of surrounding communities." Examining data from four facilities in EPA Region IV (Southeast region), government researchers found that the populations in three of the four surrounding areas were primarily black. African Americans comprised 52 percent, 66 percent, and 90 percent of the population in those three communities. In contrast, African Americans made up no more than 30 percent of the general population of the states involved. In addition, the study found that the communities hosting waste facilities were disproportionately poor when local poverty levels were compared to state averages.

The third, and most often cited, empirical study was published in 1987 by the Commission for Racial Justice (CRJ) of the United Church of Christ. The CRJ study had two important components: an analytical survey of commercial waste TSDFs and a descriptive analysis of uncontrolled toxic waste sites. Both statistical studies

> *"Staten Island . . . is considered a 'minority' community even though over 80 percent of its residents are white."*

were designed to determine the extent to which African Americans and other minority groups are exposed to hazardous wastes in their communities. By using population data (based on five-digit zip codes) as well as information gathered from the U.S. Environmental Protection Agency (EPA) and other sources, CRJ researchers isolated three variables: the percent of minority population, mean household income, and mean value of owner-occupied housing.

The CRJ study revealed a correlation between the number of commercial waste facilities in a given community and the percentage of minority residents in that community. Specifically, the CRJ found that the percentage of "nonwhites" within zip codes with one waste plant was approximately twice that of zip codes without such a facility. For areas with more than one waste plant, the percentage of minority residents was on average three times greater than that of communities with no facilities. Critically, the United Church of Christ found that race was statistically more significant than either mean household income or mean value of owner-occupied housing. This suggested that race was a more likely determinant of where noxious facilities were located than socioeconomic factors. Combined, these results led the CRJ to conclude that there are "clear patterns which show that communities with greater minority percentages of the population are more likely to be the sites of commercial hazardous waste facilities."

A final study which deserves mention was published by the National Law Journal (NLJ) in September 1992. Unlike the research discussed above, which focused on the location of industrial and waste facilities, the NLJ study examined racial disparities in EPA enforcement and remediation procedures. The findings indicate that significant disparities exist in the fines levied against polluters in white communities and those in minority areas. Likewise, the study found that EPA took longer to clean up waste sites in poor and minority communities than in more affluent neighborhoods. The NLJ researchers concluded that "the federal government, in its cleanup of hazardous sites and its pursuit of polluters, favors white communities over minority communities under environmental laws meant to provide equal protection for all citizens."

Research Flaws

While the studies discussed above have been widely cited by environmental justice advocates, all suffer from serious methodological difficulties. The first major criticism of the present research centers on the definition of the term "community." Defining minority communities as any area where the percentage of nonwhite residents exceeds the percentage found in the entire U.S. population means that a community may be considered "minority" even if the vast majority of its residents are white. Based on this methodology, for example, Staten Island—home of the nation's largest landfill—is considered a "minority" community even though over 80 percent of its residents are white. In fact, Staten Island is the "whitest" of New York City's five boroughs.

Another instance of this is evident in a *National Law Journal* study which ranked communities according to percentage of white residents. The term "white community" was used to refer to the top quartile of all affected communities, while "minority community" referred to the bottom quartile. Interestingly, the "whitest" of the "minority communities" had a higher percentage of white residents (84.1 percent) than the general population of the United States, which is 83.1 percent white.

A second, but related, problem is that these studies ignore population densities. Merely citing the proportion of minority or low-income residents in a given host community does not provide information about how many people are actually exposed to

> *"The percentage of minorities living in neighborhoods with commercial [hazardous-waste] facilities is no greater than in areas without such facilities."*

environmental harms. For example, given that blacks presently comprise approximately 16 percent of the nation's population, a host community of 1,000 residents, 20 percent of whom are black, would be considered "minority," while a host community of 6,000 residents, 15 percent of whom are black, would not.

By overlooking population density, the studies fail to point out that more blacks (900 versus 200) would be exposed to the pollution in the second, "non-minority" community, than in the first.

Aggregation Errors

In addition to the problems associated with proportionality and population density, the environmental justice studies cited above often define the affected area in geographic terms that are too broad. Much of the prior research is based on zip-code areas, which are frequently large units established by the U.S. Postal Service. As a result, the data likely suffer from what statisticians call "aggregation errors." That is to say, the studies reach conclusions from the zip-code data which would not be valid if a smaller, more consistent geographic unit were examined. A study released by the Social and

"Legislative proposals to combat environmental inequities may result in greater harm to minority and poor residents."

Demographic Research Institute at the University of Massachusetts, Amherst (UMass), confirms that an analysis of census tracts—small geographic units with relatively fixed boundaries—yields strikingly different results.

The UMass study compared the social and demographic characteristics of census tracts that contain commercial TSDFs with those tracts that do not have TSDFs. Contrary to conventional wisdom, the UMass researchers found that the percentage of minorities living in neighborhoods with commercial facilities is no greater than in areas without such facilities. Indeed, in the 25 largest metropolitan areas studied, commercial hazardous-waste facilities are slightly more likely to be in industrial neighborhoods with a lower percentage of minorities and a *higher* percentage of white working-class families. According to Douglas L. Anderton, director of the UMass project, "We looked at smaller neighborhood areas and found that facilities are more often located in census tracts that are white working-class industrialized neighborhoods. Even other census tracts nearest to those with facilities had no higher percentage of minorities." The results of the UMass study—the most comprehensive analysis of environmental justice to date—cast serious doubt on many of the research claims of proponents of environmental justice.

Unsubstantiated Risks

A third flaw in the existing environmental justice studies is that they imply rather than explicitly state the actual risk presented by commercial TSDFs. While the research attempts to disclose the prevalence of commercial waste plants in poor and minority communities, there is no corresponding information about the dangers associated with living near such facilities. The regulatory requirements regarding the building and operation of industrial and waste facili-

98

ties in the United States are among the most stringent of any industrialized country in the world. These requirements, along with the voluntary efforts of industry, significantly reduce the noxious emissions of commercial waste plants and other facilities.

Moreover, health risks are a function of actual exposure, not simply proximity to a waste facility. The environmental justice advocates' claims of negative health effects are not substantiated by scientific studies. In fact, many of the legislative proposals to combat environmental inequities may result in greater harm to minority and poor residents than the emissions from noxious facilities themselves. By reducing the incentives for businesses to locate in poor and minority areas, these measures may exacerbate local problems of poverty and unemployment—conditions far more unhealthy than the minute risks associated with waste disposal facilities and industrial plants.

Finally, existing research on environmental justice fails to establish that discriminatory siting and permitting practices caused present environmental disparities. While the studies match the location of industrial and waste facilities with the current socioeconomic and race characteristics of the surrounding neighborhoods, they do not consider community conditions *when the facilities were sited*. Furthermore, they fail to explore alternative explanations for higher concentrations of minority and low-income citizens near undesirable facilities. Thus, none of the studies prove that the siting process actually caused the disproportionate burden that poor and minority communities purportedly now bear. These gaps leave open the possibility that other factors may lead minorities and the poor to move into areas of high industrial activity.

The Media Disregard White Crime Victims

by David Horowitz

About the author: *David Horowitz is the president of the Center for the Study of Popular Culture in Los Angeles.*

Just after midnight on October 17, 1995, the day after black supremacist Louis Farrakhan's "Million Man March," two white men, returning from a reunion, were stopped by black police officers in a black Chicago suburb where they had strayed on the way home. The police officers took one of the two white men—the driver of the vehicle—into custody as a dead-beat dad, and impounded his car. They left his passenger, 32-year-old Richard Will, to walk home. Fifteen minutes later, Will was found near death on the ghetto street. He had been beaten and set on fire by two black thugs and died a few hours later. Later, one of the residents of the neighborhood he was killed in blamed the victim: "What was he doing here?' What was a white man doing walking down the street?"

Unreported Racial Murders

You probably did not read this story in your local press. Not a single newspaper reported the story for ten days, until it was broken by Chicago columnist Mike Royko, who asked whether there would be such disinterest in the story if the victim was black and the lynchers white. It took the *New York Times* another week before the story appeared in its pages on Nov. 5, 1995, buried on page eight, and with a headline that did not mention the racial dimension of the case. The *Los Angeles Times* didn't report the story until Nov. 27, and then only on page 27 of its little-read Saturday edition. Its headline—"Death of Man Left by Police in Crime-Ridden Area Probed"—also failed to note that race was involved.

The same week the *L.A. Times* story appeared there was another racial murder, even more horrible. An estranged black father and his new girlfriend, also black, killed the two white children of his former lover while sparing the black son they had together. The pair then cut open the pregnant mother's womb to rescue the black infant before killing the mother.

Reprinted from David Horowitz, "Identifying Black Racism: The Last Taboo," *Orange County Register*, December 10, 1995, by permission of the author.

The press did not ignore this gruesome incident but failed to make anything of its racial dimension. Imagine the public outcry and editorial hand-wringing if the two murdered children and the murdered mother had been black, and the children spared had been white.

The Media Ignore Black Racism

These silences are not unique. In January 1991, Mark Belmore, a white student at Northeastern University in Boston, was murdered by Robert Herbert, who told police that he and three other blacks had agreed to kill the first white person they saw. The story was strictly local news.

In February 1991, a black man named Christopher D. Peterson was arrested in Indiana for killing seven whites with a shotgun. Explaining his crime to police, he said he had "a deep-rooted hatred for white people." The incident was hardly noticed.

In 1991–1992, a trial was held in Florida for members of the "Yahweh" cult. Like Louis Farrakhan, the leader of the cult, Hulon Mitchell, taught his followers that white people were devils. To be initiated into the cult, new members had to kill a white person and cut off an ear as proof of the kill. At the time of the trial, seven persons were known to have been killed. Like the burning of Richard Wills in Chicago, the trial of the Yahweh cult leaders went largely unnoticed.

"Robert Herbert . . . told police that he and three other blacks had agreed to kill the first white person they saw."

The same may be said of the lynching of Yankel Rosenbaum by a black mob in Crown Heights which chanted "Kill the Jew!" as Rosenbaum was stabbed to death by a black man. The killer confessed to the crime but was then acquitted by an all-black and Puerto Rican jury, who gave a party for the defendant when the trial was over.

Hate Crimes Against Whites

Silence—as anti-AIDS activists are quick to point out—sometimes does equal death. Is it an accident that the group whose demonization is most acceptable to our intellectual elites—whites and white males—has become such a target of racial injustice? According to the Uniform Crime Reports of the U.S. Department of Justice for 1994, hate crimes against whites actually exceeded the number of hate crimes against homosexuals, Jews, Native Americans, Asian and Pacific Islanders, and Hispanics.

Sixty percent of black Americans, according to a CNN/Time Poll, believe that Louis Farrakhan "speaks the truth." Is it any wonder that in 1994 50 percent of all racially motivated murders were committed by blacks? (This statistic was reported by the liberal Southern Poverty Law Center.)

Or that, according to U.S. crime statistics, the probability of a black offender selecting a white victim is higher than 50 percent? (The probability of a white offender selecting a black victim, according to the same statistics, is only 3 percent.)

Race hatred is a poison no matter who dishes it out. It's time to put an end to the taboo that protects race-haters if they're black, or that invokes a double-standard by excusing crimes committed against whites as "payback" for "injustices" committed in another time and place.

Chapter 3

Does Affirmative Action Remedy the Effects of Racism?

Chapter Preface

In November 1996, voters passed the California Civil Rights Initiative (CCRI), a measure that forbids the use of race, gender, or ethnicity as criteria in state hiring or public university admissions. The CCRI, which is expected to encourage similar legislation throughout the country, has already created controversy due to declining minority enrollment at California public universities.

CCRI supporters promote the measure as a gain in civil rights, arguing that before the CCRI was implemented, white or Asian applicants were sometimes turned away in favor of less-qualified black or Hispanic applicants. According to CCRI proponents, affirmative action is discriminatory in that it judges applicants based on their race, not their merit. Furthermore, proponents argue, affirmative action programs stigmatize minority students by implying that they need special treatment in order to succeed. Advocates insist that the CCRI will eliminate these injustices.

Opponents of the CCRI, however, allege that affirmative action provides a needed boost to minority students, many of whom come from inadequately funded high schools and poverty-ridden neighborhoods. Moreover, CCRI critics contend that the initiative inhibits diversity on college campuses. When Fall 1997 admissions of African Americans dropped to almost nil at the University of California's Boalt Hall law school, commentators blamed the CCRI, claiming that it bars blacks and other minorities from the most common route to success—higher education.

The CCRI debate highlights some of the main disputes over affirmative action. The following chapter discusses these and other issues in greater detail.

Affirmative Action Stigmatizes Minorities

by James L. Robinson

About the author: *James L. Robinson is the author of* Racism or Attitude? The Ongoing Struggle for Black Liberation and Self-Esteem, *from which the following viewpoint is excerpted.*

Affirmative action has long been a sacred cow of the civil rights community. Yet affirmative action has always exacted a price from its beneficiaries, a price which has sometimes appeared to be as high as the supposed reward. It is this "price" that I plan to discuss in this viewpoint. And it is this price which many civil rights advocates are loath to discuss. At the outset, I would like to say, by way of confession, that I am the product of an affirmative action program at the University of California at Los Angeles (UCLA). I confess to being an affirmative action student at UCLA in the same manner as did professor Stephen L. Carter in *Reflections of an Affirmative Action Baby.* Carter, now teaching at Yale Law School, states that he was admitted to Yale Law School because he was black. I was admitted to UCLA for similar reasons. Actually the scenario, in my case, is more complicated than that.

Carter was an excellent undergraduate student at Cornell University before he ever applied to Yale. Yet, as he says, he might not have been admitted to Yale Law School if he had not been black. My undergraduate career was not as distinguished as Carter's. In fact, my situation smacks of a Horatio Alger story. I dropped out of high school at sixteen and finally got my diploma from Los Angeles Adult High School. I then attended a community college, where I was not exactly an exemplary student. I made it to California State College, a four-year college, only by the skin of my teeth, but I was highly successful there during my last two years. When I applied to UCLA's graduate school of political science in 1968, I had excellent grades in political science, but modest scores on the Graduate Record Exam. I was admitted anyway, and I have often wondered if I would have been admitted if I had been a white student with a similar background. I guess I will never know. I excelled at UCLA and had a highly successful graduate experience. I benefitted from affirmative action by being admitted to a major university with a full scholarship. The price I paid and even continue to pay is a sense that perhaps I did not belong at the university. As Professor Carter states in his book, I, too, will always wonder if I could have been successful on my own, without help from some "special minority program."

The Price of Affirmative Action

Many proponents of affirmative action would argue that the "price" I paid was low, considering I got into UCLA and was ultimately successful in obtaining my Ph.D. Yet they will never know how it felt or feels to sit next to non-affirmative-action students and wonder if they see you as their intellectual equal. Even more important, you wonder if you are their intellectual equal. The fear of "not being smart enough," which haunts all students, becomes even more pronounced for you, as an affirmative action student, because you didn't get there on an equal playing field. What would be the response of black college basketball players if affirmative action became a goal of the National College Athletic Association and each team had to have a certain number of white players? More important, how would the white players who joined the teams under those conditions feel? Would they feel equal to the black players? Most people believe that if two athletes compete, all things being equal, the better athlete will win. However, affirmative action as it worked for Professor Carter, for me, and for countless others did not say that the "best" would win, only the best black. How good is the best black student? Is he or she as good as the best white student or only the average white?

While most blacks stop short of opposing affirmative action outright, an influential few suggest that the concept needs rethinking. Outright quotas, the flash point of white opposition, are increasingly rejected as counterproductive because of how whites administer them. Says Larry Thompson, deputy general counsel of Wall Street's giant Depository Trust Company, "Most of us who have benefitted from or participated in minority recruiting would be against numerical goals and quotas because all they lead to is taking the first 10 dark faces that walk through the door instead of taking people who are qualified." Most important, preference programs seem to have only a minimal effect on breaking the cycle of ghetto poverty. As Professor Carter

> *"The fear of 'not being smart enough,' which haunts all students, becomes even more pronounced for . . . an affirmative action student."*

argues in his book, "What has happened in black America in the era of affirmative action is this: middle-class black people are better off and lower-class black people are worse off. . . . The most disadvantaged black people are not in a position to benefit from preferential admission."

On the other side of the argument are liberal social commentators, like Stanley Fish, who believe in the utility of affirmative action. Fish argues that the objection to affirmative action denies the historical racism and discrimination that blacks have suffered. He rejects the position put forth by opponents that if it was wrong to treat blacks unfairly, it is wrong to give blacks preference and thereby treat whites unfairly. In a 1992 article entitled "Reverse Racism or How the Pot Got to Call the Kettle Black," he wrote, "This objection is just another version of the forgetting

> *"Affirmative action has reinforced a self-defeating sense of victimization among blacks."*

and rewriting of history. The work is done by the adverb 'unfairly,' which suggests two more or less equal parties, one of whom has been unjustly penalized by an incompetent umpire. But blacks have not simply been treated unfairly; they have been subjected first to decades of slavery, and then to decades of second-class citizenship, widespread legalized discrimination, economic persecution, educational deprivation, and cultural stigmatization. They have been bought, sold, killed, beaten, raped, excluded, exploited, shamed, and scorned for a very long time. The word 'unfair' is hardly an adequate description of their experience, and the belated gift of 'fairness' in the form of a resolution no longer to discriminate against them legally is hardly an adequate remedy for the deep disadvantages that the prior discrimination has produced. When the deck is stacked against you in more ways than you can even count, it is small consolation to hear that you are now free to enter the game and take your chances."

Preferences Promote Racial Tension

Yet as Shelby Steele stated in a 1991 *Time* magazine interview, "Any time you have one group of preferred people and another group of unpreferred people, you are laying the groundwork for racial tension. [Preferences] stigmatize blacks in the workplace and in universities. They make black people wonder if they would be there if not for the color of their skin—wonder whether they have the competence to really compete with whites." As an English professor at California's San Jose State University, Steele has emerged as the most eloquent proponent of this view. He asserts that affirmative action has reinforced a self-defeating sense of victimization among blacks by encouraging them to pin their failures on white racism instead of on their own shortcomings. Says he, "Blacks now stand to lose more from affirmative action than they gain."

Many blacks have decidedly mixed views about the effectiveness of affirmative action. According to recent Gallup polls, 77 percent feel that minorities should not receive preferential treatment to make up for past discrimination. But even Steele and Carter are not opposed to some form of affirmative action. The reason for the ambivalence blacks feel toward affirmative action is the mixed results one sees from such programs. For example, how would one evaluate the following two cases of affirmative action at work? In one case, for Mignon Williams, aged forty-two, a black marketing executive in Rochester, New York, affirmative action meant opportunity. She was recruited by the Xerox Corporation in 1977 under a pioneering plan to hire women and minorities and rose from saleswoman to division vice-president in just thirteen years. While Williams attributes her success mainly to hard work and business savvy, she acknowledges that her race and her sex played a role in her rapid rise. Affirmative action, she says, "opened the door, but it's not a free pass. If anything, you feel like you're under a microscope and have to constantly prove yourself by overachieving and never missing the mark."

However, for Roy V. Smith, aged forty, a black eighteen-year veteran of the Chicago police force, affirmative action means frustration. Since 1973, court-ordered hiring quotas and the aggressive recruitment of minorities have expanded black representation on the 12,000-member force from 16 percent to 24 percent. Smith contends, however, that gender and race have not opened doors for him but shut them. Ironically, he has been denied promotion to sergeant so that Hispanics and females who scored lower on exams could be given the higher-ranking positions set aside for those groups. In a strange role reversal, Smith is in a position similar to that of white officers and perceives himself to be hurt by affirmative action. In the fall of 1994 he joined a reverse-discrimination lawsuit against the City of Chicago by 313 police officers, mostly white. "I am not anti-affirmative action," he

> *"You feel like you're under a microscope and have to constantly prove yourself by overachieving."*

says. "I am just against the way it is being used. It's something that started out good and now has gotten out of hand."

Smith's situation was inevitable because there are other groups that also have legitimate grievances regarding representation on Chicago's police force. And when you start to make hiring or promotional decisions based on race—or, in this case, on race and gender—someone has to lose. The losers, like Smith, are not going to be happy and will feel discriminated against.

How Effective Is Affirmative Action?

The cases of Williams and Smith reflect an increasingly acrimonious debate among African Americans about the effectiveness and desirability of affirmative action. On one side of the argument, a small but widely publicized group of black neoconservatives contends that efforts to combat racial discrimination through quotas, racially weighted tests, and other techniques have psychologically handicapped blacks by making them dependent on racial-preference programs rather than on their own hard work. In response, some scholars, like William Julius Wilson, wonder whether socioeconomic class ought to augment race, or even replace it, as a criterion in affirmative action. Proponents say that would be fairer and, in a society of limited resources, more effective. They add that it might diminish backlash, especially if preferences went to poor whites as well. Stephen Carter is far from alone in perceiving affirmative action as primarily a middle-class boon. Larry Thompson, of Wall Street's Depository Trust Company, who has recruited for his college, Yale, and his law school, Berkeley, says prestige institutions fared far better in the 1960s and 1970s in empowering the poor. Now, he argues, they enroll the children of black alumni. This outcome, too, was, I believe, inevitable because these institutions want those they enroll to be successful, and who better than the children of alumni?

> *"White businesses always wonder if you got the contract because you were good or a minority."*

Princeton admissions dean Fred Hargadon allows that prestige schools are not finding enough of the disadvantaged, black or white: "None of us are yet so successful with affirmative action that we can spread resources to other social problems." Whatever the best universities and largest corporations do, however, affirmative action programs are fated to remain distant from the problems of the ultra-poor. Says Eleanor Holmes Norton, a former chairman of the U.S. Equal Employment Opportunity Commission, "Affirmative action is now essentially a tool for getting people better jobs rather than for bringing the economically excluded into the system." This results from what economist James Smith, author of a U.S. Labor Department study on the problem, labels a "proskill bias." Most such programs operate at colleges and graduate schools or in private business. By the time impoverished blacks are of an age to deal with these institutions, many of them have been overwhelmed by a combination of inadequate schools, troubled homes and neighborhoods, an environment of drug use, and other social ills. Even those with the will to work often need remedial training far beyond any corporate internship.

College recruitment has proved to be of limited value unless accompanied by tutoring and counseling to help disadvantaged students all the way through. Since 1976, according to Reginald Wilson, who tracks minority affairs for the American Council on Education, the share of black high school graduates attending college has dropped from 35.4 percent to about 30.8 percent, as opposed to 38.8 per cent for whites, primarily because of higher dropout rates for blacks. "The tragedy on many campuses," says Wilson, "is that recruitment of minority students gets a lot of attention but remedial programs necessary for them to succeed do not."

Affirmative Action Harms Minorities

I found this lack of support for remediation also to be true at Rutgers University. . . . This mixed bag of affirmative action in education also exists in other race-specific programs, such as so-called minority set-asides. My father-in-law, who has run a general contracting business in Los Angeles for forty years, believes that minority set-asides only hurt black contractors. He says that there is a stigma attached to these kinds of contracts which makes it harder for a "minority" business to move into mainstream contracting. According to him, "White businesses always wonder if you got the contract because you were good or a minority." Many civil rights leaders would call this response by white business to affirmative action set-asides "racist." Yet the minority-owned firm is at a disadvantage in trying to prove that it obtained the contract on merit, not just race. Many beneficiaries of affirmative action largess have this basic lingering doubt about competence. Why was I chosen instead of someone else? If I was hired solely because of race, what does that say about my basic worth and competence?

When I sat in my UCLA political science graduate classes, I always felt a slight uneasiness, a feeling that perhaps I didn't really belong there. To my absolute amazement, many of my white colleagues expressed similar doubts about their ability to "make it" through the graduate program. Over the years, since leaving UCLA, I have come to believe that this feeling of "incompetence" is a natural feeling, shared by many in academic life and elsewhere. However, those who came into the academic process through traditional ways had been validated numerous times along their journey. They competed openly with all others and were given no particular advantage. Affirmative action beneficiaries have not been validated in this manner and have actually suffered nonvalidation by being admitted or enrolled into a program for one reason: race.

Affirmative Action Is Unjust

by Pete Wilson

About the author: *Pete Wilson, a Republican, is the governor of California.*

Our state and nation are engaged in a debate that goes to the very foundation of the American dream. The question before us: Is preferential treatment based on race or gender consistent with the American dream of equality under the law?

This is a charged issue that has been confused by emotionalism on all sides. But we cannot avoid taking a stand. We cannot sidestep this issue or pretend that it doesn't exist. For it goes to the heart and soul of the nation.

"Special Privileges for None"

The success of the civil rights movement—against enormous odds—was very much based on its appeal to our heritage that this nation was founded on the principle, as Thomas Jefferson said, of "equal rights for all, special privileges for none." That principle, however, is slipping away from us when we allow affirmative-action programs that grant preferential treatment based on race or gender.

As originally conceived by President John F. Kennedy, affirmative action merely prohibited discrimination by federal contractors. But by 1970, the federal government established regulations which required affirmative action through "goals and timetables." While unintended in conception, in practice, these too often encouraged preferential treatment for members of the group being recruited and hired. And ultimately, affirmative action became expressly based on preferential treatment in the form of quotas and other efforts that made race and gender determining factors in employment, admissions and contracting decisions.

Those who proposed such steps felt then (and some persist in feeling so today) that any member of a group that suffered historic discrimination is entitled to special opportunity as compensation—even though a member of that group has not as an individual suffered discrimination.

Reprinted by permission of the *Washington Times* from Pete Wilson, "The False Promise of Affirmative Action," *Washington Times*, June 5, 1995, page A19.

The argument is that it is perfectly permissible and right to impose wrongful discrimination upon members of one group to compensate members of another. However natural this compensatory urge may have been in the immediate post-discrimination period of the 1960s and 1970, the validity of the need for such compensation has steadily faded ever since.

Inequality Does Not Bring Equality

President Lyndon Johnson compared the effort to a footrace in which those who had once been shackled must be given some advantage—the inside track or even a bicycle—to keep up with other runners. Johnson sought to justify preferences by this metaphor, which appealed to our fundamental sense of fairness. Government gladly played the role of enforcer. A full-court press was made to persuade Americans that mandating and practicing inequality could bring equality. But, of course, it can't.

> *"Instead of treating every American as an individual, [affirmative action] pits group against group, race against race."*

The contest simply isn't fair if we grant preferential treatment to some of the contestants based not on past discrimination, but simply on being born into a protected group. Even the architects of this system of special preferences never intended that it would last forever. No one, in fact, envisioned that redressing two centuries of unfairness would launch a whole new era of unfairness. But it has.

Rather than uniting people around our common core, this system of preferential treatment constantly reminds us of our superficial differences. Instead of treating every American as an individual, it pits group against group, race against race.

Affirmative Action Denies Opportunity

But worst of all, this system is eroding the American ideal that anyone who works hard and plays by the rules has an equal chance to achieve the American dream, an ideal that has attracted generation after generation to our shores.

Most Americans, of all races and creeds, recognize the need to end preferential treatment for protected groups. For whatever good it may have done in the past, they see the harm it is doing to our nation today.

They see that the current system of special privilege based on race and gender is breeding resentment from those left standing on the sidelines.

Parents watch as their children are denied the opportunity to attend the school of their choice or find the job for which they've been trained—not because they don't have what it takes or haven't worked hard all their lives, but because they don't belong to a particular group that enjoys a special advantage.

We cannot ignore the unfairness and pretend it doesn't exist. We must change what's wrong and set it right. We must replace the discredited policies of preferential treatment with a new vision based upon justice, upon individual merit, and upon the fundamental civil rights principle of equality under the law.

A New Vision

We must make hard work, self-reliance, individual initiative and merit—not group membership—the basis for success in America. This new vision rests on three basic pillars:

• Everyone must be prepared to compete. Life is a competition. We shouldn't cancel it through affirmative action. We should ensure that every child is given every chance to grow up to be an individual prepared to compete in life, through preventive programs that prepare children for school, education reform to improve the quality of our schools, and financial aid to help students get the higher education they need to succeed in life.

• Zero tolerance for discrimination of any kind. We can't pretend that discrimination against women and minorities doesn't still exist. We must conscientiously and vigorously enforce the laws that prohibit and punish unlawful discrimination. Wherever bigotry rears its insidious head, we must condemn it, and we must punish it.

But we must also recognize that preferential treatment based on group membership is also discrimination and that it too must end. Discrimination is wrong regardless of who the victim is.

• Government alone can't do the job. Finally, we must recognize that government alone cannot achieve the goal of a society that rewards merit and ignores the color of someone's skin. Parents must teach their children tolerance and self-reliance. Schools must teach right from wrong. And children must learn that hard work is rewarded and responsibility is expected from all.

Making these changes won't be easy. But the future of our nation demands that we make them.

Eliminating Preferences

We've begun eliminating special preferences from state hiring and the award of contracts in California. And I am supporting the California Civil Rights Initiative to enshrine in our state constitution the principles of equal opportunity. [The initiative, which prohibits using the criteria of race, gender, or ethnicity for state hiring and public university admissions, was passed in November 1996.] But because the most egregious preferential practices are required and promoted by federal law, I urge President Clinton and Congress to waste no time in ending these discriminatory practices.

> *"Discrimination is wrong regardless of who the victim is."*

This is not the first time America has faced this fundamental question about the equal rights of individuals in our nation. In the dark days when Abraham Lincoln was searching for a way to avert a civil war over the question, he looked to a passage from the Bible and told the nation: "A house divided against itself cannot stand."

We are again a house divided against itself. We are divided by a system that offers preferences and privileges to some, but not to others. We are divided by a system that flies in the face of the American notion of fairness.

Generations of Americans have grown up believing that in this country, if you strived and worked hard, you'd have the chance to achieve anything within the grasp of your God-given ability. We grew up believing that everyone had an equal shot at the prize.

An America without that hope is simply not America. We must no longer allow our laws to deny that hope to any child in our country.

Affirmative Action Violates Free Market Ideals

by Dinesh D'Souza

About the author: *Dinesh D'Souza is John M. Olin Scholar at the American Enterprise Institute and the author of* The End of Racism.

Before adopting a course that will determine the future of race relations into the 21st century, Americans must step back from the sound and fury of the affirmative action issue long enough to consider the four basic policy options for dealing with the continuing problem of racial discrimination.

The first approach is to preserve racial preferences, based on the logic of proportional representation. This is the Clinton administration's preferred route, and despite recent Supreme Court decisions it remains the regnant practice. Absent discrimination, our laws expect minorities to fan out into the work force at roughly their proportion in the population. Companies that fail to maintain the proper ethnic breakdown of workers are guilty until proved innocent: The Civil Rights Act of 1991 places on employers the burden of proving that they are not discriminating.

But over the past generation the basic flaw in proportional representation has become apparent: Merit, no less than the old racism, produces inequality— inequality between individuals and among groups. There is no reason to expect that equality of rights for individuals necessarily translates into equality of results for groups. If different groups of runners hit the finishing tape at different times, it does not follow that the race has been rigged. Our current civil rights laws, therefore, are built on an intellectual foundation of quicksand.

In addition, proportional representation fails the test of social justice. Columnist Michael Kinsley argues that race is a "rough and ready shorthand for disadvantage," but that does not hold true any more. The African-American community has bifurcated into a middle class and an underclass.

There is no justification for giving a university admissions preference to the black government official's son who attends a private school in Washington over the daughter of a white Appalachian coal miner or a Vietnamese refugee. Moreover, proportional representation unfairly subsidizes the children of new immigrants, who have played no part in American history, at the expense of the sons and daughters of native-born citizens.

A Matter of Unfairness

Proportional representation also erodes the principle of equality of treatment under the law, the only unifying principle for a multiracial society. People can live with inequality of results if they are assured equality of rights, just as we can endure losing a contest in which all competitors played by the same rules. Majorities, no less than minorities, need the assurance that they are being treated fairly; otherwise they are sure to mobilize through democratic channels to affirm their interests.

Finally, proportional representation ensures an unceasing balkanization and racialization of American society. At least the old discrimination existed anomalously with the American creed; the new discrimination, enshrined into law, corrupts the nation's institutions and makes them purveyors of injustice.

The only prop sustaining affirmative action today is the liberal conviction that the social outcomes produced by merit alone would prove painful and humiliating for blacks. For example, studies have shown that if the University of California at Berkeley selected students solely based on grades and test scores, the percentage of blacks would fall to between 1% and 2%. Similarly, blacks would be scarce in some professions. Proportional representation will end only when we have the courage to say that we are willing to live with these outcomes until blacks are able to raise their own standards to compete at the highest levels.

Preferences for Blacks

A second option, favored by some scholars, is to abolish racial preferences for all groups except African-Americans. Eugene Genovese, for example, argues that blacks have faced a unique history in this country and should be permitted to identify themselves as culturally black and benefit from a carefully selected range of preferences.

This approach has the benefit of acknowledging the absurdity of preferring newcomers from Mexico City over locals from Kansas City. It sensibly seeks to narrow the range of beneficiaries to the group that has suffered the evils of slavery, segregation and widespread discrimination. It would preserve preferences as exceptional, rather than typical. And it would continue to view them as temporary.

> *"There is no reason to expect that equality of rights for individuals necessarily translates into equality of results for groups."*

The problem with this attractive strategy is that it is increasingly unsustainable in a multiracial society. If we are going to insist that middle-class blacks deserve preference for admissions and jobs over the poorest members of all other groups, this will not only produce acute resentment, it will probably stigmatize African-Americans as inherently inferior. Whites, Hispanics, Asians and Native Americans would all be competing together, with a kind of Special Olympics reserved for blacks. The moral and psychological damage would almost certainly outweigh any tangible short-term benefits, so that the only workable scheme is one proposed by sociologist Lawrence Fuchs: Limit affirmative action now to African-Americans and set a date, perhaps 2010, when "all counting by race should be phased out."

A Colorblind Policy

The third option is a blanket nondiscrimination rule, which requires the enforcement of colorblind principles both in the private and public sectors. This is the approach that Martin Luther King Jr. favored, and the one that was written into law in the Civil Rights Act of 1964. Liberals such as Jim Sleeper, Randall Kennedy, William Julius Wilson and Clarence Page as well as conservatives such as Newt Gingrich and Jack Kemp are trying to revive this approach, typically combined with a demand for class-based affirmative action.

The benefit of this colorblind strategy is that it would use a single standard to implement civil rights laws. Whites and blacks would enjoy the same degree of protection, and so would other groups. Resources currently invested in promoting proportional representation could be more sensibly invested in strictly enforcing antidiscrimination laws.

> *"The only prop sustaining affirmative action today is the liberal conviction that the social outcomes produced by merit alone would prove painful and humiliating for blacks."*

Yet the cardinal weakness of the broad-based colorblind rule is that, if applied even-handedly, it would require the government to outlaw minority companies from giving preferences to members of their own group. Peek into a Korean grocery store and what you often see, in the back, is other Korean workers. Similarly, black-owned businesses may seek out African-American employees. Should the government prohibit these obvious displays of minority ethnocentrism? Such interference makes no sense, particularly considering the fact that earlier generations of ethnic minorities such as Jews have advanced by helping their own people.

The limitations of the previous three policy options invite us to consider a fourth, which is based on the distinction, crucial to a liberal society, between the public and the private sphere. This approach holds the government to a rigorous standard of colorblindness, while allowing private actors to be free to discriminate as they wish. In practice, this means uncompromising race-neutrality in government hiring and promotion, criminal justice and the drawing of voting districts. Yet individuals and companies would be allowed to discriminate in private transactions such as selecting a business partner or hiring for a job. Am I calling for a repeal of the Civil Rights Act of 1964? Actually, yes. The law should be changed so that its nondiscrimination provisions apply only to the government.

In a recent book, legal scholar Richard Epstein argues that "discrimination laws represent the antithesis

> *"[Ethnocentrism] is a desirable and in some cases even admirable trait."*

of freedom of contract." Mr. Epstein asserts that people should be free to hire and fire people for good reason, bad reason, or no reason at all. He challenges the strongly held belief of many Americans that they have a right not to be discriminated against: In a free society, he counters, they have a right to enter into voluntary transactions that other parties should be at liberty to accept or refuse.

Without putting it this way, Mr. Epstein is defending ethnocentrism as not only natural but also justifiable. He implies, and I agree, that this is a defensible and in some cases even admirable trait. What is the argument for preventing people from giving jobs and benefits, which are theirs to give, to those whom they prefer? Admittedly in some cases the job goes to the nephew of the boss. This, in the boss's mind, is his nephew's "merit"—to be related to him. Such nepotism, although reprehensible in the public sector where the government has an obligation to treat citizens equally, is entirely appropriate in the competitive private sector where the economic cost of selecting the less competent falls on the individual or company making the selection.

I can already hear the gasps of civil rights activists. Absent legal penalties, they will warn, many companies would simply refuse to hire blacks even when they have demonstrated that they are the best qualified candidates for jobs. Since such behavior makes no economic sense, we can expect it will be relatively infrequent in a competitive market.

Discrimination Is Economically Irrational

To see why markets tend to eliminate irrational discrimination, consider sociologist Christopher Jencks's example of what would happen if every baseball team in America refused to hire blacks. Blacks would suffer most, because they would be denied the opportunity to play professional baseball. And fans would suffer, because the quality of games would be diminished. But what if only a few teams—say the Yankees and the Dodgers—refused to hire blacks? African-Americans as a group would suffer hardly at all, because the best black players would offer their services to other teams. The Yankees and the Dodgers would suffer a great deal, because they would be deprived of the chance to hire talented black players. Eventually competitive pressure would force the Yankees and Dodgers either to hire blacks or to suffer losses in games and revenue.

On the other hand, some forms of discrimination—rational discrimination based upon statistically accurate group judgments that are nevertheless unfair to some members within the group—are likely to persist. Yet anyone familiar with today's work force knows that discrimination against blacks has declined dramatically and is now furtive and largely anecdotal, while discrimination in favor of blacks is systematic, openly practiced and legally sanctioned.

Consequently, if faced with the alternative of an enforced colorblind approach, many African-Americans who recognize the pervasiveness of contemporary preferences in their favor might well prefer to see those benefits continue, and thus would be willing to pay the price of tolerating a few relatively isolated employers who would refuse to hire blacks. Thus we arrive at a supreme irony: The best way for African-Americans to save private-sector affirmative action may be to repeal the Civil Rights Act of 1964.

Affirmative Action
Is Racist

by K.L. Billingsley

About the author: *K.L. Billingsley is a staff writer for* Heterodoxy, *a conservative newspaper published by the Center for the Study of Popular Culture.*

One day in January 1995 a number of companies in San Diego, California, woke up to find that they had a "deficient work force." This new designation, which had literally come overnight, had nothing to do with the intelligence of the workers in these companies or with their levels of education and skill, their attendance record, or their dedication. It did not mean that the employees were unable to write computer programs, repair jet engines, run DNA tests, or even clean toilets. Rather, it meant that under San Diego's new Equal Opportunity Ordinance, the companies were guilty of "a statistically significant underutilization of ethnic or gender groups in any occupational category."

A guilty company must file a Work Force Report, which "indicates the number of males and females in each identified ethnic group by occupational category," and submit to a Work Force Analysis in order to determine whether "the contractor's total work force exhibits a statistically significant underutilization of any identified ethnic or gender groups in any occupational category." If Equal Employment Program Manager Deborah Fischle-Faulk has "reasonable cause to believe that a contractor has a deficient work force," she will file a Deficient Work Force Notice, which shall "describe the nature of the statistically significant underutilization." (Interestingly, of Ms. Fischle-Faulk's own 17 employees, 14 are women.) The ordinance provides that a Plan Violation Notice shall "describe all remedial actions required to permanently correct the violation and establish time frames for completion." As for the statistically deficient company, they have a scant 10 days to appeal, and if they miss the deadline, the Deficient Work Force Notice shall ripen into a Final Administrative Order of the city.

"It is definitely a case of Big Sister Is Watching You," says one San Diego politician. "The courts nixed a similar plan in 1993, but no one said that building an American apartheid would be easy." But while it seems Orwellian, the San Diego plan actually pales beside other grandiose racial preference schemes, which have become the status quo throughout the state and nation, especially in education. For example, during the 1980s, supposedly the heyday of Reaganite laissez faire and educational reform, the California legislature mandated that student enrollments at the massive 20-campus Cal State system and the nine-campus University of California be based not on the students' grade or achievement but on the eth-

> *"The underlying philosophy behind affirmative action is the notion that blacks and Hispanics aren't that smart."*

nic proportions of graduating high-school seniors. [This mandate has since been overturned by the California Civil Rights Initiative, which prohibits the use of race, gender, or ethnicity in determining public university admission.] But for the state's quota politburo, even this was not enough. In 1991, California Speaker of the House Willie Brown sponsored a bill mandating that college students must not only be admitted but must graduate according to racial proportionality. The bill, which held faculty accountable for implementing the plan and let them know it would be part of their performance evaluations, drew little press coverage before being vetoed by Gov. Pete Wilson. . . .

Affirmative Action Is Racist

Fred Lynch, professor of government at Claremont-McKenna College and author of *Invisible Victims: White Males and the Crisis of Affirmative Action*, has chronicled the stories of scores of affirmative action victims, many of them liberals who, terrified of being branded with the scarlet *R* (for racist) and mistakenly believing that affirmative action enjoyed popular support, caved in to their own racially based punishment. Perhaps such self-laceration would be tolerable if someone indeed benefited by it. But the alleged beneficiaries of the institutional discrimination also suffer, as Shelby Steele described so poignantly in *The Content of Our Character.* Black journalist and media consultant Deroy Murdock, whose parents were impoverished immigrants from Costa Rica, echoes some of Steele's ideas when he notes that there are three kinds of racism: the David Duke and Adolf Hitler brand based on hatred, the Archie Bunker strain based on ignorance, and, last but not least, the racial bigotry born of patronization. "The underlying philosophy behind affirmative action is the notion that blacks and Hispanics aren't that smart and aren't prepared. We must help these little brown people, and the blacks. That's where affirmative action programs come from."

One minority worker who made it on his own in and out of government heard of a proposal to make the Equal Employment Opportunity Commission a cabinet-level agency and responded, "What are they going to call it, the 'Department of the Inferior'?" The quip hits the bull's-eye. Inferiority is the *a priori* assumption of affirmative action plans. Rutgers President Francis Lawrence, an energetic implementer of affirmative action, recently provided a textbook case of this attitude in his statement that blacks suffer from genetic defects that keep them from being high achievers in college. Mr. Lawrence should have taken a class with black economist Walter Williams, who says that "affirmative action is demeaning in many ways and even those who support it would find it insulting if told that the reason they have a job is because of affirmative action."

Forty-eight prominent black writers lobbied the Pulitzer committee to give novelist Toni Morrison an award. But Morrison said that such lobbying caused her stress: "It was too upsetting to have my work considered as an affirmative action award." Iconoclastic University of California Regent Ward Connerly, who remembers the humiliation of having to drink from "colored only" water fountains in the Louisiana of his youth, is now labeled an "affirmative action businessman," which he says is almost as bad because it keeps him from being judged by the quality of his work.

"People are competing very well on their own without preferred programs, and they carry the burden of people saying they got there by preference," Connerly says. "It is time that we allow those people to walk with dignity." And Connerly backs up his words with deeds. He owns half of his consulting business, while his wife, who is white, owns the other half. If he owned 51 percent, he could feast on the gravy train of affirmative action work, but he turns it down, along with offers from venal white contractors to be their "minority partner."

Who Benefits from Affirmative Action?

Black economist Glenn Loury, who earned his Ph.D. at MIT and has taught at Harvard, says that Connerly is an example of someone "tired of being treated as presumptively defective." This treatment is something Loury has experienced firsthand. After he gave an economics lecture at the University of Texas the school sent him a certificate describing him as "historically disadvantaged" in the evident belief that he would wear this definition as a badge of honor. According to Loury, affirmative action played a negligible role in the rise of the black middle class throughout the '80s, a claim often made by its promoters to justify the spread of quotas. "The longer historical view," Loury says, "suggests that shifts in occupational distribution from low pay to professions, the increase in college going, the improvement of primary and secondary education, all pre-date affirmative action and even the civil rights laws of

"People are competing very well on their own without preferred programs."

1960s. You can trace real movement in the relative position of blacks back into the 1940s." Walter Williams agrees, pointing out that the growth of black income for five years before affirmative action was the same as five years after. Williams attributes the growth of the black middle class to the elimination of legal discrimination that set up barriers to education and business opportunity.

This begs the question: *Cui bono?* Who really benefits from affirmative action policies?

William Mellor of the libertarian Institute for Justice argues that most benefits of affirmative action go to educated middle-income minorities: "It helps those who need it the least. For those in the inner city, it's at best useless and at worst creates a climate of hostility from other workers." Ward Connerly agrees that affirmative action is a jobs program, but for a special kind of person: "The people in Watts don't know a goddamn thing about affirmative action." Connerly adds that affirmative action promoters are "simply there to protect their own interest. They are a handful of folks who eat at the trough by reason of their class and they don't want to lose that."

> *"The people in Watts don't know a goddamn thing about affirmative action."*

San Diego provides a case in point. A city in the midst of budget cuts and suffering unemployment as a result of military downsizing, it nonetheless carries on its employment rolls the annual salary of the equal opportunity program's administrative analyst, who gets $107,998 plus a generous benefit package. This top-drawer jobs program also pays the "associate analyst" $86,386. And a similar affirmative action nomenklatura exists in every major city in the country, not to speak of its entrenchment in the university. It is probably no accident that the University of California keeps no budgetary figure for the costs involved with its swollen affirmative action bureaucracy. But some observers estimate that it must exceed $10 million annually.

But neither the expense of affirmative action programs, their failure to improve the economic conditions of their supposed beneficiaries, nor the antagonisms they have engendered have caused their supporters to have second thoughts. The affirmative action bureaucrats have instead argued what all bureaucrats argue: that the program will work if we just have more of it. They increase their own power and job prospects by finding yet more historical disadvantage and new groups of accredited victims.

Seeking New "Victims"

The city of San Francisco gives preference to gays in hiring and is exploring new protections for transsexuals and cross-dressers, alleged victims of straight society. The federal government's Office of Management and Budget and House Census Committee has been holding hearings on whether the designations "black," "white," and "Hispanic" are too broad. They have heard calls to count light-skinned and dark-skinned blacks separately, to split the Hispanic label six ways, to swap the current "Pacific Islander" for "Native Hawaiian," and to include everyone from Kurds to Bedouins under a "Middle Eastern" category. "Deciding who fits into such new categories could put government into a business chillingly akin to eugenics," says Deroy Murdock. "Can ethnicity in-spectors—armed with eye-color charts and DNA testing gear—be far away?"

It sounds fanciful. But that is where we are heading in government, the academy, and the workplace, all arenas where a racial and gender spoils system reigns. The truth of affirmative action is even stranger than this fiction. In order to increase the number of Hispanic patrolmen, for example, the California Highway Patrol has even recruited among Mexican nationals. On a national level, the Federal Communications Commission offers "bidding credits" of 25 percent for minority and female-owned firms, which al-lows them to bag a $1-million auction bid for the bargain-basement price of $750,000.

> *"The affirmative action bureaucrats have . . . argued what all bureaucrats argue: that the program will work if we just have more of it."*

Affirmative action has become the insatiable hunger and the expanding maw. Ward Connerly says that at a recent University of California Board of Regents meeting, affirmative action "was presented not to remedy past discrimination but to promote educational diversity. It has become a goal in and of itself. There will never be an end to it." Connerly has discovered by experience what Thomas Sowell showed in *Preferential Policies: An International Perspective*—that affirmative action policies around the globe always claim to be temporary measures but invariably wind up as permanent policy.

Arguments Against Affirmative Action Are Based on Misinformation

by Clarence Page

About the author: *Clarence Page is a nationally syndicated columnist and the author of* Showing My Color: Impolite Essays on Race and Identity, *from which the following viewpoint is excerpted.*

Most newspapers and broadcast news operations in America were not much interested in hiring black reporters or photographers when I graduated from high school in 1965. Nevertheless, I asked the editor of the local daily if he had any summer jobs in his newsroom. I knew I was good. I was an honors graduate and feature editor at the local high school's student newspaper. I had a regional award already glistening on my short resume. Still, I was not picky. I would be delighted to mop floors just to get a job in a real newsroom.

And it was not as if I did not have connections. The editor had known me since I had been one of his newspaper's carriers at age twelve. Still, it was not to be. He told me the budget would not allow any summer jobs for any young folks that year. Then the very next day I found out through a friend that the newspaper did have an opening after all. The editors had hired a white girl a year younger than I, who also happened to be a reporter under my supervision at the student newspaper, to fill it.

Don't get mad, my dad advised me, just get smart. Get your education, he said. "Then someday you can get even!"

My saintly, interminably patient schoolteacher grandmother, dear old Mother Page, also helped ease my tension. "Son," she said, "just prepare yourself, for someday the doors of opportunity will open up. When they do, you must be ready to step inside."

Little did she know that that very summer, riots would erupt in the Watts section of Los Angeles. More than four hundred riots would explode across the nation over the next three years. Suddenly editors and news directors across the country were actively looking to hire at least a few reporters and photographers who could be sent into the "ghetto" without looking too conspicuous.

"Tokenism"

Many of the black journalists hired in that talent raid, much of it waged on the staffs of black publications and radio stations, would bring Pulitzers and other honors to their new bosses, dispelling the notion that they were mere "tokens" and confirming the depth of talent that had been passed over for so long. Women soon followed. So did Hispanics, some of whom had worked for years with Anglo pseudonyms to get past anti-Latino prejudices; Asians; and Native Americans. . . .

Yet it is significant that I and other "first blacks" hired in the nation's newsrooms felt pretty lonely through several years of "tokenism" before affirmative hiring—or, if you prefer, "diversity hiring"—policies began to take hold at the dawn of the 1970s. The message to us journalists of color was clear: White managers did not mind hiring a few of us now and then, but they didn't want to make a habit of it, not until policies came down from the top stating in military fashion that "you *will* hire more women and minorities."

So, of all the arguments I have heard various people make against affirmative action, I find the least persuasive to be the charge that it makes its recipients feel bad. Stanford law professor Barbara Babcock

> *"Nothing in affirmative action law calls for the unqualified to be hired regardless of merit."*

had the proper response to that notion when President Jimmy Carter appointed her to head the civil rights division of the Justice Department. When she was asked in a press conference how it felt to think that she had gotten the job because she was a woman, she replied that it felt a lot better than thinking that she had *not* gotten the job because she was a woman.

True enough. Most white males have not felt particularly bad about the special preferences they have received because of their race and gender for thousands of years. Why should we? Believe me, compared to the alternative, preferential treatment feels better.

Nor have I heard many express a nagging doubt about their ability to "hack it" in fair competition with others. Quite the opposite, privileged groups tend to look upon their privilege as an entitlement. Whatever guilt or misgivings they may have are assuaged by the cottage industry that has grown up around bolstering the self-esteem of white people. Books like Charles Murray and Richard J. Herrnstein's *Bell Curve* are intended, at bottom, to answer this deep yearning. Much is made in the book about how whites perform fifteen percentage points higher on average than blacks do on standardized tests and that this may easily explain why whites earn more money than blacks. Little is made of how Asian

Americans perform fifteen percentage points higher than whites, yet they have hardly taken over management or ownership of American corporations.

Or, as one of my black professional friends put it, "Since we all know that hardly any of us is really all-black, I want to know how come we only got all the dumb white folks' genes?"

Racist Presumptions

The notion that Babcock should feel bad about her appointment is based on the pernicious presumption that, simply and solely because she is a woman, she must be less qualified than the man who normally would be preferred simply because he was a man.

Charles Sykes, in *A Nation of Victims: The Decay of the American Character* (1993), says that those who insist on affirmative action really are arguing that "minorities" (he speaks little of women) cannot meet existing standards, and that ultimately affirmative action forces all minorities to "deal with the nagging doubt that its policies stigmatize all successful minority individuals."

Another critic of affirmative action, Dinesh D'Souza, resident scholar at the American Enterprise Institute, goes so far as to say in his inflammatory *The End of Racism: Principles for a Multiracial Society* (1995) that most of us middle-class blacks should be stigmatized because we owe our prosperity, such as it is, to affirmative action. He then speculates that middle-class blacks must suffer "intense feelings of guilt" because "they have abandoned their poor brothers and sisters, and realize that their present circumstances became possible solely because of the heart-wrenching sufferings of the underclass."

> *"Hesitant to tell applicants the awful truth that they are not going to be hired, some job interviewers use affirmative action as a scapegoat."*

Affirmative Action Does Not Lower Standards

Yet nothing in affirmative action law calls for the unqualified to be hired regardless of merit. Even "special admissions" minority students are selected from among those who already have met the standards required to do the college's work.

Affirmative action calls only for "merit" standards to be more inclusive. Affirmative action, properly implemented, *widens the pool* of qualified candidates who will be considered. This often benefits qualified white males, too, who would otherwise have been bypassed because of nepotism, favoritism, and other unnecessarily narrow criteria. My favorite example is the University of Indiana Law School's decision in 1969 to broaden its acceptance criteria to open doors to bright, promising applicants who showed high potential but, for the present, had not scored as well as other applicants in a highly competitive field. The goal of the program was to offer a second chance to disadvantaged students like those who could be found in abundance in Gary and other urban centers, but the program was not limited to them. Several white students got in, too. One was a well-heeled De Pauw University graduate named J. Danforth Quayle. He later became vice president of the United States. He apparently had not scored well enough to qualify for the law school under existing criteria, but, like him or not, he did have potential. Some people are late bloomers.

> *"Affirmative action, when it works properly, guarantees only equal opportunity, not equal results."*

The Privilege of White Skin

Despite America's new "atmosphere of tolerance" cited by Sykes, white skin still has its privileges. Sociology professor Andrew Hacker of Queens College recounts in his book, *Two Nations,* that he has posed to his white students the hypothetical proposition of being turned black overnight. When he asks them how much compensation they would ask for whatever inconvenience they might suffer, they tend to ask for millions of dollars for every year of their life expectancy. Who wouldn't? We all love money. The point is that none of the students presumes he or she would *not* be penalized in some fundamentally significant way by nonwhite skin. . . .

Is there less prejudice today? It is certainly less obvious, and what remains of it is mostly denied. If the words "racism" and "sexism" have lost their sting with white America through overuse, so has the phrase "I'm not prejudiced" for those who have been victims of prejudice, for it is inevitably followed by a qualifier—"I'm not prejudiced, but . . ."—that prepares listeners to brace themselves for an announcement of the speaker's prejudices. A page-one *Wall Street Journal* feature in June 1995, for example, described the reluctance of many immigrant entrepreneurs to hire blacks, even when their clientele is black. One Chinese-American owner of a Los Angeles toy company "says he isn't prejudiced," but nevertheless expects to fill his next job opening with a Mexican immigrant, probably recruited by his workers, because blacks have a "negative image" and "don't mix well with workers of other backgrounds," the story reported. Not prejudiced? Right. He's not prejudiced. He just doesn't like black people.

Reverse Discrimination Is Exaggerated

The wrongs committed by affirmative action are constantly overblown. At the newspaper where I work, I have received mail from people who allege episodes of reverse discrimination. Since I have experienced the sting of racial discrimination in jobs, housing, and public access, I sympathize with them, but not by much. After all, if they have a legitimate complaint, they can do the same thing I would do. They can file a complaint with the proper federal, state, or local authorities. Many white males do, and many win. Many receive sizable judgments. Some even have famous Supreme Court cases like "Bakke," "Weber," and "Crosson" named after them. So I called my readers' bluff. I challenged them to send me examples they have *personally* experienced. The mail fell to a trickle, all of which came from white males who described job interviewers who had turned them down saying something like, "Too bad you're not a woman or a minority." Why, I wondered, had they not filed a complaint? More important, if the company had not been looking for women or minorities, would this particular complaining individual have stood a ghost of a chance of getting the job instead? Or would some other white male have gotten it? Was the complainer really certain the company had any jobs available anyway? Was the job interviewer just trying to let the applicant down easy by passing the buck? I called my letter writers who included their telephone numbers and asked. They did not know. I think the worst foes of affirmative action have not been Ronald Reagan, Jesse Helms, or David Duke. They have been job interviewers. Hesitant to tell applicants the awful truth that they are not going to be hired, some job interviewers use affirmative action as a scapegoat. Some actually have been told by their superiors to keep an eye out for more women or minorities because, in many cases, their own year-end bonuses depend on showing improvements in their hiring numbers. This is not a bad thing, since the companies that do this tend to be companies that have dismally low numbers in the first place. An *affinity impulse* drives most of us, when given a chance, to prefer hiring people who look and sound like us. Sometimes the best way to break through the affinity impulse is to put somebody's paycheck in the balance.

Nor does it settle the argument to say affirmative action is unfair to "meritocracy," America's cherished tradition of rewarding effort by "deserving" individuals. Americans have always had a wide array of exotic standards for determining "merit." For example, I have a blond-haired, blue-eyed friend of Scandinavian descent who is a Washington lawyer; he told me, jokingly, that he "got into Harvard thanks to affirmative action for Nebraskans."

> *"Affirmative action . . . asks nothing more of interviewers than a widening of the [hiring] criteria and the search pool."*

Another, who happens to be a Greek-American college professor, tells me he is "convinced I got into Dartmouth because I was the only application they got from Albuquerque that year. I'm sure some talented Jewish kid from New York was kept out so I could get in."

Indeed, geographic diversity was practiced by college and university admissions officers long before affirmative action came along. Few people would deny Harvard the right to choose from a broader pool of qualified applicants than just Philips Exeter graduates from New England. Nor have I seen valiant efforts put forth to dismantle preferences for promising athletes or the children of alumni or major contributors. But let a university's admissions criteria take race or ethnicity into account, and suddenly the alarms are sounded.

A Level Playing Field

Then again, I have been asked, "Would you want to be treated by a doctor who got into medical school through affirmative action?" As I once heard Yale's Stephen Carter argue back, "I would care less about how that doctor got into medical school than how he or she came out." Contrary to what some critics say, affirmative action, when it works properly, guarantees only equal opportunity, not equal results.

A Georgetown University law student, for example, kicked off a scandal there in the late 1980s by revealing to the student newspaper confidential files that showed most of the law school's black students had scored lower on their admissions tests than some qualified white applicants who had been turned down. Horrors, exclaimed conservative critics in a high state of dudgeon. The critics gave little attention to some other relevant facts. For one, admissions tests have never been and probably never will be the sole criterion on which colleges' admissions are based. Experts agree that their ability to predict performance drops off sharply after the first academic year. For that reason, as well as the simple enriching virtues of diversity, colleges use many criteria to select their students, including geography and areas of interest. Most important, no one could argue that the black students, despite having scored lower than the white students who were accepted, were not qualified to enter the school. The critics conveniently overlooked the fact that the black students who were accepted still scored higher test scores than most other white students who applied. Despite myths to the contrary, affirmative action is not intended to promote people who are not qualified. It is intended to widen the criteria for those who are chosen out of the pool of the qualified.

> *"[The] fundamental preference for white males in the employment marketplace . . . has not gone away."*

Affirmative action is, at bottom, intended to do what its advocates say: level the playing field. Unfortunately, government inevitably does a pretty heavy-handed job of it, especially in a country as diverse as this one is, and heavy-handed enforcement of any kinds of laws, regulations, or guidelines always raises the threat that innocents will be penalized. White men are not accustomed to feeling racially vulnerable. Affirmative action has given them a taste, a tiny taste, of it. They don't like it, they want to get rid of it, and they don't want to feel it again.

Recruitment, retention, and promotion of women and minorities leads to lowered standards only when cynical managers resort to "bean counting" and impose quotas *of their own* without regard to individual merit. For example, the biggest political enemies of affirmative action are job interviewers who don't want to admit to white male applicants that there are no jobs, so instead they say something like, "Gee, it's too bad you aren't a woman or a minority. I could hire you right now."

They could, but would they? In most cases, they wouldn't. But it doesn't matter. Every applicant who hears that excuse feels cheated about what might have been, if not for that darned pesky affirmative action.

In fact, affirmative action properly conducted asks nothing more of interviewers than a widening of the criteria and the search pool by which companies do their hiring. An excellent example is offered by Clifford Alexander when he was secretary of the army under President Jimmy Carter. Sent a list of candidates for promotion to general, he sent it back with a demand for more women and minority candidates. One of the names added to the second list, and a name that he approved, was Colin Powell.

President George Bush also boldly promoted diversity in his Cabinet and set high numerical goals for female and minority hiring at the Pentagon, among other agencies, despite his public protestations against "quotas." Bush promoted Powell over other generals with higher seniority to make him the first black chairman of the Joint Chiefs of Staff. Was that an affirmative action decision? No one could say for sure, since he obviously was qualified, judging by, among other criteria, his performance during Operation Desert Storm.

> *"America will not have racial equality until opportunities are equalized."*

I sympathize with those whites and males who feel they have been or might be victimized by affirmative action. Even though I think their fears are overblown, I sympathize because I can empathize. Long before there was affirmative action for women and minorities, there were racial and gender preferences for white males. This fundamental preference for white males in the employment marketplace may have diminished in these more enlightened times, but it has not gone away. None of us is immune from the fundamental affinity impulse that causes us to prefer the company of people who are as much like us as possible. . . .

A Success or a Failure?

Opponents of affirmative action have had the luxury of having their argument both ways: Some say affirmative action has failed, therefore it should be ended, while others argue that affirmative action has *succeeded,* therefore it should be ended. Here, again, the truth runs somewhere down the middle. Affirmative action has succeeded, but not enough to say it should remain unchanged. It has also failed, but not enough to say it should be eradicated. Andrew Hacker offers the example of his alma mater, Amherst College, where his own graduating class of 250 had only two black members, "not even 1 percent," he notes in an essay for the *Nation*. In 1996, Amherst classes tended to be about 8 percent black, at least partly because the college adjusted its admissions criteria to create a more diverse student body. The eight Ivy League schools together had 5,471 black students out of their total enrollment of 95,204 in 1996. Without affirmative action, will these schools return to their old 1 percent days? At least one study Berkeley conducted forecast a two-thirds drop in its black enrollment if affirmative action was ended, a possibility that caused one conservative black member of the state university system's board of regents to concede that perhaps some affirmative action should be retained. . . .

America will not have racial equality until opportunities are equalized, beginning at the preschool level, to build up the supply of qualified applicants for the new jobs emerging in information-age America. The American ideal of equal opportunity still produces rewards, when it is given a real try. It needs to be tried more often. Affirmative action is not a perfect remedy, but it beats the alternative, if the only alternative is to do nothing.

Affirmative Action Is Essential to the Success of Hispanics

by Roberto Santiago

About the author: *Roberto Santiago is a contributing writer for* Hispanic *magazine.*

In the daily struggle for equal opportunity, Affirmative Action was always the third of a three-legged argument. Businesses should hire and work with minorities because it's good business and it's the right thing to do. These arguments usually preceded any discussion of Affirmative Action. Companies may say they support "diversity," but in practice, the challenge of diversity still exists. For this reason, the federal government took the leadership on the issue, demonstrating how to become an equal opportunity employer. But when the Supreme Court opted not to hear the *Hopwood* v. *University of Texas* case, which states that race can no longer be considered for college admission, it rendered Affirmative Action, if not dead, certainly terminally ill and with time quickly running out.

Affirmative Action is under attack not because the majority of Americans are against it but because conservative critics have effectively distorted its definition, say Hispanic experts on Affirmative Action. "In recent years, the definition of Affirmative Action has been deliberately twisted by its opponents to provoke racial hostilities against minorities," says Central Michigan University's Angela Haddad, who headed the university's Affirmative Action efforts. "Their distortion has been so effective that many white Americans now hear Affirmative Action and think: preferential treatment, reverse discrimination, white displacement. Many whites silently define Affirmative Action as the hiring of unqualified minorities over qualified whites."

Nothing could be further from the truth. First, Affirmative Action, as defined by the American Association of Affirmative Action, is any measure and effort

Reprinted from Roberto Santiago, "Critical Condition," *Hispanic*, August 1996, by permission of the author.

beyond simple termination of discrimination to bring about equal opportunity. "In other words, Affirmative Action recognizes that outlawing discrimination in the workplace or university has not eliminated institutional racism against minorities," says Chicago State University's Pedro Martinez, who heads the university's efforts. "Affirmative Action recognizes the impact of racism and makes employers and universities accountable for it by actively encouraging the hiring and enrollment of minorities."

"Qualified Minority"

Second, minorities hired through such Affirmative Action efforts are not unqualified, as conservative critics concur, but members of the most qualified group of candidates. "It bothers me every time I hear people using the term 'qualified minority,'" Haddad says. "You never hear the term 'qualified white.' Why? Discrimination in this country is such that people will automatically assume a white to be qualified and a minority to be unqualified—even before examining their credentials.

"All Affirmative Action does is give the most talented minorities the opportunity to compete. Whites can accept losing a job to another white, but not to a minority. Their sense of privilege cannot accept that a black or Latino was better qualified than they."

This realization may be hard to accept, but is nevertheless true. A 1992 study by the Urban Institute and a 1995 study by the U.S. Department of Labor found that virtually all so-called reverse discrimination suits were "thrown out of court because they are brought by frustrated [white] job applicants who are less qualified than the chosen woman or minority candidate." The distortion of Affirmative Action is so great that many minorities buy into insidious conservative myths that suggest people hired by Affirmative Action are not qualified.

Minorities Must Be Proud of Affirmative Action

Juan Figueroa, president and general counsel of the Puerto Rican Legal Defense and Education Fund (PRLDEF), is troubled by minorities who refuse to credit Affirmative Action efforts for their success. "Every time I hear a black or Latino professional say, 'I got here because I am qualified, not because of Affirmative Action,' I cringe," Figueroa said before a group of university educators and administrators in Connecticut. "How can we defend Affirmative Action if we buy

"Many whites silently define Affirmative Action as the hiring of unqualified minorities over qualified whites."

into the myths? We are all products of Affirmative Action, and we must be proud to say it."

Figueroa, Martinez, and Haddad all agree that Affirmative Action must be reclaimed from conservative forces that blame Hispanics for all the ills of this nation. "The Pat Buchanans, the Pete Wilsons, the Bob Doles of this country are racially dividing the country," Gonzalez says. "They have white Americans believing that they lost their jobs because of Affirmative Action—not because we live in a global economy and American manufacturing takes place all over the world."

Haddad agrees. "Its much easier to blame a Mexican immigrant for your unemployment than rich white corporate leaders who export thousands of manufacturing jobs overseas every year," she says.

Affirmative Action Makes a Difference

Gilbert F. Casellas, chairman of the U.S. Equal Employment Opportunity Commission—the only federal agency devoted to civil rights enforcement—writes that Affirmative Action in higher education and employment is necessary to ensure that Hispanics will not remain an underclass into the next century. Does Affirmative Action make a difference? Casellas cites a 1989 study by the Urban Institute which used job applicants with equal qualifications and credentials as test applicants in companies that had no Affirmative Action policies. The white applicants received 23 percent more interviews and 52 percent more job offers than did the Hispanic applicants.

"Whites can accept losing a job to another white, but not to a minority."

Among other EEOC data, Casellas cites that Hispanic men in 1992 earned 64 cents for every dollar earned by white men while Hispanic women earned only 55 cents. Hispanic women with college degrees earn less than white men with only high school diplomas. In March 1995 the EEOC published the findings of a bipartisan committee called the Glass Ceiling Commission that, among other things, proved that a glass ceiling still exists for women and minorities, that white women have benefited more than blacks or Hispanics from Affirmative Action, and that most of the progress made by minorities and women would not have been made without "vigorous enforcement" of anti-discrimination laws.

"Sadly, many Americans are not aware of the persistence of discrimination," Casellas writes. "We must continue to remind people that these persistent patterns rob us of our rightful place in America, and they rob America of our contributions. So we must not be ashamed of or apologize for Affirmative Action."

A Latino Issue

In testimony before the U.S. Senate in September 1995, Georgina C. Verdugo, regional counsel for the Mexican American Legal Defense and Education Fund (MALDEF), said, "All too often, Latinos are overlooked as the debate over Affirmative Action focuses on African Americans and women, recognizing Latinos only when the issue blends with controversy over immigration. But Affirmative Action is a Latino issue, and its resolution will have profound implications for this fast-growing minority and economically vital portion of the U.S. population."

Although the Census places the Hispanic population at 10 percent, a September 1995 study by the Rand Institute on Education and Training estimated that the Hispanic population will be 20 percent by the year 2020. The Rand Institute found that equal access to higher education for Latinos

> *"[Latinos] must not be ashamed of or apologize for Affirmative Action."*

would boost productivity for the U.S. economy. For example, "If high school completion rates and college participation rates for the current generation of Latinos were equal to the rates for whites, the increase in federal tax revenues would be on the order of $13 billion per year."

Economic Advantages

But the fact is that high school and college completion rates among Hispanics are at crisis level, with more than half dropping out of high school and only one-third enrolling in college. A policy paper by MALDEF found that if conservative policies against Affirmative Action recruitment and scholarships in higher education were enacted, Hispanics would not be able to fully contribute to this country. "Conservatives don't realize that by denying higher educational and employment opportunities to minorities they are perpetuating the growth of an underclass," Haddad says. "In trying to preserve the status quo for whites, they are destroying the economic growth of this country and making the nation a lesser player in the world economy."

Although conservatives would be hard-pressed to believe it, Affirmative Action benefits universities and corporations as much as it does the African Americans and Latinos who are enrolled and hired. A 1994 study by the U.S Department of Labor stated that "companies with the best equal opportunity/ Affirmative Action records have the highest profit margins." And according to a policy paper by MALDEF; university presidents such as Gerhard Casper of Stanford University; business leaders such as Edwin L. Artzt, CEO of Procter and Gamble Company; the American Council on Education; the Business Roundtable; and the National Association of Manufacturers applaud Affirmative Action efforts for helping promote growth in their institutions.

But the evidence of how good Affirmative Action is for America continues to be stifled by campaigns of misinformation by conservatives. Their distortion has already given rise to much-publicized efforts to eliminate Affirmative Action from higher education.

On May 3, 1996, Ward Connerly, a regent on the University of California Board of Regents, submitted a proposal entitled, "Elimination of Race-Based Financial Aid." Connerly was instrumental in winning support in 1995 for a measure to end the university's use of Affirmative Action. He orchestrated the campaign for a state ballot initiative, misnamed the Civil Rights Initiative, that would end Affirmative Action from California's public institutions if approved by voters in November 1996. [The initiative has since passed.]

This is by no means the only case. On April 23, 1996, Georgia Attorney General Mike Bowers called on state colleges and universities to end policies that "favor racial minorities." And on April 8, 1996, Robert Berdahl, president of the University of Texas at Austin, announced the end of Affirmative Action funding for all students. This was a result of the alleged reverse discrimination case of *Hopwood* v. *University of Texas*, in which four defendants, three white men and one white women, claimed that admissions policies at the university gave preferential treatment to African American and Hispanic students. According to the ruling of the U.S. 5th Circuit Court of Appeals, the university could not justify its affirmative action program on the grounds that it helped rectify past discrimination. Affirmative Action, according to the court, had run its course and societal discrimination did not alone justify government programs that give preference to minorities.

The Texas case was appealed to the United States Supreme Court because it challenges the decades-old *Bakke* v. *University of California* ruling, which upheld Affirmative Action as a necessary antidote to racism. The U.S. Supreme Court, however, opted not to hear the case. Because there was no ruling by the court, the case does not set nationwide precedent but it will set the stage for other universities to call into question their own admissions policies.

The "Equal Opportunity" Act

The anti–Affirmative Action hysteria has even taken on Orwellian doublespeak. In early 1996, Florida Republican Congressman Charles Canady, along with Republican presidential candidate Robert Dole, proposed a bill called H.R. 2128—which would prohibit all Affirmative Action in federal government contracting, hiring, and administering federally conducted programs or activities.

Unbelievably, Dole and Canady named their bill "The Equal Opportunity Act." The attacks on Affirmative Action alarm many people, among them a Latina college student from New York named Taryn Fernandez, who is a sophomore at Bentley College in Massachusetts: "I have benefited tremendously from Affirmative Action," Fernandez says. "My Latina status helped me to be accepted here by early decision. I am an INROADS intern and have worked for Pitney

> *"Equal access to higher education for Latinos would boost productivity for the U.S. economy."*

Bowes, Inc., for the last two summers. The mission of INROADS is to place and develop talented minority youth in business and industry and prepare them for corporate and community leadership. What's wrong with that?"

Nothing at all. But as the attacks on Affirmative Action wage on from conservatives, Hispanic experts warn that Hispanics should not fall victim to the infighting that often comes about between minorities when initiatives that promote their progress are reduced or threatened.

"Some will argue that Affirmative Action has benefitted white women for the greater part, and that should not be. Others will argue that dark-skinned blacks and Latinos are overlooked in favor of light-skinned or white Latinos, and that should not be," says Martinez. "It's divisive when you have minorities fighting over the crumbs like this because we wind up defeating ourselves by pettiness. People struggling for progress need to work together—not accomplish the work of those who want us to remain at the bottom."

Affirmative Action Is Needed to Counter White Male Advantage

by Deborah A. Cooksey and Marilyn K. Easter

About the authors: *Deborah A. Cooksey practices law in Oakland, California. Marilyn K. Easter has a doctorate in education and teaches at several universities in the Bay Area.*

We hate to admit it, but some of the stereotypes about African Americans are true. In fact, the authors of this viewpoint fit the disturbing profile of girls in the 'hood. We are young, black, raised in the inner city in large families and broken homes. Many of our homies are locked up, cracked up, or smacked up. We've had close encounters with the welfare system and one of us has been doing battle with the court system for most of her adult life. The other has been in school for what seems like an eternity and just can't seem to get out. One has enough kids to fill a classroom and the other sometimes doesn't even know where her ol' man is. We think of ourselves as assertive; others call us domineering and combative. On the job we're labeled as "quota hires" or "affirmative action babies"—everything except qualified.

Now that we've got the attention of those who think you know us based on the above profile, here's the truth behind the stereotypes. The protracted stint in academia has netted one author a doctorate in education. She is a college professor whose "kids" fill her classrooms to capacity; her courses have a one-year waiting list. She is married to a dentist with his own practice. The other author is a practicing attorney specializing in labor and construction litigation. She earned her law degree from an Ivy League school back east and also is married to a successful professional, a corporate attorney who travels extensively.

In short, we are the beneficiaries of affirmative action. And we are fed up with the hype that says undeserving minorities are "getting over" at the expense of whites. The implication is that minorities no longer need affirmative action because (1) it has served its intended purpose of leveling the playing field in education and employment and/or (2) attempting to right past wrongs is unfair to the white majority.

We recently interviewed over 700 people of all races in a research study to find out just how level today's playing field is. What we discovered is that affirmative action has opened doors for women and minorities but has not been able to overcome the unfairness of white male affirmative action, otherwise known as racism, elitism, and nepotism.

Racial Perceptions

Many African Americans in corporate settings and higher education find themselves resented and referred to as "quota hires" in the workplace. It is as though their hard-earned credentials are no more than consolation prizes in the affirmative action sweepstakes. In general, while white professionals are likely to be held in high esteem even if they graduated at the bottom of their class from a nonaccredited university, African American professionals are prejudged as possessing "tainted" degrees even though they graduated from Ivy League schools.

No amount of power positioning seems to overcome racist perceptions. In the courtroom, for example, one author is usually mistaken for a legal assistant or court reporter, despite the fact that she sits at counsel's table beside her client. The other author starts each new university course by entering the classroom and writing her name and title on the board. Students nevertheless assume she is a teaching assistant rather than a professor.

Grandfathering the Privileged

Despite the politically correct lip service paid to equal employment and a color-blind society, entrenched elitism continues to be a barrier. When one author earned her doctorate in education at 35, after more than 10 years of practical experience, she was informed that she would need at least 20 years of work experience to qualify for an entry-level university teaching position. She challenged the obvious unfairness of the situation; many currently working white teachers and some high-level university administrators had neither a doctorate degree nor 20 years' work experience. The explanation given is that many academics were "grandfathered" into teaching and administrative positions. In many sectors of society, grandfathering allows less qualified administrators to set arbitrary standards they themselves are not required to (and in some cases, could not) meet. Grandfathering can make it impossible for women and minorities to gain equal access to employment.

> *"White professionals are likely to be held in high esteem even if they graduated at the bottom of their class."*

Phony Affirmations

There are those who argue (with a straight face!) that affirmative action should be abolished because it is unfair to whites, particularly white males. They ignore the fact that white males have always had their own peculiar form of affirmative action. Consider the 1960s, when white college students, sons of prominent politicians and leaders of industry, were routinely awarded draft deferments. Other examples of white affirmative action include tax breaks for corporations, the bailouts of savings and loans, red-lining to keep white suburbs homogeneous, prep-school connections, and membership in exclusive clubs . . . just to name a few.

> *"Grandfathering can make it impossible for women and minorities to gain equal access to employment."*

The creation of phony companies is one way powerful whites have used affirmative action laws to their own advantage. Businesses throughout the country have established separate entities headed by a minority or a woman (often the wife or a female relative of the CEO of the parent company). The new company boasts a racially diverse work force, which qualifies it to bid on those portions of government contracts earmarked for women- and minority-owned businesses. However, the new company is not actually competing with its sire and has no real autonomy; the parent company continues to control the new company's board of directors and finances.

Chips off the Old Block

Nepotism is perhaps the oldest and most subtle form of white affirmative action. Our research subjects told of countless situations in which business owners and corporate executives hire, retain, and promote family members and friends, regardless of their qualifications, training, or abilities. Qualified minority applicants, who because of historical discrimination have no relatives in high places, are often out of luck.

White affirmative action is a part of the fabric of American life. It is hypocritical and wrong to call for the eradication of affirmative action for minorities while accepting affirmative action for bankers, high-level managers, and other white men in power as normal entitlements.

After 30 years of affirmative action, the playing field is far from level. For all the angry white males who want to abolish affirmative action for women and minorities, we say, *"No problem."* But while you're at it, don't forget to eliminate racism, elitism, nepotism, and the other forms of white affirmative action. They too must go!

Affirmative Action Promotes Diversity

by Chang-Lin Tien

About the author: *Chang-Lin Tien is a professor of mechanical engineering at the University of California at Berkeley and served as the university's chancellor from 1990 to 1997.*

In 1956, I came here for graduate studies, a virtually penniless immigrant from China with a limited grasp of the language and customs of the U.S. A teaching fellowship was my income. To stretch my frugal budget, I walked across town to eat at the least expensive restaurants and scouted out the lowest-cost washing machines and dryers.

As a result of the wonderful educational opportunities I have enjoyed, I have contributed to America. My research in heat transfer has enhanced our engineering expertise in many critical technologies, including nuclear reactor safety, space shuttle thermal design, and electronic systems cooling. My former students teach and conduct research in America's top universities and industries. I was privileged to head the university with the largest number and highest percentage of top-ranked doctoral programs in the nation.

Yet, along with opportunity, I have encountered the harsh realities of racial discrimination that are part of America's legacy. Like it or not, this history of racial division is linked with the debate over affirmative action. Although the U.S. has made great strides, race still divides our society. It is part of the debate over how we afford equal opportunities to everyone.

My first months in the U.S. reflect how opportunity and racial intolerance can be linked. I served as a teaching fellow for a professor who refused to pronounce my name and only referred to me as "Chinaman." One day, the professor directed me to adjust some valves in a large laboratory apparatus. When I climbed a ladder, I lost my balance and instinctively grabbed a nearby steam pipe. It was so hot it produced a jolt of pain that nearly caused me to faint, but I did not scream out. I stuffed my throbbing hand into my coat pocket and waited until the class ended. Then I ran to the hospital emergency room, where I was treated for a burn that completely had singed the skin off my palm.

My response seems to fit the Asian model minority myth: Say nothing and go about your business. My silence had nothing to do with stoicism, though. I simply did not want to endure the humiliation of having the professor scold me in front of the class.

Racial Divisions

Today, after four decades of major civil rights advances, members of racial and ethnic minorities like me no longer are intimidated into silence. Still, serious racial divisions remain. Those of us who are of Asian, Latino, or Middle Eastern heritage have become accustomed to having passersby tell us, "Go back to your own country." More typical is the polite query: "What country do you come from?" It makes no difference if you are first-generation or fifth-generation. If you have Asian, Latino, or Middle Eastern features or surname, many Americans assume you were born in another country. The ancestors of a professor in the university's School of Optometry left China to work in California during the 1850s. Even though his roots run far deeper than those of the vast majority of Californians, people invariably ask him where he was born.

Our nation cannot afford to ignore the racial strife that continues to divide America. Nor should we forget that the U.S. is a great democracy built by diverse peoples. It is critical to attack the problem of racial division and build on national strengths. The finest hope for meeting this challenge will be America's colleges and universities.

These institutions launched affirmative admissions programs to open their doors to promising minority students who lacked educational and social opportunities. Over time, the composition of America's college students has changed. Campuses are more diverse than at any time in history.

Critics of continuing race or ethnicity as a consideration in student admissions argue that affirmative action unfairly discriminates against white and Asian-American applicants who worked hard in high school and received top grades. They further maintain that it no longer is needed to provide opportunities. Although I agree that affirmative action is a temporary measure, the time has not yet come to eliminate it. Educational opportunities vary dramatically in U.S. public schools.

The inner-city student can find illegal drugs more readily than computer labs and after-school enrichment courses. In contrast, the more affluent suburban student is hooked into the Internet, enrolled in honor classes, and looking forward to summer instruction.

"The U.S. is a great democracy built by diverse peoples."

Given this reality, it is fair and equitable to consider race and ethnicity as one factor among many—including test scores and grade-point averages—in admitting qualified youths to highly competitive universities. Such an approach remains the most effective way to make sure America does not turn into a two-tiered society of permanent haves and have-nots.

Assisting promising students is not the only reason for preserving affirmative action. The diversity of students, faculty, and staff that it inspired is one of the most exciting and challenging phenomena in American higher education today. All students stand to gain, whether they are whites, Asian-Americans, or traditionally underrepresented minorities.

The Need for Diversity

I believe students on campuses that lack diversity can gain just a limited, theoretical understanding of the challenges and opportunities in a highly diverse nation. A lecture on Toni Morrison's novels or the theater of Luis Valdez is not enough.

No career or profession will be untouched by the rapid socio-demographic change. For instance, consider how America's diversity will affect those in U.S. colleges and universities. Education students will teach many youngsters born in different countries. Medical students will treat many patients with beliefs and attitudes about medicine that differ from the Western outlook. Students of engineering and business will work for major corporations, where they will be expected to design, develop, and market products that sell not just in the U.S., but in markets

> *"The inner-city student can find illegal drugs more readily than computer labs and after-school enrichment courses."*

around the world. Law students will represent clients whose experience with the judicial system in their neighborhoods and barrios is distinctive from the way middle America regards the law.

Diversity in colleges and universities benefits all students, not just the underrepresented minorities. Our experience at Berkeley shows the promise of affirmative action. Every time I walk across campus, I am impressed by the vibrant spirit of our diverse community. Nowhere do you see this better than teeming Sproul Plaza, where dozens of student groups set up tables representing a wide range of social, political, ethnic, and religious interests.

At Berkeley, undergraduates are about 40% Asian-American; 31% non-Hispanic Caucasian; 14% Hispanic; six percent African-American; and one percent Native American, with the rest undeclared. About one-quarter of freshmen come from families earning $28,600 a year or less: another quarter from families that earn more than $90,000. The median family income reported for 1994 freshmen was $58,000.

Young people from barrios, comfortable suburbs, farm towns, and the inner city come together at Berkeley to live and study side by side. Not surprisingly, they find first-time interactions with students from different backgrounds occasionally fraught with misunderstanding and tension. . . .

Today, our campus faces a major new challenge. The University of California Regents have voted to end the use of race, ethnicity, and sex as a factor among many others in student admissions at its nine campuses in 1998. At first, the Regents' decision stunned me. I questioned whether we could preserve the diversity which is so important to our campus after losing an important tool for achieving student enrollments that reflect California's wide-ranging population.

Yet, I quickly realized the importance of the Regents' reaffirmation of their commitment to diversity even though they discarded affirmative action. So, I decided to take the Chinese approach to challenge. In Chinese, the character for crisis actually is two characters: One stands for danger and the other for opportunity. For me, times of crisis present both challenges and opportunities.

The end of affirmative action at the University of California gave us the impetus for trying new approaches to improving the eligibility rates of high school students traditionally underrepresented in higher education. At Berkeley, we set to work right away to turn challenge into opportunity. We realized our efforts would be doomed unless we worked even more closely with the public schools. Within weeks of the affirmative action decision, I joined the superintendents of the San Francisco Bay Area's major urban school districts to announce our new campaign to diversity: The Berkeley Pledge.

The announcement made it clear that our campus would not shirk its commitment to diversity. Instead, we pledged to step up the drive to support the efforts of disadvantaged youth to qualify for admission and preserve access to higher education. I committed $1,000,000 from private gifts, and we are seeking additional private support to fund this innovative approach.

America has come a long way since the days of Jim Crow segregation. It would be a tragedy if our nation's colleges and universities slipped backward, denying access to talented, but disadvantaged, youth and eroding the diversity that helps to prepare the leaders of the 21st century.

> *"Diversity in colleges and universities benefits all students."*

I find one aspect of the debate over affirmative action to be especially disturbing. There seems to be an underlying assumption that if it is eliminated, the nation will have solved the problems associated with racial division. Nothing could be further from the truth. It is critical for America to address the issue of how people from diverse backgrounds are going to study, work, and live in the same neighborhoods together in harmony, not strife.

This is the challenge in higher education. It demands the collaboration of students, faculty, staff, and alumni at universities and colleges across America. All must work together to maintain the diversity that is essential to excellence.

Chapter 4

How Can Racial Problems Be Resolved?

Chapter Preface

In 1954, the Supreme Court decision of *Brown v. Board of Education* judged segregated schools to be unconstitutional. Three years later, President Dwight D. Eisenhower moved to enforce the Court's ruling by dispatching federal troops to accompany nine black students through the doors of Central High School in Little Rock, Arkansas. At the school's entrance, the black teenagers were punched, threatened, and spit upon by a riotous mob of segregationists. Melba Patillo Beals, one of the Little Rock Nine, stated that at the end of the day she could "wring spit from [her] dress."

Despite its violent inception, many saw the integration of Central High as a pivotal victory in the civil rights movement, predicting that it was the first of many strides toward racial equality. Forty years later, however, social critics are disappointed by the questionable progress of integration; as one civil rights lawyer reports, "[The races] are much more separated today than [they] were 40 years ago." The failure of integration has often been attributed to the exodus of many whites from the cities since the 1950s—some of whom fled to escape de-segregated schools. Though busing programs were later instituted to combat the effects of residential segregation, the majority of these programs were abandoned in the 1980s and 1990s due to objections by both blacks and whites.

The dismal results of desegregation efforts have caused some to reject integration altogether. While segregationists have traditionally been white racists, among recent supporters are some younger African Americans. Frustrated with a system they perceive as being hostile to blacks, they view Martin Luther King's dream of integration as "naive." Citing the success of African Americans who attended the all-black schools existing prior to *Brown v. Board of Education*, these segregationists declare that separation, not integration, benefits blacks.

Many others, however, hold that integration is essential. Integrationists maintain that segregation isolates black children in poor, low-quality schools. In addition, says one proponent of integration, "[black] students don't get to know whites their own age, and white students . . . have hardly any knowledge of black youngsters." This ignorance, integrationists claim, creates a society in which racial harmony is impossible.

Addressing the issue of segregated public schools is central to finding a resolution to racial problems in America. This and other potential solutions will be discussed in the following chapter.

Whites Should Acknowledge Their Role in Racial Problems

by Harlon L. Dalton

About the author: *Harlon L. Dalton is the author of the book* Racial Healing, *from which this viewpoint is excerpted.*

"America has a race problem." Those five words seem innocuous enough, perhaps even a bit bland. But I can still recall how they surged through me the first time I encountered them. I was in my early teens, I think, and was hanging around the house waiting for dinner. While thumbing through the latest issue of *Ebony* magazine, I happened upon a serious-looking essay by historian Lerone Bennett, Jr. Instead of skipping over it in favor of something a bit lighter, I decided to check it out. I'm not sure I ever got to the essay's main point, for I was mesmerized by something Bennett said early on. He said, in essence, that we Negroes should stop thinking that *we* have a race problem and start recognizing that *America* has a race problem.

The effect on me was electric. Until that moment, I did not realize how thoroughly I had bought into the notion that racial injustice was "the Black man's burden." Sure, we could implore White America to set things straight, but weren't we the ones who were suffering? It was a short step from thinking that we had a problem to believing that we *were* the problem, and I was already in mid-stride. Lerone Bennett understood how psychologically debilitating such beliefs can be, and he reached across the printed page to save me.

Thinking of race as "the Black man's burden" is also debilitating to Whites. It leaves them powerless to effect change. It deprives them of the opportunity to be moral agents and to participate in the cleansing of this nation's great stain. It reinscribes a vertical relationship, even for people who are philosophically committed to equality. Moreover, sitting on the sidelines virtually guarantees that America's future will be bleak. We don't have a person to waste. We cannot build a healthy modern economy while disempowering and undervaluing a large segment of the workforce. We owe our children more; not just a thriving economy and a clean environment, but also a nation free of permanent divisions and human decay. As a practical matter, people of color cannot do it alone. We are busy enough just getting by. Besides, the scale of the problem is such that we need all hands on deck. In order to redistribute advantage and rethink how we relate to one another, everyone's participation is needed.

Disowning Race

So it is imperative that White folk accept joint ownership of America's race problem. But first they must *un*learn the many ways in which they commonly *dis*own race. For example, Whites often excuse themselves from taking an active role by engaging in a heightened rhetoric of Black responsibility. Sometimes it seems as if every race conversation gets turned into a discussion of what Black people need to do to get their own house in order. "They" need to become more ambitious, to take education more seriously, to be willing to meet Whites halfway, to stop victimizing each other.

An especially galling version of table turning is "let's talk about Black-on-Black crime." I do not mean to suggest that Black-on-Black crime is not a serious issue. On the contrary. The Black community has viewed it as critical for years. Part of the reason that Louis Farrakhan is held in such high esteem in the Black community in spite of his many failings is that he has steadfastly taken the community to task for preying on its own. Similarly, Jesse Jackson has preached for years that there is nothing manly or honorable about victimizing one another. The same message has echoed from pulpits, podiums, and street corners in Black neighborhoods across America for at least a decade. Since 1993, Black-on-Black crime has topped *Ebony*'s annual readers' poll as "the most pressing issue facing Black America."

Given all that, there is something deeply insulting about the implication that Black people have not focused on the issue, or worse, that we aren't concerned about it, or worse still, that we wouldn't be concerned about it if White folk did not wave it in our faces. Moreover, there is something

> *"It is imperative that White folk accept joint ownership of America's race problem."*

passing strange about the sudden interest in Black-on-Black crime to the seeming exclusion of Black-on-*White* crime. In any event, the dominance of this and other issues of Black responsibility serve to deflect attention away from our joint obligation to transform America's relation to race.

The Role of Personal Responsibility

A second way in which White folk sometimes disown the race problem is by treating Black people as if they were fully in control of their own fate. "Why don't they just . . . ?" Why don't they just go get a job? Why don't they just move out of the inner city? Why don't they just stop having babies? Why don't they just exercise more control over their children? Why don't they just take the bull by the horns? (Does anyone ever say what you are supposed to do with the bull once you've grabbed hold of it?)

The problem is that such questions are often posed rhetorically. Moreover, even when serious answers are sought, some answers seem to fall outside the pale. Thus, it just wouldn't do to respond, "Because you wouldn't

> *"We do not have to choose between doing right by one group and doing right by another."*

hire them," or "Because you wouldn't be interested in having them as next-door neighbors." Yet there is much truth in these answers. Black people do not, in and of themselves, control the real estate market, the job market, the economy, the welfare system, the school system, or the streets. The problem with the questions and the anticipated answers is that they assume a false world in which Black people are both the problem and the solution. The net effect is that the posing of such questions tends to deflect attention away from the possibility of joint ownership of both.

"Reverse" Racism

A third way in which White people sometimes avoid dealing with the impact of racism on Black America is by turning the tables. In particular, the notion that White men have suffered greatly at the hands of people of color (and White women) has been responsible for the death of many trees of late. "White, Male and Worried," proclaimed *Business Week*. "White Male Fear" graced the pages of the *Economist*. Perhaps less surprisingly, *Playboy* ran a two-part series entitled "The Myth of Male Power." And *Newsweek* hit the nail on the head with "White Male Paranoia." Actor/director Michael Douglas has even managed to create a virtual cottage industry with his portrayals of victimized White males.

Assuming for the moment that *Business Week, Newsweek,* and the rest are onto something terribly important, we make a mistake in allowing it to drown out or eclipse our concern for the plight of people of color. Justice is not a limited resource. We do not have to choose between doing right by one group and doing right by another. Nor are the aspirations of White men (or women) necessarily in conflict with those of people of color. If we were to take joint responsibility for cleaning up the racial mess, we could search for creative solutions that expand opportunities for everyone. Moreover, upon reflection thoughtful Whites might discover that sometimes less is more. That has certainly been my experience as a male. Ceding the right to, as Humphrey Bogart put it in *Casablanca,* "make the decisions for both of us" has been enormously liberating. Similarly, in a very real sense Black liberation holds the promise of White liberation as well.

The attention given to the "victimization of the White male" is troubling in a second respect. It is insensitive to power and position and ignores issues of quality and scale. Several years ago, lesbian and gay male students at a small private law school in the Northeast which shall remain nameless were the victims of a series of belligerent acts. Someone had ascertained their sexual orientation (by, I suspect, taking note of who received a rather distinctive party invitation) and placed hateful messages in their student mail slots. Vulgar graffiti directed at lesbians were scratched into an elevator wall. Threatening messages were slipped under at least one student's dorm-room door.

Eventually, the law school's dean called a town meeting at which students, faculty, and staff could come together as a community to share information and express solidarity with those who had been attacked. As it happens, the president of the university was in the building that afternoon, and was invited to join the rest of us in the courtyard. After listening to several gay students speak of how frightened, vulnerable, and angry they felt, he approached the microphone. "I know how you feel," he told the students, or words to that effect (I am paraphrasing from memory). "I know what it is like to be under attack." He then proceeded to describe the ongoing labor strife between the university administration and the clerical and technical workers' union and to emphasize how personally stung he had been when workers in the heat of passion had called him names.

The students stared at him dumbstruck. Although he claimed to be empathizing with them, it was obvious that the president had been unnerved by their emotionalism and was indirectly urging them to respond with more dispassion. But beyond that, how could he dare equate his experience with theirs? He was the president of an exceedingly wealthy university that historically had treated its clerical and technical workers as if they were vassals. He should be able to handle a little negative feedback. The gay students, on the other hand, were being stalked by an anonymous assailant simply for being who they were. They had no ready way to defend themselves, no sense of when the belligerence would end, and no idea how far things might go.

Equating the current plight of the angry White male with that of historically oppressed people of color is a little like that. Although the contrasts are not as sharp and the parallel is less than perfect, the error is the same. The comparison only makes sense if

> *"Race and class are sometimes interrelated in complex ways."*

you sweep aside issues of hierarchy and control. Somehow, despite his vaunted victimization, the angry White male seems to have done rather well for himself in effecting a political sea change in 1994. Meanwhile, America's hidden wound continues to fester.

A fourth way in which the race problem is disowned is by simply removing race from the picture. "Wouldn't you agree," I am often asked, "that these days the problems of Black people have much more to do with class than race?" Before I can even object to the leading question, a follow-up is posed: "Wouldn't it make more sense to formulate social policies that target class concerns rather than racial ones?"

The Problem of Class

These statements (dressed up as questions) suffer from at least two fundamental defects. First, they assume that race and class are independent of one another and can be readily teased apart. Sociologists have long known, however, that race and class are sometimes interrelated in complex ways. It's often difficult to determine whether what one is observing is a race effect, a class effect, a combination of the two, or an interaction between the two. (Not to mention the effect of mass culture. When it comes to watching the Super Bowl or purchasing Nike shoes, we are probably all more American than anything else.) Second, the sentiment that we should really be focusing on class either assumes that a forced choice is required or is a disguised way of saying that race is irrelevant. After all, if we aren't artificially limited to one choice, and if racism is indeed alive and well, then the simple answer is that we should focus on both.

> *"Race-related indifference is largely responsible for our unwillingness to . . . improve the lot of the poor."*

As is too often the case, my fellow pointy-heads in the academy bear a measure of responsibility for stirring the pot. For some time, social scientists have been asking, in one form or another, the following question: to what extent can differences between the races (in attitudes, in behavior, in social location) be explained by class? The answer usually comes back that when you control for class, many or even most (depending on the study) racial disparities disappear. I do not quarrel with these results. I simply question what they mean.

Which disparities remain, and are they significant in the life of the Black community? Does statistically controlling for class tell us anything at all about what would happen in the real world if we sought to make the Black class structure mirror that which presently exists for Whites? How would we go about doing that? Would we, for example, employ economic (as distinct from racial) affirmative action? What would be the impact of this class shifting on Whites? If we could simply wave a magic wand and equalize the class structures, why not use it to eliminate racism as well? More fundamentally, why does the difference in class structure exist in the first place? Might not racism have something to do with it? And if so, what reason is there for believing that we can just focus on class without also focusing on race?

In fairness, I should note that some who suggest that we worry less about race and more about class are making a rather different point. They might well concede the case that is powerfully made in Ellis Cose's *The Rage of a Privileged*

Class—namely, that racism remains a problem for Blacks who break through the class barrier. They question, however, whether racism is an important concern of the so-called Black "underclass." Surely for the folk who can't afford to buy Cose's book, runs the argument, class is much more important than race. Therefore, by continuing to focus on race, we favor the relatively well-off Black middle class over the much more numerous and needy underclass.

Despite its surface appeal, this position is seriously flawed. Of course the problems of the underclass are largely economic. But that doesn't mean that the poor don't also suffer from racism. It may well take a different form than is true for the middle class. An underemployed single mother in the inner city is a hell of a lot less likely to be concerned about bumping against a glass ceiling than about being left behind. But the cause of her predicament is not solely her class position, for the racial pecking order is largely responsible for the fact that Blacks are massed at the bottom of the economic pile. And race-related indifference is largely responsible for our unwillingness to do what is necessary to improve the lot of the poor. Furthermore, while the material position of inner-city Blacks may not be appreciably different from that of, say, many rural Whites, the color line serves to divide economic like from like, thus increasing the likelihood that nothing will be done to improve their lives.

> *"To contemplate that one might have contributed to or benefited from [other people's pain] is not easy."*

I honestly believe that many who push the "it's all class" line have the best of intentions. I also happen to believe that many others are simply looking for a way to get off the race hook. But either way, the practical effect is the same: to deflect attention from the enduring problem of race, with only the most theoretical of payoffs in return.

Conditional Participation

Finally, rather than disown the race problem altogether, many Whites simply make their participation in bringing about change conditional. I can't tell you how many times I have heard, "I'd be willing to help, if you would only . . ." Be less shrill. Get your own house in order first. Meet me halfway. (Guess who gets to determine where that point is.) Inevitably, I experience these preconditions as a kind of muscle flexing or throwing down of the gauntlet. In case I forgot, I am being shown who is still in charge.

That White folk would resist owning the race problem is perfectly understandable. Dealing with race takes a considerable psychic toll, especially on those who are most attuned to the felt grievances of people of color. To recognize other people's pain and to contemplate that one might have contributed to or benefited from it is not easy. It is no wonder that genuinely decent White people sometimes try to make race disappear. How do you make peace with the fact that people like you have subordinated others in your name?

Then there is the small matter of coping with change. For most of us change is anxiety-producing even when it promises to serve us well. I suspect that most White folk would be in favor of marked progress for people of color if they could be guaranteed that their own lives would not be significantly affected. But that is not in the cards. We all must change if we are to promote racial healing and aspire to racial justice. All of our lives will be altered in some respects—for example, our neighborhoods may change complexion and our employment prospects may differ—but the biggest changes will be in how we think. And abandoning old attitudes and familiar patterns of belief is never easy.

The Moral Vacuum in Black America Must Be Filled

by Joseph H. Brown

About the author: *Joseph H. Brown is an editorial writer with the* Tampa Tribune *and a columnist for* Headway.

He returned as a hero, not as the convicted rapist he is. Mike Tyson, former heavyweight boxing champion, was the recipient of all kinds of hosannas at a Harlem rally in his honor following his release from prison. Predictably, the crowd absolved him of his crime and made yet another victim of "the system" instead.

What was most damaging about this spectacle was the letter of support Tyson received from fifty-two churches. So in addition to the many prominent "leaders" who unsurprisingly wished him well such as Al Sharpton, Percy Sutton (former Manhattan borough president), and Benjamin Hooks (former head of the National Association for the Advancement of Colored People [NAACP]), many black ministers in the community also heaped praise on the convicted former champ.

Moral Decline

Black ministers used to be the moral and spiritual leaders of black communities. It was they who would shake their fingers at those who weren't on the straight and narrow path of righteousness. It was they who would admonish those who crossed the line between right and wrong. But this is increasingly not the case.

It would have been appropriate if some ministers had joined a group of black people who held a vigil against violence toward women, but their moral cowardice wouldn't allow them. The entire affair was symbolic of the moral decay that has engulfed the black community during the last three decades. Thirty years ago a black man, heavyweight champion or not, could never have raped a woman, be totally unrepentant for his act, and then have a rally in his honor upon his release, as did Mike Tyson. Look at Jack Johnson, the first black heavyweight champ. His public behavior, which included drunkenness and cavorting with white women, was deemed unacceptable by leaders like Booker T. Washington. That is why when Joe Louis became the second black man to hold that title in 1937, he promised to conduct himself in such a manner that the race could be proud of him in and out of the ring. But no such code

> *"What we have today in many black communities is a moral vacuum."*

of conduct exists anymore. As the words of the Cole Porter song convey, "anything goes." Nature, proverbially speaking, abhors a vacuum, and what we have today in many black communities is a moral vacuum.

This moral vacuum was created more by silence than by anything else. There is not enough righteous anger and public denouncement of things like black-on-black homicide, open-air drug dealing, and irresponsible parenting. We do not condemn these evils the way we should. Even when racism and segregation were in their heyday, it was never like this. So when did it start? I believe we have to go back thirty years to the Moynihan Report to get the answer.

The Moynihan Report

Thirty years ago, Daniel Patrick Moynihan spoke the perfect truth when he said: "From the wild Irish slums of the 19th century Eastern seaboard to the riot-torn suburbs of Los Angeles, there is one unmistakable lesson in American history. A community that allows a large number of young men to grow up in broken families, dominated by women, never acquiring any rational expectations about the future—that community asks for and gets chaos."

Moynihan's remarks were a call to arms. As assistant secretary of labor in 1965, he saw all of the signs and issued a report warning of the consequences if the trend continued. At that time, the social climate was generally temperate—by today's standards. Out-of-wedlock births and drugs were far less pervasive. But cracks were beginning to appear in the black community's ethical and moral fortifications.

Rather than take Moynihan seriously and begin to patch up those cracks, black ministers, intellectuals, and community leaders circled the wagons in defense. They denounced both the message and the messenger. They revised history and said that single-parent black families were a residual effect of slavery. It was the beginning of the code of silence of declining moral standards in black America. The cracks in our ethical foundations soon became gaping holes.

The Silence of Black Leaders

The voices of righteousness have been muted for over thirty years now. Black ministers, civil rights leaders, and scholars have formed what political scientist

Martin Kilson called an ethic *cordon sanitaire* around the black experience in America. They have basically adopted what amounts to a code of silence on such touchy issues as black crime, unwed parenthood, and inferior academic performance. These disappointments are either blamed on white racism or simply ignored. Blacks who break this code and question this official story are labeled "traitors," and whites who address these problems are automatically presumed "racist."

The result is a psychological slavery to replace the chattel form under which black Americans once suffered. The victimhood that goes along with this new form of enslavement is in many ways more devastating than its predecessor. In the slavery of old, most blacks looked for ways to escape. With the new form, many believe that they are permanently trapped in their current socioeconomic situation.

It is most disappointing to see and hear the so-called black leaders when they address the many social ills that afflict the black community. Their lack of vision, their unwillingness to publicly stand firm against self-destructive behavior, their moral cowardice, their refusal to foster self-reliance, and their blatant worship of popularity is simply appalling.

For example, everyone knows that low-income babies born out of wedlock stand a better than average chance of always living in poverty, and that these mothers virtually condemn themselves and their children to a lifetime of hardship. You don't

> *"Black crime, unwed parenthood, and inferior academic performance . . . are either blamed on white racism or simply ignored."*

need Moynihan's report to know this, just common sense. Yet, the so-called leaders lack the nerve and sense of morality to tackle this issue. Why? Because such talk is unpopular and would take away from the notion that all of this is the fault of the white man. "We can't let white folks off the hook," they say. But we black Americans are the ones left hanging.

If these same "leaders" who are always on the scene when a racial incident takes place would instead go on the stump about illegitimacy and other issues that lead to self-destruction, many black girls would pay attention. And some would change their behavior. But these same racial-political ambulance chasers won't do that because they don't want to be accused of putting down "the people."

Individual Responsibility

Think about what a difference it would make if ministers and other traditional community leaders stopped complaining and started telling young black men to take care of their children, to take school seriously, that crime is wrong under any circumstances, and to take any job, even minimum wage, rather than be unemployed for any long period of time. It would change the moral climate in a way that no government social program ever could. But none of these officials wants to be accused of saying anything negative about black people, and so they leave it out of their public agenda.

Instead they do what Reverend Jesse Jackson did in August 1995. He led a march to the Cook County Jail in my hometown of Chicago, a structure that incarcerates over 9,000 inmates, most of whom are black. There he and others demanded a national urban policy that emphasizes jobs and education over the "jail-industry complex." Jackson's march is an example of the continued use of protest politics rather than emphasis on individual responsibility. By demanding that the government provide jobs and self-esteem to young black men instead of these same leaders going out into the community themselves and rallying the masses with appeals to pride and heritage, they prove that they are either unable or unwilling to lead.

Black America is currently deprived of the ability to solve many of its problems because there is a reluctance even to talk about them. Hewing to the old adage of not airing one's "dirty laundry" in public has harmed us to the point that we remain silent even though an orgy of self-destruction is going on right under our noses. But how can dirty laundry become clean unless it's taken out of the hamper? Sadly, avoiding bad press has taken precedence over solving problems, and we suffer for it.

The moral vacuum that currently exists in black America must be filled. We simply cannot continue to live like this. It is beneath our heritage. We must know that there is no hope for us to change without concerted moralizing. We must distinguish behavior that is self-evidently wrong from that which is self-evidently right. If as a people we insist on being too bashful to say out loud what we know to be true—that the advancement of the race hinges on a reaffirmation of personal responsibility and moral law—then we will continue to pay the price. And all of those black Americans who died—during centuries of fierce struggle—in order to make us free and to enable us to take our rightful place in this society, will have perished in vain. We cannot let that happen.

Society Must Work to Become Racially Integrated

by John A. Powell

About the author: *John A. Powell is on the faculty of the University of Minnesota Law School, where he directs the Institute on Race and Poverty.*

The roles of segregation and integration have been central to understanding and maintaining or destabilizing white privilege. Much of the discussion about integration and segregation has been fought out with poignant focus on school and education. This is understandable, in that school plays a central role in the formation of the American citizenry. Common schools are the crucible of American identity. They are the place where our children spend a tremendous portion of their lives, where their values and identities are shaped. In my discussion about integration and segregation, however, I will start, not with schools or even housing, but by rethinking what we mean by integration and segregation and how our misunderstanding of these limits our imagination and practice with respect to racial issues in this country. What I am suggesting, then, is that our collective conceptual error has important implications for the movement toward a racially just society, a racial democracy. Recognition of this error should play an important role in our thinking about integration and segregation in the educational context.

Defining Integration and Segregation

Today, there is requestioning of the relative benefits of integration and segregation. Despite this questioning, much of the discussion around these issues remains largely unreflective. The debate about the relative merits of integration and segregation has a long, rich history in the Black community. The pros and cons of each approach were thoughtfully and often sharply debated by W.E.B. Du Bois and Booker T. Washington at the turn of the century. Washington posited that Blacks should rely upon themselves for self-help, whereas Du Bois thought the most talented Blacks should learn from whites, and then bring these attributes back to the Black community. Much of today's discussion draws on

Reprinted from John A. Powell's remarks addressing the symposium question, "Is Racial Integration Essential to Achieving Quality Education for Low-Income Minority Students, in the Short Term? In the Long Term?" *Poverty and Race*, September/October 1996, by permission of the author.

some of the ideas raised by Washington and Du Bois without the benefit of the depth of thought they used to support their conclusions.

In order to deepen the discussion today, it is important to give pause and reflect on what integration and segregation mean in contemporary terms and what the implications for these two strategies are in the 21st Century. Part of the difficulty is that scholars and others have not been clear about what we mean by the words integration and segregation. Indeed, I would suggest that in recent times the debate has not focused on integration and segregation, but assimilation and segregation. The attack on integration, then, has largely not been an attack on integration but an attack on assimilation.

Assimilation Versus Segregation

Assimilation is problematic because it is a product of racial hierarchy. Although there have been many distinct versions of assimilation and segregation, both of these concepts have been framed primarily by the dominant white society and operate under the implicit assumption that there is something wrong with the racial "other." The less extreme assimilationist would *fix* the racial other by acculturating him or her to the dominant culture. The more extreme assimilationist position is that the racial other must intermarry into the dominant race and cease to be. In either scenario, the voice of the minority is either ignored or eliminated.

The white segregationist shares this belief in white racial hierarchy. The segregationist also believes there is something defective about the racial other. But unlike the assimilationist, the run-of-the-mill segregationist takes the position that the racial other must prove that he or she has been fixed or modified before segregation can end. A more extreme segregationist view is that the racial other cannot be fixed,

> *"[An] extreme segregationist view is that ... affiliation with [other races] will diminish and contaminate whites."*

and affiliation with any of them will diminish and contaminate whites. The idea that one drop of African blood contaminates white blood is closely associated with this view. Both assimilationists and segregationists are disturbed by the otherness of the racial other. The extreme segregationist is also concerned about the other as well as otherness.

One may protest that this is the position only of the dominant society. What about racial minority groups that want to segregate themselves from the dominant society? While theoretically one can imagine that a racial minority might, for positive reasons, want to segregate itself despite openness from the dominant society, this is simply not the history of racial politics in the United States. Indeed, when Washington called for self-segregation, it was in part because he accepted the position that Blacks were unfit and must prove themselves to whites before segregation could end. The reality is that many African-

Americans have adopted segregation as an accommodation and protection from white racism. While this is understandable, from a self-survival point of view, the problem is that it does not destabilize white hierarchy and it also has very little practical benefit. When one looks at middle-class Blacks who choose to live in Black neighborhoods, among the prevalent reasons cited is the desire to have space to retreat from white racism and the frustration of dealing with whites in the workplace. This does not mean that there are not positive things about the Black community or Black culture. This is another variation of the assimilationist position. What I am suggesting is that when one examines the roots of segregation, either self-imposed or imposed by the dominant society, white racism is central to understanding it.

Transforming Racial Hierarchy

Social interaction is constitutive of the individual and the collective identity of the community. Assimilation envisions the absorption of minorities into the mainstream. Real integration is measured, however, by the transformation of institutions, communities and individuals. Real integration involves fundamental change among whites and people of color, as people and communities. Segregation is not just the exclusion of people, but also the limitation of their opportunities and economic resources. It creates and maintains a culture of racial hierarchy and subjugation. Integration, as a solution to segregation, has broader meaning: it refers to community-wide

> *"Real integration is measured . . . by the transformation of institutions, communities and individuals."*

efforts to create a more inclusive society, where individuals and groups have opportunities to participate equally in their communities. Inclusion gives us tools to build democratic communities, the ability to approach complex issues from a multitude of perspectives. Integration, then, transforms racial hierarchy. Rather than creating a benefactor-beneficiary distinction along lines of race and class, true integration makes it possible for all groups to benefit from each other's resources. Homogeneous education fails to prepare students of all races for a multicultural society. Integrated education necessarily implies a curriculum that respects and values cultural difference, while building a community of equals.

The Case of Native Americans

Although I cannot do justice to this issue in a short viewpoint, it is important to consider the situation of Native Americans. There is a strong feeling among American Indians that if they integrate, they will lose their culture and be overwhelmed by the dominant society. The discussion about segregation and assimilation in many ways is not germane for Native Americans. First of all, the issue of segregation and assimilation is a discussion that takes place within a nation. The debate for Native Americans is about how to build or maintain a nation within a nation. Native Americans have not been pushing to be part of this nation, but rather to preserve their own nation. If they cannot maintain their nation, it is likely that these other issues will become more important. In addition, when one asserts that Native Americans or other groups that are not allowed to segregate may lose their culture and identity, one is essentially making a claim that if not allowed to segregate, a group may be forced to assimilate. Given the two alternatives, maybe segregation is more desirable.

> *"Segregation prevents access to wealth accumulation by residents of isolated, poor communities of color."*

But this is not the issue that Blacks face in large numbers. While it may be possible for a few African-Americans to assimilate, that is not possible for large numbers. Blacks in the United States are unassimilable—what one writer calls "the designated other." This leads us to segregation or something else.

Before considering something else, I want to assert that segregation is morally, pragmatically and ontologically flawed. It is morally flawed because it cannot be reconciled in our society with the fundamental value of equal respect and dignity of all people. It is pragmatically flawed in that it can never produce equal life chances for whites and "others." It is ontologically flawed in that it damages and distorts the identity of all members of the racist society where segregation is practiced.

Problems Caused by Segregation

Segregation prevents access to wealth accumulation by residents of isolated, poor communities of color, thereby establishing barriers to market participation. Lack of educational opportunities, poor job accessibility and declining housing values in isolated, low-income communities are symptoms of the problem. Further, racial and economic segregation damages the whole metropolitan region, including both the urban cores and the suburbs. Segregation geographically polarizes metropolitan communities along lines of race, income and opportunity, and separates urban centers from the surrounding suburbs. The experience of attending desegregated schools is likely to increase participation in desegregated environments in later life. When students attend integrated schools, they are more likely to attend desegregated colleges, live in integrated neighborhoods, work in integrated environments, have friends of another race and send their children to integrated schools. Conversely, students from segregated schools are more likely to avoid interactions with other races and generally conduct their lives in segregated settings. As Peggy McIntosh points out in her article "White Privilege: Male Privilege," her schooling as a white attending an all-white school led to strained interactions in the workplace as an adult. Once she entered an integrated work space, she realized she wouldn't be able to get along if she asked her non-white co-workers to adapt to her worldview. One thing is clear to me: that racial neutrality or "color blindness" is more likely to work toward maintaining the status quo than destabilizing it.

Toward Incorporation

Traditionally, desegregation in education has meant either removing formal barriers or simply placing students in physical proximity to one another. These remedies are limited. Segregation is not just the exclusion of people, but also the limitation of their opportunities and economic resources. Properly conceived, integration is transformative for everyone involved. Integration embraces a multi-cultural concept of social interaction. Much of the focus on the benefits of integration has been on how integration will benefit Blacks and other "others." What has been missing is an understanding of how integration, as well as segregation, affects us all. If we are to be successful at integration, we move much closer to David Goldberg's notion of incorporation. He asserts that, "incorporation, then, does not involve extension of established values and protections over the formerly excluded group. . . . [T]he body politic becomes a medium for transformative incorporation, a political arena of contestation, rather than a base from which exclusions can be more or less silently extended, managed, and manipulated." Incorporation allows the views and experiences of both the dominant group and minority groups to meet, informing and transforming each other. With incorporation, no experience is the exclusive one. In this respect, incorporation clearly differs from assimilation and desegregation models. The ultimate goal of integration is this transformative incorporation Goldberg describes.

If we accept this reconstituted way of viewing integration, it provides a positive strategy for how to start thinking about integration in relationship to schools as well as a critical perspective on how integration in the past has failed. Most of the efforts of the past and even today are halfhearted, leaving students de facto segregated or token assimilated. Too often the assumption is that if we can fix the other by having them go to schools with whites without addressing the underlying assumption of white privilege, including cultural privilege, we have successfully integrated. In assessing integration efforts, we too often look at the racial composition of a school, and not at what happens in the school. But if we look at integration in the way suggested above, it requires that we look at what goes on in school as well as outside of school. It requires that we link housing, school, employment and cultural opportunities. Linking housing and education policies, rather than focusing solely on integrating schools, directs attention to the importance and benefits of racial integration in multiple settings. By contrast, the approach of desegregating schools in isolation from other important institutions disregards the signifi-

> *"Integration embraces a multi-cultural concept of social interaction."*

cance of building and strengthening communities. A qualitative analysis of the social effect of integration makes clear that achieving broad integration remains a central goal in, and a necessary step toward, making a fully participatory democracy a reality. The social value of integration embodies the founding ideals of this country. Making it possible for everyone to participate actively in our democracy should be a fundamental goal woven into the fabric of the nation's public policies. Another necessary element of participation is for residents to feel connected to the community as valued members of the polity. Segregated society has continued to exclude community members, even when formal rights to participate exist. The school setting provides both academic and social tools for participating in society. The less formal environment of our neighborhoods and social circles provides equally important tools for everyday life. Integration of both schools and housing demonstrates for all of us how the practice of living and learning together can inform our understanding of the world.

> *"Integrating schools while simultaneously creating greater housing opportunities makes true integration the goal."*

The Legacy of *Brown*

More than forty years ago, the Supreme Court, in *Brown v. Board of Education,* recognized the unique harm experienced by Black students forced to attend racially segregated schools. The Court declared the circumstances unacceptable. Today, after a halfhearted effort at best, most American schools remain segregated. While the explicitly segregationist policies of the *Brown* era seldom exist today, a more subtle network of social and institutional barriers persists, working to maintain segregation in our schools and communities. Desegregated schools may be the only institutions in which African-American and Latino students have access to the abundance of college and employment contacts that whites and wealthy students take for granted. William Julius Wilson and other social scientists have noted that the greatest barrier to social and economic mobility for inner-city Blacks is their isolation from the opportunities and networks of the mostly white and middle-class society. School desegregation has a profound impact on Blacks' ability to acquire knowledge that would enhance their academic and occupational success via social contacts and integrated institutions. Integration can be a tough concept to embrace when one considers that it cannot claim many examples. Integration has been attacked by both ends of the political spectrum. In 1995, in his concurring opinion in *Missouri v. Jenkins,* Justice Clarence Thomas noted that "[I]t never ceases to amaze me that the courts are so willing to assume that anything that is predominantly Black must be inferior." Several Afrocentrists recall early attempts at integration that resulted with assimilation. The implications of assimilation have appropriately been criticized by a number of scholars.

Chapter 4

The Link Between Housing and Education

The spatial isolation of minority poor students concentrates the education disadvantages inherent to poverty. Racial segregation, moreover, denies all students the benefits of an integrated education. For parents fortunate enough to be able to choose where they live, their selection is often determined by the quality of public education for their children. America's metropolitan areas increasingly have become characterized by a poor minority core, with a white, middle-class suburban ring. More often than not, the public schools considered best are in the middle-class and upper-middle-class neighborhoods. Negative perceptions about urban schools contribute to the unwillingness of white families to move to urban neighborhoods. Part of the reason urban schools have a poor reputation is, of course, because they are segregated by race and class. The two most commonly expressed concerns about integration are "white flight" and mandatory busing, both of which can weaken communities, resulting in the drive for many school districts to return to neighborhood schools. The return to neighborhood schools, for which many policy makers are now calling, may, in fact, maintain or increase the racial segregation of communities that are isolated by race and class. Integrating schools while simultaneously creating greater housing opportunities makes true integration the goal, while it recognizes the social and economic barriers to integration. Building more integrated communities seems possible and desirable when people of different racial and economic groups begin to recognize that, without ignoring their differences, they share many goals and concerns. When housing and school policies work together, integrated communities maintain a stable, yet diverse, population.

African Americans Should Practice Limited Separation

by Roy L. Brooks

About the author: *Roy L. Brooks is the author of* Integration or Separation? A Strategy for Racial Equality, *from which the following viewpoint has been excerpted.*

Throughout the nation's history, African Americans' sentiment has swung back and forth between racial integration and racial separation. The inclination of many African Americans today, even those within the moderate middle class, is in favor of racial separation. Racial integration is not working satisfactorily for the majority of African Americans. On the other hand, full-blown racial separation is merely a dream that would be problematic even if it could come true. What other solutions are there to the American race problem? I wish to propose a specific policy, limited separation in alliance with racial integration, to advance such a solution.

By "limited separation" I mean African Americans coming together to support each other, but not for the sake of promoting racial kinship, as in some 1960s Black Nationalism replay; the group in this case would seek to promote the welfare of the *individual*. African American public schools, businesses, and communities would be created or redesigned to further self-interest: "It is not from the benevolence of the butcher, the brewer, or the baker that we expect our dinner, but from their regard to their own interest," as Adam Smith wrote in *The Wealth of Nations II*. Each person employs his own felicific calculus; each African American seeks to maximize her own personal happiness. Limited separation, quite simply, is *cultural and economic integration within African American society.*

Like total separation, limited separation is significantly different from racial segregation in that it is voluntary and designed to create a nurturing racial environment. Unlike total separation, limited separation does not preclude racial mixing. It does not presuppose black nationhood or exclude whites from participating in African American institutions. Furthermore, under limited separation internal exploitation or subordination would not be tolerated. There would be little room for the racial romanticism of total separation, in which it becomes quite acceptable to sacrifice individual rights for the good of the "nation" or the good of the "cause." The individual is king in the realm of limited separation. . . .

This policy is not, however, intended to supersede racial integration. Rather, it is designed to temper racial integration's tendency to place policy before people. Under limited separation, defenseless African American children would not be used for liberal educational experimentation, and there would be no neglecting the special needs of poor and working-class African Americans left behind in racially isolated communities after the civil rights movement. Limited separation provides an option to scores of African Americans who do not have the superhuman strength or extraordinary good fortune to make it in racially hostile, predominantly white mainstream institutions. Racial integration and limited separation should be viewed as different paths to racial equality.

The Benefits of Limited Separation

Limited separation not only provides a needed option to racial integration, but it can also be a dependable ally. It can lead to two-way racial mixing among whites and African Americans, something the nation has yet to experience. Nurtured in understanding and supportive environments, African American students and professionals will be able to compete toe-to-toe with whites in predominantly white mainstream institutions without the aid and hence the stigma of affirmative action. But the purpose of limited separation is not to keep the races (already significantly separated) separated or to subordinate or stigmatize any race or individual. Rather, it is to create a supportive environment for African Americans in counterpoint to that of debilitating white racism.

"The individual is king in the realm of limited separation."

True, individual whites may, on occasion, be denied an opportunity. But such denial—what in law we call the use of an exclusionary or restrictive racial classification—could only happen under extraordinary circumstances. For example, a white student could be denied admission to an African American public school located in an inner city if the school has so many white students already in attendance that the enrollment of the additional white student would cause it to lose its institutional identity or focus. Under these circumstances, the use of an exclusionary racial classification is bona fide, and its legality can be argued not only by analogy to current anti-discrimination law (which permits the use of exclusionary classifications based on religion, gender, national origin or age in the workplace), but also on constitutional grounds. But, realistically speaking, most whites will have about as much interest in sending their children to an

African American inner-city public school as they might have in voting in the dog catcher's election in Sparks County, Alabama.

Three Conditions

A more realistic problem is whether limited separation, as an optional civil rights policy, will apply to other minorities, women, and even whites. My response is yes, provided that they observe three conditions equally applicable to African Americans. First, the group seeking limited separation must be able to demonstrate the need for a supportive environment free of debilitating racism or, in the case of gender, sexism. If our mainstream institutions practice the type of racial subordination against other groups that they do against African Americans, if other groups can point to educational, socioeconomic, or political disadvantage due to race or gender, then they satisfy the first condition. White males will have a difficult time meeting this condition because even the "angry" ones are not disadvantaged on account of their race or gender. A distinct white male group must show that its purpose is not to maintain racial or gender domination.

Second, institutions that operate under limited separation must not unnecessarily trammel the interests of other individuals or groups. This means that gratuitous discrimination is prohibited. The institution that chooses limited separation must grant access to individuals from outside the group, so long as these individuals are willing to support the institution's primary objectives. For example, a

> *"[The purpose of limited separation] is to create a supportive environment for African Americans in counterpoint to that of debilitating white racism."*

white student should be allowed to attend a Historically Black College or University (HBCU) so long as he understands that the institution's primary objective is to attend to the special educational needs of African American students. Likewise, an African American lawyer should be allowed to practice law in a small Korean law firm so long as she understands that the law firm's primary objective is to serve the surrounding Korean community, and a Latino graduate of Harvard Business School should not be denied employment with a Wall Street investment banking firm so long as it is understood that the primary objective of the firm is to service large multinational corporations.

Third, the only time an individual can be denied an opportunity on account of his or her race (or gender)—the only time a restrictive classification can be used—is when race (or gender) is a bona fide selection qualification "reasonably necessary to the normal operation of the particular [institution]," to borrow from analogous civil rights law. Race, for example, would constitute a bona fide selection qualification (or "bfsq") if an African American institution were in danger of losing its identity or focus by the admission or hiring of an additional white applicant. Under these very limited circumstances, limited separation remains faithful to its principle of nonsubordination. It does not unnecessarily trammel the interests of others even while it uses racial or gender classifications.

Limited separation is radical yet reasonable. It is the former because it challenges the received tradition—racial integration—as the nation's only legitimate civil rights policy. It is the latter mainly because it is surely needed, given the sad state of racial relations. Not only is it reasonable to ask civil rights organizations to try something new and to invite the Supreme Court to rethink its civil rights stance; it is also time for African Americans to put a constructive policy into action without waiting for a governmental rescue or the goodwill of whites. . . .

Effects on Education

In the area of education, limited separation gives all parents of all races the option of sending their children to publicly financed integrated or separate schools. The goal is to ensure that all students, especially African American students, will leave public school academically and emotionally prepared to make life better than they find it—that is, "to live more abundantly," as the great African American educator Carter G. Woodson put it. To achieve this objective, public schools will have to change. I ask the reader to visualize education in computer terminology: money is the hardware and academic programming is the software. The academic failure of well-funded public schools in places like Kansas City and Detroit underscores the importance of both hardware and software.

To secure the educational hardware—public financing—of integrated and separate schools, I favor a "revenue" funding system in which schools operating more expensive educational enrichment programs for the poor would receive more public funds on a weighted per pupil basis than other schools.

Regarding educational software, students in both schools will study the best of American culture in addition to the "three Rs." Because we are, as Walt Whitman said, "a nation of nations," the study of American culture is the study of multiculturalism, a reasonable blend of Western civilization, African American heritage, the cultures of other ethnic groups, and women's studies. Tracking and ability grouping will be prohibited. In integrated schools white and African American students will work and play together, and principals and teachers will be taught in ongoing courses how to foster healthy racial relations in the classroom.

> *"It is . . . time for African Americans to put a constructive policy into action without waiting for a governmental rescue or the goodwill of whites."*

Separate schools must observe the three conditions of limited separation discussed earlier. They can only be established if there are no available integrated schools to address the *special* educational needs of a particular racial group: a concern that will reflect the modifications of the software. Separate schools are acceptable only because education is more important than integration. White students or teachers will not be excluded, but they cannot alter the educational software, the mission of such schools, which is to address the special needs of African American children. The software components include parental and community involvement to bridge the gap between home and school; teachers who understand the needs and conflicts African American children face; multiculturalism; a stronger emphasis on African American pride and heritage; and specialized programs for African American boys and teenagers who are most at risk.

> *"Separate schools are acceptable only because education is more important than integration."*

Higher education too will be offered in both integrated and separate schools. At predominantly white colleges and universities I would replace affirmative action with the "whole-person theorem" or "public interest affirmative action" (at least until limited separation is firmly in place in the elementary and secondary schools); base financial aid and academic support on need rather than race; require courses in race relations; and encourage multicultural student centers rather than "black houses" or other race-specific centers or dorms. Limited separation certainly embraces the continuation and fostering of Historically Black Colleges and Universities (HBCUs). These institutions of higher education provide opportunities for many African Americans that integrated colleges and universities do not. This is particularly true in the South, where "Blacks and Hispanics still lack equal access to public colleges and universities . . . even though the Supreme Court outlawed segregated schools four decades ago," as stated by the Southern Education Foundation. Justice Clarence Thomas's eloquent and effective defense of HBCUs in *United States v. Fordice* merits serious attention.

Impact on Culture

Limited separation will have its greatest impact on housing and employment. Rather than fighting a frustrating and demeaning battle against housing and employment discrimination, African Americans, like white immigrant groups, should use their residential isolation as a catalyst for individual and group success in America. In the housing context, limited separation means that middle-class African Americans will run toward rather than away from working-class and poor African Americans. The hope is that the human and economic capital withdrawn from African American communities during the civil rights movement, when America's integrationist drive was in high gear, will return to these communities. Separation will establish a physical as well as a cultural and economic basis for worldly success. It will give to African Americans a sense of belonging and with it a foundation on which to build individual and group pride, economic independence, and political strength.

Limited separation will enable poor and underclass African Americans to jettison a self-defeating and dysfunctional culture and adapt to a more middle class, African American culture. Here I disagree with African American conservatives who argue that African Americans as a whole must undertake a cultural adaptation to the white mainstream. I disagree, for example, with Thomas Sowell, who finds a deficiency of human capital among African Americans, and Shelby Steele, who assumes that African American culture is limiting or impoverished. Both writers totally ignore socioeconomic stratification within African American society. Had they taken class stratification into account, I believe they would agree that the solution to the internal problems of African Americans—welfare, crime, drugs, and teenage pregnancy and motherhood—lies in acceptance rather than rejection of African American culture, a culture that is both shared and unique and that I identify as tripartite: a general or shared American culture; a generic African American culture; and a class-based African American culture.

Economic Effects

In the economic sector, limited separation will promote economic integration—by which I mean African Americans of all classes coming together as financiers, entrepreneurs, employers, employees, and customers in a complex interchange that is necessary to achieve economic independence. Proceeding from this premise, I will propose a program of African American economic integration and independence centered in small businesses and the Black Church. Small businesses are important because they open employment opportunities for the African American labor force; circulate money within the communities; foster a sense of pride, self-confidence, and optimism, all of which work to reduce crime, welfare dependency, and other social pathologies; provide a new class of positive role models for the African American youth; and promote the entrepreneurial spirit (constructive risk-taking). One instance of the sort of venture I have in mind is the Family Campus Initiative, a joint project run by Yale University and the City of New Haven to turn abandoned buildings (schools, stores, and others) in the poorest communities into "family campuses" housing an array of social services such as health care, child care, and adult education. These campuses could be supported by the city, private businesses, and free services from African American professionals.

"Limited separation will have its greatest impact on housing and employment."

Networking, I argue, is the most effective way to obtain the capital and expertise for creating successful small businesses. The Black Church, as a market maker, can bring people with the talent and desire to start or operate a business together with those with funds to invest—entertainers, sports figures, business executives, and professionals. I also propose networking to secure the services of experienced management consultants and to set up educational programs. My proposal will find prototypes in the American immigrant experience and models in the African American past.

Again, limited separation in housing and employment does not necessitate the exclusion of whites from African American communities or businesses: I reject Black Nationalism and its variants. But, as with public schools and HBCUs, African American communities and businesses will attempt to address issues of importance to African Americans. Whites would have to accept that the main purpose of these efforts is to pursue African American institutional objectives.

To be sure, cultural and economic community integration is not for every African American. Some will eschew it altogether, finding integration fulfilling. And others may use it as a stepping stone to racial integration rather than as a permanent way of life, or as a temporary respite from the harrowing experience of racial mixing.

Political Power

Voting or political power is the final area in which limited separation is applied. The right-to-vote problem is best dealt with by traditional piecemeal litigation under the Voting Rights Act. Unfortunately, this is the only way to enforce compliance with a law that is generally clear and effective. Of course, some of the problems associated with voting may dissipate on their own in African American communities built in the spirit of cultural and economic integration. Presumably, African Americans will be in charge of the election apparatus in such communities.

> *"The solution to . . . welfare, crime, drugs, and teenage pregnancy and motherhood lies in acceptance rather than rejection of African American culture."*

The voting power problem would be rectified by a two-pronged approach: cumulative voting together with political coalitions buttressed by the Black PAC, or political action committee. My endorsement of cumulative voting—a race-neutral electoral device that allows voters to cast more than one vote for a candidate, depending on the number of contested seats—is conditioned upon its separation from proportionality, which provides that African Americans are entitled to a certain percentage of seats on the governing body. I favor cumulative voting because it favors the success of the individual. In this case, as in the case of all forms of limited separation—separate public schools, HBCUs, and cultural and economic integration—racial kinship is a distant second to individual opportunity; the latter is never to be sacrificed to the former. This puts me at odds not only with civil rights attorney Lani Guinier, but also with the Black Nationalists of the 1960s.

Although cumulative voting can increase the ability of African Americans to express their individual political preferences as well as elect the candidates of their choice to office, it cannot completely resolve the voting power problem.

Like racial redistricting, cumulative voting only ensures the election of marginalized African American politicians. They are always outnumbered and hence outvoted in their respective deliberative bodies.

To further build African American political power, I propose cross-racial political coalition building and the Black PAC. Admittedly, such coalitions have had limited success, Jesse Jackson's Rainbow Coalition being a prime example. But they will look very different in the context of an overall strategy of limited separation. The probability of success of these coalitions is substantially increased when our most racially divisive issues—such as busing and racial preferences—are taken out of the mix. As an expression of limited separation, the Black PAC is nothing more than a political action committee like the others. With local and national offices, the Black PAC will raise money (in large part from African American businesses and wealthy individuals), refine political ideology beneficial to most African Americans, influence white candidates and office-holders at all levels, and run its own candidates if necessary.

Whites Must Pay Economic Reparations to Blacks

by Richard F. America

About the author: *Richard F. America is adjunct lecturer at the Graduate School of Business Administration at Georgetown University in Washington, D.C.*

To properly define any current race related economic problem, including affirmative action, in employment, contracting, and lending, we first need to understand how past slavery and discrimination produced unjust enrichments to the Haves, including the business classes, at the expense of the Have Nots, primarily the "truly disadvantaged" and the working poor. That means that housing, education, affirmative action, employment, health, crime, and business development problems cannot be understood and solved if we avoid addressing them in the context of reparations.

Fortunately, the American people, generally, have decent instincts. So a moral case, which is the key to solving the problem, stands a good chance of prevailing in the court of public opinion. The restitution principle, as applied to affirmative action, has a politically realistic chance to succeed. But even if it did not, the principle should be the basis for arguing the matter. In the end, whatever might be the current political climate, this principle will emerge as the basis for redistributive justice in race relations.

The Restitution Principle

There is a consensus that slavery and discrimination were wrong. Because this is so, it is clear that it is also wrong to receive benefits from those practices. This is the *restitution principle*. It says that income and wealth produced by past transactions that violate current norms should be returned, as a practical matter, and affirmative action is one way to make restitution.

Reparations—for slavery and for later discrimination—are becoming a serious public policy concept. It used to simply be an emotional rallying cry.

We can now define and measure the current benefits from past slavery and discrimination. Slavery coercively diverted income and wealth from blacks to

Reprinted from Richard F. America, "Has Affirmative Action Repaid Society's Debt to African Americans?" *Business and Society Review*, Summer 1995, by permission of the author.

whites. So did discrimination in labor, housing, education, and capital markets. These past practices produce an unjust enrichment currently to the Haves, as a class—the top 30 percent of the income distribution—those earning over $45,000 annually.

We can estimate these benefits. Then we can use the normal tax and budget system—"tax and spend"—to redistribute income from the wrongful beneficiaries to the classes that have been exploited, excluded, and discriminated against. And this can be done in ways that satisfy victims, strengthen the overall economy, and serve the general public interest. Explaining these realities is the key task of corporate leaders who want to engage the race issue in ways that will have lasting value.

Until the idea that there is a debt—that whites owe blacks money—is clearly established, there is only altruism and compassion, and vague notions of the general public interest to support claims that are redistributive. And affirmative action is redistributive. That's why there is an argument and a serious problem requiring courage and vision from business leaders.

Redistributing Wealth

As a practical matter, we can accomplish reparations through taxation and budgeting targeted to education, training, economic, and community development. As we better understand the concept of "unjust enrichment," the necessary public policy remedies, to be financed through progressive taxation, will become broadly acceptable.

Employees and other stakeholders resist affirmative action and other interracial income redistribution because, in part, the Haves say they believe they are entitled to keep what they have. They say they think that they have earned it fairly, and received it justly. But if, in fact, income and wealth distributions are based in part on past injustices and transactions that violate current norms such as slavery, then corporate policies should acknowledge that.

In one recent year, African Americans were 12 percent of the U.S. population. Had they received 12 percent of total income instead of the 7.2 percent they actually received, they would have earned $264 billion instead of $159 billion.

We may estimate that about half of that $105 billion gap was a result of discrimination in employment, so $52 billion was diverted to whites as an unjust enrichment.

If we go back through the centuries, the present value, adjusted for price changes, of the benefits from such discrimination is in the range of $5 trillion to $10 trillion. Some might counter that any social debt has been repaid through transfer programs and The Great Society, including social security, unemployment compensation, public assistance, and other direct money transfers, as well as in-kind programs. And we have provided business set-aside

"Whites owe blacks money."

and assistance programs and private charity.

But even allowing some such transfer payments and social programs as off-sets, it appears that less than 20 percent of the debt has been repaid. Before the 1930s, transfer payments were nil. And community development spending was too. So even generous allowances for payback leaves a conservative esti-mate at more than $500 billion for the period 1929 to the present day.

> *"What was wrongfully diverted to whites by slavery and discrimination was capital."*

Furthermore, we should not count subsistence payments. Black people managed to subsist historically on their own. What was wrongfully diverted to whites by slavery and discrimination was capital. It would have been used to build black savings and wealth in all forms—institutional, human, physical, and financial. Instead, it was wrongfully appropriated to build white wealth. So only capital transfers count against the debt, not welfare.

Economic Justice

Surveys and polls show that widespread anger over injustice undermines the respect that is needed between leaders and followers. Resentment corrodes our economy. We cannot progress if so many people are convinced that the system is unfair, and that they are victims of a massive historic injustice that could be corrected through honorable dealings.

We want to draw everyone into the work force and help all people find satis-faction, growth, security, achievement, a sense of pride and self-worth, and a valued place in the community. And we want everyone to understand the issues so they can vote intelligently and participate in the public life from a position of strength. But our income and wealth distributions are badly skewed toward the upper end. And that is corrosive.

If we want broad economic stability and improvement, it will require eco-nomic justice. Schools produce ill-prepared youngsters; factories are idle, un-dercapacity, and obsolete; streets are dangerous. It does not have to be that way. The restitution principle—meaning acknowledging, measuring, and repaying unjust enrichments currently enjoyed, based on past wrongful practices—can help focus corporate and public policy on practical redistributive remedies. And it is the strongest basis for affirmative action.

Blacks Must Forgive Whites

by George A. Kendall

About the author: *George A. Kendall is a columnist and the author of the book* Spirit and Community: Essays on Soul and Society.

The emergence of some serious public debate concerning the iniquitous government policies lumped together under the term "affirmative action" suggests two things: first, that our country's race war is far from over; second, that more and more serious people would like to bring it to an end. The problem is how. I do not pretend to be able to give a detailed answer to this question, but I would like to suggest that before the war can be ended, we are going to have to collectively recognize some obvious realities about the situation. Of these, one of the most obvious is this: that no group has the right to hold a perpetual mortgage on a society because that group was treated unjustly in the past. These "mortgages" have to come to an end sooner or later, or they end up being a disease, a kind of social cancer, which eats away at the society until it dies.

A rather interesting edition of the CNN talk show *CNN and Company* did a lot to clarify this issue. On that particular day, the show featured, among other guests, the infamous Sinead O'Connor, the rock star who once tore up a picture of the Pope on *Saturday Night Live.* I would never have dreamed that I might find myself even somewhat ambiguously on the same side of an issue as Sinead O'Connor. And yet that day on CNN she actually made a little bit of sense. The topic, as I remember, had something to do with the rage of blacks over the first trial of Rodney King's alleged attackers, and the Reginald Denny trial held in Los Angeles. It focused, in other words, on the issue of racism. One of the other panelists was a black woman named Julianne Malveaux, a syndicated columnist who appears to make a living absolving blacks of any responsibility for their lives because, after all, they are nothing but victims. She is, in my judgment, about the closest thing to a black racist one is likely to encounter.

O'Connor obviously had her mind filled with some kind of nebulous New

Reprinted from George A. Kendall, "Ending America's Race War," *Wanderer*, July 6, 1995, by permission of the author.

Age spirituality, and did not exactly express herself in a way most of us would consider a model of articulateness, yet she did not wholly miss the mark on the day in question. While Malveaux argued that racial conflict takes place solely because blacks lack money and power, O'Connor tried, not very successfully, to say that the underlying problems are spiritual, not just economic and political. She then provoked an outburst of rage and hatred from Malveaux by suggesting that, sooner or later, black people are going to have to forgive white people for their history of mistreatment of blacks. It is true that she vitiated what she said by adding a bit of psychobabble to the effect that white people are going to have to forgive themselves, but, as a character from *The Mary Tyler Moore Show* once said, when a donkey flies, you don't get mad because he doesn't stay up very long.

Letting Go of Past Injuries

O'Connor was absolutely right in the first part of what she said. Forgiveness is not just a mushy sentimental emotion, it is something essential to the maintenance of a social and political order. Sooner or later, people have to let go of grievances or there can never be any peace at all and we would totally destroy one another. The New Testament Greek word *aphiein*, which we translate as "forgive," basically means to loose or to let go. When I forgive someone, I let go of the claim that I have on that person for a past injury, I let go of the debt he owes me for that injury. I do not do that just for the other person's sake, but for my own as well, because it would be profoundly destructive for me to spend the rest of my life tied to the grievance. In letting the other person go, I let myself go as well, and I become free to forget about the injury and go ahead with the real work of my life, to love and serve God and neighbor.

People who cling to a grudge forever and ever are sad cases. They live stunted, constricted lives, because all their efforts go into holding onto the grudge and seeking revenge. We need to forgive and be forgiven every day of our lives simply so that life can go on at all. Sooner or later, people have to call a halt to their grievances. Just think of these miserable families who get involved in blood feuds that last for generation after generation. The killing never stops, because every time someone gets killed, that person's family or clan feels it has to kill someone on the other side to re-

> *"Forgiveness is . . . essential to the maintenance of a social and political order."*

establish justice, but justice never does get re-established. Everyone born into one of the feuding groups is born into the grievance, and hence is never really free. Sooner or later, the people on both sides have to give up (let go of) their right to vengeance. If not, the killing never stops.

A sad case of people who will not let go of a grievance is what has happened to many Jews, especially those who were in Hitler's death camps, since World

War II. Many of these people, who were young at the time of the Holocaust, are old now and have basically devoted their lives to tracking down Nazi war criminals. Certainly, no one can deny the justice of their grievance. Yet by hanging on so tenaciously to it, many of these people have blighted their own lives, and now it is too late. It may be shocking to say so, but sooner or later the Jews, for their own sake, are going to have to forgive the Nazis.

> *"People who cling to a grudge . . . live stunted, constricted lives."*

Otherwise, we will end up with a situation like the 1915 Turkish mass murder of Armenians. There is hardly anybody left today who was alive and an adult at the time of the Armenian Holocaust. Yet Armenian terrorists are still killing innocent Turks over a grievance that neither was party to. In a situation like that, no one wins. Forgiving one's enemies is not just a sentimental emotion that we are supposed to feel if we are to be good Christians. It is absolutely necessary for the survival and healthy growth of any decent human community.

Here in America, it is time to call a halt to the racial war. It is time for both sides to say no to measures like slave reparations and affirmative action. It is time for whites to be forgiven for the crimes committed by their ancestors, and it is time for blacks, who were freed some years ago from all institutional and legal barriers to their advancement, to get on with the business of actually living their lives, and to turn away forever from a way of life characterized by perpetual grievance and perpetual victim status.

The Free Market Will Solve Racial Problems

by Michael Levin

About the author: *Michael Levin is a professor of philosophy at the City College of New York.*

Everyone over the age of three knows there is a race problem in the U.S. Actually, there are race problems: fault lines separate whites from blacks in education, employment, housing, crime, demographic growth, and welfare dependence, and issues superficially unrelated to race, such as homelessness or the changing character of sports, often have a tacit racial dimension.

The first step in addressing a problem or problem-cluster is to describe it precisely, so what counts as a solution is clear. The symptoms of the race problem are all too familiar: a black unemployment rate several times the white (excluding the many black males who leave or never enter the workforce); black schoolchildren performing far behind white and Asian, and dropping out more frequently (the dropout rate for non-European Hispanics being even higher); skyrocketing black illegitimacy, with half of all female-headed black households supported by welfare; blacks, at 12% of the population, committing most of the violent crime and constituting more than half the prison population; black drug use; the seemingly inevitable decay of black neighborhoods; a huge cohort of black urban derelicts. What is the underlying disease?

Not inequality per se. Most people understand that individuals or groups have varying traits which yield varying life outcomes. They are not outraged that an opera singer earns more than the rest of us because he was born with a powerful voice. Only wrongful inequality is a problem.

Is the problem, then, that racial inequality is caused by "racism"? Again, no. Discrimination against blacks is now illegal, while preferences favoring blacks are ubiquitous. Many large cities have elected black mayors, and Martin Luther King enjoys the status of a secular saint. Movies, television, and advertising, all run by whites, carefully present blacks as intelligent, competent, and authorita-

Reprinted from Michael Levin, "How the Free Market Can Solve the Race Problem," *Rothbard-Rockwell Report*, January 1996, by permission of the author.

tive. By any measure, "racism" is less prevalent now than a half-century ago. Yet the race gap in criminal behavior, illegitimacy, and unemployment has widened in that time, and the gap in educational achievement has not narrowed.

Intrinsic Racial Traits

That racial inequalities grow as discrimination declines suggests that they are due to intrinsic traits of the races.

As soon as this is said, a battle dependably erupts as to whether race differences are wholly environmental or partly genetic in origin. As I have defended "hereditarianism" elsewhere, I won't press it here. In fact, as we will see, one virtue of the market is its utter unconcern with where race differences come from. But thinking of race in largely genetic terms does define the race problem, which becomes: how to minimize friction when two groups differing in intelligence, emotional intensity, and time horizons occupy the same geographical territory.

Flawed Approaches

The non-market approaches of the left—civil rights, racial preference, busing, magnet schools, job training, Head Start—have failed absolutely. I suspect that even their advocates privately realize this by now, and that, when they recommend midnight basketball leagues or some other harebrained scheme, they are trying to buy time. But time runs out, leaving the real issues to be faced.

Some of the approaches of the right are equally unpromising, interventionist, or peculiar. To forestall a "custodial state," Richard J. Herrnstein and Charles Murray would simplify society so the less intelligent and self-restrained can grasp its rules and find meaningful niches. I seldom agree with Stephen Jay Gould, but he is right to call this proposal "almost grotesquely inadequate."

There has been talk, perhaps born of desperation, of separating the races, but to execute such a proposal would mean the forcible relocation of enormous numbers of people; plainly, we had better look elsewhere. There has also been talk of eugenics. Surely, however, no friend of liberty wants the state preventing anyone from having children, or dangling taxpayer money as a breeding incentive. Of course, private parties are free to bribe able individuals to have children and less able individuals to refrain, but such efforts are unlikely to work on a large scale. Anyway, as we will see, the market all by itself has welcome demographic effects.

> *"That racial inequalities grow as discrimination declines suggests that they are due to intrinsic traits of the races."*

By default, then, if for no other reason, it is time to consider the market solution: return to people the freedom they have surrendered over the last half-century, and let the chips fall where they may.

Even without elaboration this idea has a liberating zest, since, unlike interventionist nostrums, it aims at no predetermined result. A "good" market outcome is not one in which blacks and whites each get a set portion of jobs or wealth, or live happily together, or live apart. A "good" outcome is simply one that results from individual choices, whatever that upshot turns out to be. At the same time, market theory predicts that this upshot will also be more equitable and yield greater net satisfaction than any alternative.

> *"The whole notion of discriminatory 'victims' is confused."*

Right now, the most extensive limits on liberty are imposed by civil rights law. This body of statutes has made it a tort for one individual to deny another a loan, or refuse to hire him, promote him, sell him a house, rent him an apartment, or deal with him in any "public accommodation" on the basis of race (or religion or sex—but here I concentrate on race). Over time, these statutes have been stretched to cover semi-private associations as well, such as clubs, restricting free association further.

It is useful to realize that "protection from racial discrimination" is a 20th-century American idea without historical precedent. Traditionally, the rights of private parties against each other have involved criminal aggression and fulfillment of contract; any further rights enjoyed by individuals protected them against the state. English common law did require inn-keepers to accept any presentable traveler, because of the danger of highwaymen—a threat that hardly faces would-be diners seeking lunch at a restaurant whose owner does not wish to serve them. Neither the common law nor tyrants of old presumed to tell inn-keepers whom they could hire as stable boys.

Harmless Discrimination

It is also important to realize that civil rights laws do not fend off harm, because *discrimination as defined by these laws does no harm.* A harms B when B is worse off after something A has done than he was previously. But when an employer turns down a job applicant, whether on the basis of race or religion or hair style, the applicant is not made worse off. He had no job when he applied, and he has no job after his offer is rejected. Apart from a bruise to his ego, the applicant occupies the very situation he was in before he presented himself.

Likewise, a would-be tenant refused an apartment for any reason is no more in need of an apartment than he was before. The whole notion of discriminatory "victims" is confused. It is not as if anyone minding his own business can be zapped out of the blue by discriminators; you cannot suffer discrimination unless you first ask a landlord, firm, or bank for an apartment, job, or loan. Not only does discrimination leave no one worse off, virtually all discriminatory exchanges must be initiated by its "victim"—and it was once a truism that no-one can claim injury from an action of his own.

What would happen if people were (again) free to decide whom to deal with?

For one thing they would *feel* free, no small thing. The suffocating sense of no escape from obsessive racial head-counting, now current, would abate. For another, letting people work and live with the company they please would end the resentment created by race-based decisions—a big part of the solution we seek. Court-ordered quotas and Office of Federal Contract Compliance Programs "goals" would no longer deny whites positions, promotions, and scholarships. Whites would no longer have reason to suspect the qualifications of black co-workers, and those whites who fail to advance for mysterious reasons would not wonder whether racial factors played a role. Blacks might initially resent the loss of privilege, but the workplace (and the campus) would on balance be more harmonious.

Effects on the Workplace

This détente would not necessarily resegregate the workplace (which, in truth, is hardly integrated now). Many people reflexively think of repealing the Civil Rights Act as "turning back the clock" to the bad old Jim Crow days, but laws against integration are equally alien to the market. Likewise, just as the market rejects laws mandating discrimination against whites, it rejects laws forbidding it. Employers who endorse affirmative action would be free to favor blacks. Whites seeking positions with such employers would presumably share this judgment; whites who bridled would be free to seek race-blind employers, or employers who favor whites—choices that do not exist when all firms must be "equal opportunity employers."

Should affirmative action prove unprofitable, i.e. inefficient, sympathetic consumers could buy the goods and services of affirmative-action firms at higher prices. Alternatively, blacks seeking to overcome resistance or compete against better-qualified whites might accept wages below those of whites. Such bargains should leave morale intact, since whites would have nothing to resent about less-qualified blacks earning less, and blacks would have nothing to resent about better-qualified whites earning more. Displaced whites could themselves offer to work for less.

The labor market, in short, is race-neutral. By indulging all racial preferences without siding with any, it permits everyone to find a position in which he is most comfortable, at least as far as race goes. It asks no embarrassing questions about the origin of group traits, and it does not require that every group bring the same traits to the marketplace. However, the market provides no guarantee that every trait will be valued equally. Neither the market nor the government can make labor more valuable than it is—nothing can do that—but there is one impediment the government can remove to less productive labor being paid what it is worth, and that is the minimum wage.

> *"The labor of so many blacks is of little value to potential employers."*

183

The basic objection to the minimum wage, that it forbids voluntary bargains otherwise likely to be struck, is unrelated to race. But the minimum wage also exacerbates unemployment among the young and unskilled, since employers will hire labor at \$4.35/hr only if it is worth that much, and that, as many economists have pointed out, is a point of contact with race. Because the labor of so many blacks is of little value to potential employers, the only jobs these blacks can hope to get pay less than the minimum. Insisting that employers pay them more insures that they will not be hired at all.

> *"It can hardly be a coincidence that black illegitimacy began its rise when welfare was liberalized."*

A minimum wage supposedly protects workers' dignity and fends off exploitation, but it is surely better to earn two dollars per hour sweeping a floor than no dollars per hour doing nothing. Like many people, I worked during high school and college at a number of menial jobs, which I never viewed as undignified because nobody told me they were. I was more than happy to be making some money. The "dignity" argument only encourages the idea, prevalent among young black males, that "dead-end" jobs are beneath them, and that the only good jobs are those that pay well for very little work. Needless to say, such jobs exist only in the imagination.

The Problem of Welfare

An actual disincentive to black workforce participation is welfare, the abolition of which is also part of the market approach. Opposition to welfare, like opposition to the minimum wage, is rooted in an ethos of liberty and is unrelated to race per se. People should not be forced to support strangers. However, 42% of recipients of Aid to Families With Dependent Children are black; black women are more than eight times more likely than white to get some form of public assistance. These facts give the welfare issue an unavoidable racial spin.

The benefits of abolishing welfare flow from a single axiom: if you know that no-one will avert the consequences of your actions, if what becomes of you is up to you, you will be more cautious than otherwise. Specifically, awareness of the possible consequences of premarital intercourse—a baby to care for with no husband to help—has in the past led women to decline. (There is no point telling men to refrain from premarital sex when the opportunity is offered; they won't listen. Sexual morality rests with women.)

AFDC and related programs changed these rules. Now that the taxpayer will foot the bill, having illegitimate babies is no longer imprudent, and it can hardly be a coincidence that black illegitimacy began its rise when welfare was liberalized during the 1960s. The *New York Times* runs articles almost weekly denying any connection between illegitimacy and welfare, but the research cited (when any) is vitiated by its restricted range. Illegitimacy may well hold constant when the value of a welfare check fluctuates by 5%; it does not follow, and it defies common sense, that illegitimacy would hold constant were welfare eliminated.

The Effects of Welfare on Society

Welfare causes other problems. Disproportionately many illegitimate boys become criminals, whether because they lack the guiding hand of a father or because they inherit a tendency to recklessness from their patently reckless parents. Welfare is thus implicated in crime insofar as it encourages illegitimacy, but it may also foster crime in its own right, by accustoming recipients to their having an unconditional right to what they want. A boy unfamiliar with working and saving for things will not know why he isn't entitled to take whatever he fancies, by force if necessary.

Welfare also plays an unacknowledged role in drug use. People who have limited funds that they must labor for are not apt to spend money they do have on narcotics. On the other hand, people who get money effortlessly spend it heedlessly. It doesn't matter that welfare "pays" less than a good job; a welfare mother will give less thought to where she directs each dollar than a wage earner. That same mother, had she worked for that dollar, and if she knew there would be no food stamps to bail her out were she to spend it unwisely, would think much longer before buying crack, and keep a sharper eye on her children's purchases. Drug use would be much reduced if anyone who wanted drugs had to pay for them from his own pocket.

For the same reason, ending welfare might improve popular culture. Many objectionable trends—baggy pants, brand-name jeans and running shoes as fashion statements, rap music—emerge from "urban youth." Relative to population size the largest movie audience are young black males, who prefer action films—i.e. violent, incoherent rubbish. These trends are not market-driven, since the funds that support them are coercively collected from taxpayers. The market imposes discipline, and while its discipline can stretch short time horizons only so far, poor adults who must secure housing and food on their own are not apt to let their children buy $125 Nikes or tickets to rap concerts.

To repeat: the problems created by welfare are not intrinsically racial, but it has acquired a racial dimension because of the responsiveness of blacks to its incentives. The black illegitimacy rate, at 70%, is five times the white. (White illegitimacy is accelerating faster than black only because the black rate cannot increase much more.)

> **"Market theory calls for repeal of 'equal housing' laws."**

And not only would such vexatious behaviors diminish if unsubsidized, ending subsidies would in the longer run induce welcome demographic change.

Poor husband material once had trouble reproducing. Women chose only likely breadwinners as mates, thereby selecting for breadwinning qualities like intelligence, reliability, and self-restraint. Improvident women were likewise at a disadvantage. Evolutionary theory predicts that supporting women no matter what mates they choose makes bad-breadwinner genes less unattractive, hence more fit and apt to spread; the state of the black slums does nothing to refute this prediction. Removing this support will reintroduce selection for breadwinning traits—eugenics without force, bribery, or "genocide."

The great practical objection to going cold turkey on welfare are the hundreds of thousands of slum inhabitants now incapable of supporting themselves. The modest changes proposed by the current Congress, chiefly the shell-game of block grants that Todd Seavey calls "decentralizing the deck chairs on the Titanic," has provoked warnings (or are they threats?) of rioting. How can mass starvation be avoided? One way is to grandfather in current AFDC recipients. A coordinate tactic would be to phase out welfare by 10% annually for a decade. Both plans would give everyone ample but not unlimited time to prepare. Retention of the minimum wage will thwart any reasonable transition, by denying people with few skills and doubtful work habits the chance to scrape by. Bear in mind, though, that reliance on the public treasury has become so entrenched that some pain may be inevitable.

The Repeal of "Equal Housing"

At the same time that the workplace is being liberated, market theory calls for repeal of "equal housing" laws and the end of subsidized housing and rent control. Once again the basic argument is race-neutral—the right of people to live where and with whom they please—but once again this right has obvious implications in American society.

Whites who prefer living among other whites would be so allowed. Exclusionary contracts would again be valid, so that any group wishing to keep its neighborhood ethnically homogeneous could do so. In many cases the invisible hand of economics would obviate the need for conscious measures. With the government no longer housing the poor (and predominantly black) where they could not afford to live on their own, "scatter-siting" the poor among the middle-class, pressuring banks to provide mortgages to uncreditworthy blacks, or forbidding rents that the affluent would be willing to pay, white neighborhoods would remain homogeneous for want of blacks able to buy their way in. (Conversely, landlords earning high profits from luxury rentals could afford to build much cheaper housing for the poor.)

At the same time, blacks and whites who wanted to live in integrated neighborhoods would also be free to do so; whites strongly committed to having black neighbors might sell or rent to blacks at lower prices than they could get from whites, or offer other financial help. Alternatively, blacks eager to live in white neighborhoods might offer to buy housing at higher than the going rates. In the end, extensive de facto segregation would almost certainly result—or rather continue, since immense government pressure has not led to integration, and blacks seem to prefer the company of their own race as much as whites do.

Repeal of open housing laws would also do much to resolve the much-agonized-over "crisis in American education."

Locally Controlled Schools

A corollary of the right to live with whom one pleases is the right to send one's children to what schools, with what racial make-up, one pleases. This freedom can be implemented in two ways. Ideally, a market-based society would dispense with public schools; people would buy education for their children just as they buy other services. If on the other hand public education were to continue, it would be understood that each locality had complete control over its schools, funding them from its own taxes and determining which if any children from elsewhere would be admitted.

Individuals would decide what comprises a locality, with localities merging and splitting as they wished. Since within any small group there is a good chance of near-consensus on educational policy, if not day-to-day decisions, locally controlled public schools approximate a private system.

Tax-funded vouchers would play no part in either a private or private/public system. The competition between schools they supposedly foster occurs spontaneously in the education market, where school choices are made by parents putting their tuition where their preferences are. No-one gains access to schools he cannot afford courtesy of the taxpayer.

> *"When the number of blacks in a school exceeds a certain minimum, personal violence increases [and] academic performance plummets."*

Once again, the basic argument for freedom of educational association is race-neutral, but the issue takes on a racial cast because of the unfortunate but undeniable link between black enrollment and school quality. When the number of blacks in a school exceeds a certain minimum, personal violence increases, academic performance plummets, and standards themselves are dropped as educators adjust to accommodate lower student abilities.

Race and Education

Performance on objective tests is highest in mostly white states, declining as the proportion of black population increases. Parents sense this: when they speak of moving to the suburbs "where the schools are still good," they mean, and everyone knows they mean, "where the schools are still white." When parents say their concern is not race but "class," or "school quality," do not believe them: their concern is race.

For this reason, most whites would probably send their children to more orderly, more demanding mostly or all-white schools. I would predict that expressions of anxiety about American education would suddenly abate, and the performance of (white) American children on objective tests would improve.

Blacks too could arrange whatever sort of schooling they preferred, excluding or inviting whites. While racially exclusive private schools would be permitted, public school segregation would be undesirable and unnecessary. As neighborhoods tend to be composed of people with similar outlooks, levels of wealth and ethnic preferences, and would be more so in a free housing market, the public schools available to whites would *be* mostly white. The invisible hand plus liberty would again do all the work. Whites who preferred integrated schools would live in integrated neighborhoods, perhaps lending blacks financial assistance to maintain integration, or, in case of too few local blacks, financing the transportation of black children from elsewhere.

As for black children in black neighborhoods, those black parents who wish a certain level of education for their children will work to attain it. If black parents do *not* create schools the average white would consider satisfactory, one can only conclude that the will or the ability is absent. Note well that no *injustice* is done when people who have more money spend it on their children; affluent whites buying better schooling take nothing away from blacks. A predominantly black school with old lab equipment would not suddenly become modernized if every suburban school with brand new equipment suddenly vanished. School quality—like that of housing, goods, and life itself—is relative. Under a market system, black schools in the U.S. are likely to be less attractive than white schools; they are also likely to be *more* attractive than schools in Africa. It is meaningless to call them good or bad absolutely.

Allowing everyone to live and work where and with whom he pleases (in both senses of "please") promises to decrease rather than increase racial antagonism. Liberals seem to imagine that racial separation leads to misunderstanding, suspicion, and hatred. Contrary to liberal fantasies, whites are not only not obsessed with grinding blacks down, whites would not think that much about blacks one way or the other were they not forced to by a network of racial laws that binds them at every turn. Left to themselves, whites and blacks have more immediate things to worry about than racial supremacy.

Society Can Solve
Racial Problems

by Kofi Buenor Hadjor

About the author: *Kofi Buenor Hadjor is a faculty member in the Department of Black Studies at the University of California, Santa Barbara. He is the coordinator and editor of* Encyclopedia Africana *and the author of* Another America: The Politics of Race and Blame, *from which this viewpoint is excerpted.*

There is no single, straightforward, overnight solution to the crisis of race relations in America or to the dire problems facing people in the ghetto. That, of course, has been said many times before, by every politician, pundit, or businessman who is asked to come up with an answer. It is true. But the reasons why it is true are not those which are usually stated.

For one thing, the reason there is no simple solution has nothing to do with a strange, ephemeral phenomenon known as "human nature." Human nature is often cited these days as a reason why a semblance of racial harmony cannot be created in America, or even as an explanation of why so many Blacks suffer in poverty. We are told that it is human nature for Whites to mistrust Blacks, or that it is human nature that makes poor Blacks prefer the world of welfare to that of work—"It is their nature, these people are just like that."

But people are not born with genes which determine that they will be a poor man or woman. When Franz Fanon said in his book *The Wretched of the Earth*, "I am rich because I am White, I am poor because I am Black," he was talking not about natural differences but about the huge disparities in wealth and facilities available to the races in colonial societies. Nor are people born with racial prejudice in their blood and bones. These social evils are the creation of human society, not human nature. They are the products of political and economic organization and action. As such, there seems no rational reason why they cannot be challenged through political and economic action of another kind. Nobody needs think it will be easy, but it is certainly not to be dismissed as "unnatural."

Another reason we are always told that there can be no simple solution for the

Reprinted from Kofi Buenor Hadjor, *Another America: The Politics of Race and Blame*, with permission from the publisher, South End Press, 116 St. Botolph St., Boston, MA 02115.

inner cities is that America does not have the money today to invest in improving the conditions of these communities. This is just so much rot. Of course, the authorities can produce some very impressive figures to show that they have already created a budget deficit of $500 billion a year. But does that paper figure prove that there is no wealth in America, the richest country on earth?

> *"[Racial prejudice is] the product of political and economic organization."*

Does the financial plight of New York City mean that there is no money around in the city of Wall Street? Does the fact that California is close to bankruptcy mean that there are no resources left in Los Angeles, a city bursting at the seams with fabulous fortunes? Or is it rather that so much of the huge wealth of America is being wasted and inefficiently spent, leaving too little for such admittedly small matters as saving the lives of the inner-city communities? As Mike Davis has noted, the $2 trillion America spent on "winning" the Cold War and bailing out the savings and loan industry could already have created a very different reality: "Spent on cities and human resources, these immense sums would have remade urban America into the land of Oz, instead of the wasteland it has become."

The major reason there truly is no simple solution has nothing to do with human nature or with a shortage of wealth. It is because dealing with the racial divide and the crisis facing Black America today involves a fundamental challenge to many practices institutionalized in the American system. And before that can be attempted, preparing the ground for such a challenge will require a mighty political struggle—a battle to turn every one of the most powerful perceptions and beliefs about race and poverty in the United States completely on its head.

Social Investment

It is high time that consideration shifted from rhetorical attempts to explain away Black poverty to practical attempts to abolish it. The deeply embedded structures of discrimination and segregation need to be taken apart, starting at the top and working downwards. The marginalization of the Black inner-city communities on the fringes of American society needs to be countered, so that these people can play a full part in the country's economic life. This will require some fundamental changes in the way that U.S. society organizes the production and distribution of its resources. There is no scope here to launch into a detailed discussion about how to address these broader structural problems of American society. But it is not difficult to suggest a few modest measures, which could be seen as small steps towards a better use of the wealth which already exists in the United States.

The key question is social investment. The poor need more. And nobody should accept the argument that there are no resources to spare for addressing this problem. The United States of America is awash with wealth, the richest nation history has ever produced. Government statistics can show how serious the budget deficit is, but they cannot alter the bottom line: there is no shortage of human, material, or financial resources in America. However, there *is* an unjust and inefficient system of concentrating control over that wealth in the wrong hands, and for the wrong purposes.

American society needs to provide the impoverished inner-city communities with real work, in order to carry out the vital job of reconstruction. Let there be no confusion here; we are not talking about another proposal for workfare. The workfare schemes all begin from the same basic assumption that the big problem with unemployment is its moral-psychological impact upon the individual. Therefore, supporters of workfare say, what is needed is to get the jobless working in some fashion—even if the "job" only means doing pointless tasks in return for their miserable welfare checks. That is an insult.

Providing the Inner City with Work

In reality, the main problem with mass unemployment in the inner cities is the poverty it creates and re-creates. Nor is poverty only a problem for the unemployed; the fact is that many people with jobs, especially women who support families alone, earn wages BELOW the miserly official poverty line. One-half of working Black mothers are in this miserable group. What good will the moral coercion of workfare schemes do for them?

> *"American society needs to provide the impoverished inner-city communities with real work."*

What people need are jobs that pay a proper wage, enough to raise their families in decent circumstances, not hovering around the official subsistence-level poverty line. And there are plenty of proper jobs that need to be done in the cities—not on some penny-pinching training scheme, but as part of a comprehensive, multi-billion dollar program designed to rebuild the urban heart of American society. Initiating such a program, and in the process creating thousands of jobs at a proper wage, is the first step the American government should take.

But where is the money to come from, ask the bean-counting critics? Let us leave aside for now the central question of a fundamental change in the pattern of wealth creation and distribution in the United States. A few minutes of thought could produce plenty of far more modest measures that might be introduced to raise the resources for an emergency reconstruction program.

After all, two planks of government spending policy during the Reagan and Bush years that helped create the huge government deficit in the first place were tax cuts for the wealthy and massive spending on defense. The consequence of prioritizing these policies was to reduce investment in social programs. In real terms, spending on welfare has been slashed over the past 20 years. Billion-dollar cuts in federal support to local government, meanwhile, have also played a major part in creating the crises of city finance, leading to service and construction cut-backs, layoffs, and more misery from Los Angeles to New York. It is high time for a change in these priorities. There are other spending programs ripe for cutting, and gaping tax concessions ready to be filled, that can generate some investment dollars for reconstruction.

Prioritizing Government Spending

Once the argument for a change in priorities is won, even a moderate reformer can find plenty of likely targets. A few possible savings are worth mentioning here, not as a blueprint, but as a small example of what you can come up with once a little imagination is applied. For example, we could (and most certainly should) de-escalate the war on drugs, while diverting some funds now spent on useless interdiction programs to treatment programs; that would save several billion dollars a year. Even squeezing the corporate rich very gently through taxation would raise enormous resources for redevelopment; for example, it has been estimated that simply by cutting the entertainment tax deduction to 50 percent, the government could raise another $16 billion over five years.

There are some slightly more ambitious targets that come easily to mind as well. After the Cold War, for example, there is an unanswerable case for truly slashing the military budget, from Star Wars downwards. And who is really in favor of America spending an estimated $30 or $40 billion a year on secret funds for the CIA and the rest of what is laughably called "the intelligence community," those patriotic runners of guns and drugs and miners of other people's harbors?

These points are not firm proposals to be incorporated into any detailed economic program. The aim of mentioning them is simply to suggest that there is no shortage of resources, and no shortage of ways to release some of them for a proper jobs-and-rebuilding program. What is missing is the political will to confront the real issues and problems. Those in authority prefer instead to retreat behind their fantastic arguments about "welfare overspending" and the supposed responsibility of a "Black underclass" for wrecking the inner cities.

This brings us to the most immediate problem: that of the current political climate. It is this culture, institutionalized by the political elites, which excuses and legitimizes the continuation of inequality and segregation in U.S. society, and which scapegoats the Black poor for the problems created by the system. If there is to be any hope of taking some practical steps to overcome these problems, the first thing

> *"[The current political climate] scapegoats the Black poor for the problems created by the system."*

that needs to be done is to alter the terms of the political and intellectual discourse about race in America. Mounting a challenge to the elitist ideologies that now dominate the public debate is the absolute precondition for changing anything in the inner cities themselves. "Today," as Bob Blauner has argued, "a contest rages over the meaning of racism." Scoring some points in that political contest will be the first step towards defeating the divisive and scapegoating war against the Black poor. . . .

Ask the Embarrassing Questions

To challenge the political climate means trying to set an independent agenda, that focuses on important issues currently being distorted or ignored. There are some questions which sound obvious enough but which seem to be entirely absent from contemporary political and intellectual debate in America. Let us start to ask them, and do it loudly.

For instance, why should crime and personal morality be treated as burning political issues, while poverty and unemployment are treated as permanent facts of life—and all but ignored?

How can it be that some of the poorest and least powerful communities in the inner cities are held responsible not just for the difficulties that blight their own areas but even for the problems facing the rest of American society?

Why is the continued reality of racial discrimination in the United States treated as if it were a thing of the past, while the kind of social Darwinism that we thought had been buried in the past is increasingly accepted as modern social theory?

> *"Black people and their behavior are not the problem facing America."*

What gives the corrupted and discredited elites of American politics and the media the right to sermonize about the morals and behavior of those whom they oppress, and to enforce their will through a police army of occupation?

And if America truly wants to consider itself a democracy, who is to control the destiny of the Black and Latino communities of the inner cities? Is their future to be decided by Washington officials, police chiefs, big-city planners, and newspaper editors? Or are they to gain some sort of control over their own lives, some chance to build a decent future for themselves and their families?

There are many more questions to be posed once the imagination is permitted to range over the largely unexplored terrain of today's pressing issues. There is a need to explore every opportunity, to start to turn some of the twisted conventional wisdoms of today on their heads and put the truth back on its feet.

Talking Openly About Race

It needs to be shouted from the rooftops and argued on every doorstep that Black people and their behavior are not the problem facing America. The problems that need to be addressed are the ways that society functions, rather than the ways that Black, Latino, or any other individuals behave because many of these social problems afflict Black people disproportionately.

It is time to start talking openly about race in American politics. It is important that America starts openly discussing the issue of race and the attitudes of those in authority and of wider society towards it. The new politics of race can only be fought out in the open, away from the shadows of innuendo and insinuation.

It is time that all of the ciphers and codes used in American politics were broken. The double-meaning discussions about the problems of crime or welfare or individual responsibility should be exposed for what they really are: largely moralistic attempts to scapegoat the poor, and especially the Black poor, for the problems of the city. The issue of race, and the reality of what Black people put up with in this country, ought to replace these dishonest debates at the center of public affairs.

> *"The entire discussion about . . . Black and Latino communities being pampered on welfare is a bizarre and bitter twisting of the truth."*

In this spirit, it is vital, too, that critically minded people should now seek to turn on its head the ever-widening discussion about "the problem of the Black underclass." The real problem is not some behavioral "culture of poverty" but poverty and repression itself among Blacks and Latinos in the inner cities.

Social and Economic Action

Tackling the dire economic circumstances of these communities should be of a paramount importance. In the first place, this action will involve challenging the ideas and the arguments that are routinely used in an effort to explain away Black poverty—primarily the various reactionary theories that center on the existence of a criminal "Black underclass" creating its own problems (and creating most of society's problems too). The first step is to start dismantling the ideological walls that the elites have used to trap many Blacks in poverty and to hold them responsible for the societal malaise. The next step is to come forward with some sort of practical proposals about how this problem might be addressed. But unless the political argument against the manipulation of the race issue has been addressed, and the post-liberal consensus challenged, there can be no hope of putting any such proposals into practice.

When it comes to discussing the economics of inner-city areas, there are powerful misconceptions, planted and watered by the elite ideologists, that need to be torn up by the roots and examined. The biggest of these is the notion that America spends far too much money on its inner-city communities—a notion that powerfully misinforms the current debate about welfare.

The undisputable fact, which should be hammered home at each and every opportunity, is that the people who live in the ghettos get far too little of the wealth and resources of American society. The entire discussion about these Black and Latino communities being pampered on welfare is a bizarre and bitter twisting of the truth. Those who use this argument are guilty of a remarkable feat of intellectual contortionism. They are accusing the poorest sections of American society of enjoying unfair privileges. This strange idea needs to be exposed as a cynical device for protecting those in positions of power, who truly enjoy massive privileges in the allegedly classless society of contemporary America.

There is plenty that the American authorities could do if they were serious about addressing the grievances of the Black poor. But at the same time, the problems are far too serious to be simply handed over to untrustworthy politicians, with our best wishes for a speedy recovery. Waiting for the solution to be handed down from government is the surest guarantee that there will *be* no effective solution to the crisis of race relations in the cities of America. There can be no administrative, colonial-style, top-down solution to the problems confronting Black communities in America. The elites who hold the reins of power have been responsible for institutionalizing and intensifying racial division. It would be naive in the extreme to imagine that they can be entrusted with the task of uniting the nation. It will require a lot of pressure from the bottom upwards before any genuine progress is made in challenging the crisis in race relations. There is a pressing need to work out some new strategies for popular political activity and to organize action towards that end.

Challenges for Black Leaders

There is a challenge for those who see themselves as leaders of the Black community: to develop a new way forward that can relate to the bitter experience of those whom they claim to represent. The question now for Black leaders is, how can the energies and sentiments of their angry constituencies be channelled into a consistent challenge to those who cause the problems?

The typical responses from Black leaders today seem to fall into two equally problematic categories. Either they depict Black people as pathetic victims of White racism, unable to do anything and in need of more protection from the authorities; or they go to the other extreme and, as in the case of the spokesmen of Black conservatism, demand that Black people stop being a burden on society, clean up their own communities, and become self-reliant chasers after the American dream. Neither of these approaches will do.

What is required are Black leaders who can cultivate a balanced outlook—one that says, Yes, Black people are oppressed, but no, we don't have to be victims. An outlook that says, Yes, Black people should develop their sense of self-respect—but in order to stand up and fight back against institutionalized discrimination, not in the forlorn hope of winning favor with the elites, which have built a system to keep them in their place.

The Black communities of the inner cities need to find their voice and make a mark on the political map, where at present they are treated as the objects, rather than the subjects, of action—as people to whom things are done, rather than people who can achieve things for themselves. This poses an important challenge to all those who put themselves forward as leaders of the Black community. Today we need Black leaders who can avoid both of the contemporary traps—conservatism, on the one hand, and victim politics on the other—and create a culture of Black people standing up for themselves in order to change the system that keeps them down.

Beyond the Black Community

The future direction of Black leadership is an issue that will need to be examined further. But it is far from the only problem in organizing political action. There is another trap which needs to be avoided—that of exclusively focusing on the politics of the Black community itself. The unavoidable fact is that the solution to racial problems does not lie in the hands of Black people alone. Whatever Black Americans do, they are a minority. The case for change will have to be taken up, and won, in the wider, Whiter American society, if anything substantial is to be achieved.

The habit of exclusively focusing our attention on the Black communities is understandable, given the wider racial climate in America. Yet it can serve to reinforce the isolation of many Black communities from the main body of American society. Of course, the pressure for proper change must come in part from Black people, from Latinos, and from other disadvantaged minorities. They have a key role to play in standing up to discrimination and repression. But however hard they were to fight, Blacks would be unlikely to succeed alone. The Black minority simply does not carry enough weight in American society. The very marginalization against which we are protesting ensures that Black people lack the clout to change things on their own. The Los Angeles riot itself demonstrated the limitations of an outburst of anger from the oppressed minorities. Such a display of lashing-out in fury can shake the system temporarily. But it cannot achieve the sort of permanent, root-and-branch changes required in U.S. society today.

If the pressure from below is to make itself count, it will almost certainly have to involve support from a significant section of the White American population. Ways will have to be found to reach outward, across the racial divide, to challenge those who have politicized the racial divide on their home turf.

Race hatred in America is a social and political construction that has been continually encouraged and exploited by those in power for their own cynical purposes. As such, it can be challenged politically. Of course, there are now many White Americans who will never be won over to the cause of racial equality and justice. They are too steeped in the modern American traditions of racial prejudice and repression.

> *"The solution to racial problems does not lie in the hands of Black people alone."*
> *"Racism . . . has a damaging impact on our whole society."*

So be it. But there are many others whom Black America would write off at its own peril. Here the emphasis must particularly be on the youth, those who have nothing invested in the busted American dream and everything to fight for in the future.

A Cause for Unity

Trying to get young White Americans to take a stand against racial politics will not be easy. But this attempt need not be, as it is often envisaged, an idealistic, utopian appeal to their altruistic instincts. These young people do have real interest in combating racial discrimination and prejudice.

Although Black people inevitably bear the brunt of oppression, racism also has a damaging impact on our whole society. It is divisive, turning us against one another and disaggregating any popular opposition to those elites who control the society in which we live and are responsible for the social problems that we all face. It is demoralizing, since it infuses White communities with reactionary, backward ideas that tie them to the forces of conservatism in American society and help hold back progress on every social issue. And it is degrading, because it ensures that we all have to live in an uncivilized environment, where the forces of law and order can beat a man to a pulp in front of a video camera and still walk the streets as upholders of the American way. Combating the politics of race is a necessity, if we want to live in a world where decency and real democracy prevail.

Bibliography

Books

Jody David Armour	*Negrophobia and Reasonable Racism: The Hidden Costs of Being Black in America.* New York: New York University Press, 1997.
Tony Brown	*Black Lies/White Lies: The Truth According to Tony Brown.* New York: Morrow, 1995.
Lincoln Caplan	*Up Against the Law: Affirmative Action and the Supreme Court.* New York: Twentieth Century Fund Press, 1997.
Jonathan Coleman	*Long Way to Go: Black and White in America.* New York: Atlantic Monthly Press, 1997.
Ellis Cose	*Color-Blind: Seeing Beyond Race in a Race-Obsessed World.* New York: HarperCollins, 1997.
Dinesh D'Souza	*The End of Racism: Principles for a Multiracial Society.* New York: Free Press, 1995.
Christopher F. Edley	*Not All Black and White: Affirmative Action, Race, and American Values.* New York: Hill & Wang, 1996.
Joe R. Feagin and Hernán Vera	*White Racism: The Basics.* New York: Routledge, 1995.
Donna L. Franklin	*Ensuring Inequality: The Structural Transformation of the African-American Family.* New York: Oxford University Press, 1997.
Steven Fraser, ed.	*The Bell Curve Wars: Race, Intelligence, and the Future of America.* New York: BasicBooks, 1995.
Jewelle Taylor Gibbs	*Race and Justice: Rodney King and O.J. Simpson in a House Divided.* San Francisco: Jossey-Bass, 1996.
Andrew Hacker	*Two Nations: Black and White, Separate, Hostile, Unequal.* New York: Scribner's, 1992.
Kofi Buenor Hadjor	*Another America: The Politics of Race and Blame.* Boston: South End Press, 1995.
Paul Harris	*Black Rage Confronts the Law.* New York: New York University Press, 1997.
Richard J. Herrnstein and Charles Murray	*The Bell Curve: Intelligence and Class Structure in American Life.* New York: Free Press, 1994.

Bibliography

bell hooks	*Killing Rage: Ending Racism.* New York: Henry Holt, 1995.
Albert G. Mosley and Nicholas Capaldi	*Affirmative Action: Social Justice or Unfair Preference?* Lanham, MD: Rowman & Littlefield, 1996.
Clarence Page	*Showing My Color: Impolite Essays on Race and Identity.* New York: HarperCollins, 1996.
James L. Robinson	*Racism or Attitude?: The Ongoing Struggle for Black Liberation and Self-Esteem.* New York: Insight Books, 1995.
Richard B. Ropers	*American Prejudice: With Liberty and Justice for Some.* New York: Insight Books, 1995.
Carl Thomas Rowan	*The Coming Race War in America: A Wake-Up Call.* Boston: Little, Brown, 1996.
David K. Shipler	*A Country of Strangers: Blacks and Whites in America.* New York: Knopf, 1997.
United States Federal Glass Ceiling Commission	*A Solid Investment: Making Full Use of the Nation's Human Capital: Recommendations of the Glass Ceiling Commission.* Washington, DC: U.S. Federal Glass Ceiling Commission, 1995.
Cornel West	*Keeping Faith: Philosophy and Race in America.* New York: Routledge, 1993.

Periodicals

John A. Barnes	"Quota Hires in Blue," *Weekly Standard,* April 14, 1997. Available from News America, 1211 Avenue of the Americas, New York, NY 10036.
Reginald G. Blaxton	"Dismantling Affirmative Action: History Drawn Full Circle," *Witness,* April 1995.
Joseph N. Boyce	"The Long Road Up from Segregation," *Wall Street Journal,* April 18, 1995.
Brian Britt	"Neo-Confederate Culture," *Z Magazine,* December 1996.
Adam Cohen	"The Next Great Battle over Affirmative Action," *Time,* November 10, 1997.
Ellis Cose	"One Drop of Bloody History," *Newsweek,* February 13, 1995.
Ron Daniels	"Racism: Past and Present," *Z Magazine,* October 1996.
Marcia Davis	"The Blue Wall," *Emerge,* November 1997. Available from One BET Plaza, 1900 W. Place NE, Washington, DC 20018-1211.
Dinesh D'Souza	"We the Slaveowners: In Jefferson's America, Were Some Men Not Created Equal?" *Policy Review,* Fall 1995.
Troy Duster	"The Hidden History of 'Scientific' Racism," *Crossroads,* February 1995.
Billie Wright Dziech	"Defusing Racial and Gender Conflicts," *USA Today,* September 1996.
Terry Eastland	"Should Washington Halt Race-Based Policies for Hiring and Contracting?" *Insight,* May 6, 1996. Available from 3600 New York Ave. NE, Washington, DC 20002.
Barry Finger	"Racism and Affirmative Action," *New Politics,* Spring 1995.

Racism

Peter Gabel	"Affirmative Action and Racial Harmony," *Tikkun,* May/June 1995.
Edward S. Herman	"America the Meritocracy: Intensifying Racism," *Z Magazine,* July/August 1996.
David Holmstrom	"Why Young African-American Men Fill U.S. Jails," *Christian Science Monitor,* October 5, 1995.
Jesse Jackson	"Dream-Busters," *Liberal Opinion,* November 3, 1997. Available from 108 E. Fifth St., Vinton, IA 52349.
Charisse Jones	"Crack and Punishment: Is Race the Issue?" *New York Times,* October 28, 1995.
Joseph C. Kennedy	"Presumed Guilty: To Racist Police, Innocence Is No Defense," *Washington Monthly,* March 1996.
Jorge Klor de Alva, Earl Shorris, and Cornel West	"Our Next Race Question: The Uneasiness Between Blacks and Latinos," *Harper's,* April 1996.
Nicholas Lemann	"The End of Racism?: An Interview with Dinesh D'Souza" *American Heritage,* February/March 1996.
Elizabeth Martinez	"Reinventing 'America'," *Z Magazine,* December 1996.
Malik Miah	"Does Race Still Matter?" *Against the Current,* May/June 1994.
Salim Muwakkil	"The Big Payback," *In These Times,* June 30, 1997.
Salim Muwakkil	"Letting Go of the Dream: African-Americans Turn Their Backs on Integration," *In These Times,* November 2, 1997.
Ron Nixon	"Crime and Punishment: How the Criminal Justice System Fails Hispanics," *Hispanic,* September 1996. Available from 98 San Jacinto Blvd., Suite 1150, Austin, TX 78701.
Barbara Reynolds	"Playing the Race Card," *Sojourners,* May/June 1995.
Jason L. Riley	"Don't Cry Wolf on Racism," *Wall Street Journal,* January 26, 1996.
David K. Shipler	"My Equal Opportunity, Your Free Lunch," *New York Times,* March 5, 1995.
Thomas Sowell	"The Nuance Excuse," *Weekly Standard,* February 3, 1997.
Shelby Steele	"Shamed by the Same Sad History," *Hoover Digest,* no. 2, 1997. Available from Stanford University, Stanford, CA 94305-6010.
Stephan Thernstrom	"Racial Bias in the Federal Courts?" *Wall Street Journal,* March 22, 1995.
Anthony Walton	"Why Race Is Still a Burning Issue," *U.S. Catholic,* October 1996.
Gordon Witkin and and Jeannye Thornton	"Pride and Prejudice," *U.S. News & World Report,* July 15 and July 22, 1996.
Don Wycliff	"Affirmative on Affirmative Action," *Commonweal,* May 19, 1995.
Troy D. Zeigler	"The Paradox of Equality," *Conservative Review,* January/February 1995. Available from 1307 Dolley Madison Blvd., Room 203, McLean, VA 22101.

Organizations to Contact

The editors have compiled the following list of organizations concerned with the issues debated in this book. The descriptions are derived from materials provided by the organizations. All have publications or information available for interested readers. The list was compiled on the date of publication of the present volume; the information provided here may change. Be aware that many organizations take several weeks or longer to respond to inquiries, so allow as much time as possible.

African Americans for Humanism (AAH)
PO Box 664, Buffalo, NY 14226
(716) 636-7571 • fax: (716) 636-1733
web address: http://www.secularhumanism.org

AAH is dedicated to developing humanism in the secular African-American community and fighting racism through humanistic education. It publishes the quarterly newsletter *AAH Examiner.*

American Civil Liberties Union (ACLU)
125 Broad St., 18th Fl., New York, NY 10004-2400
(212) 549-2500 • publications: (800) 775-ACLU (2258)
e-mail: aclu@aclu.org • web address: http://www.aclu.org

The ACLU is a national organization that works to defend Americans' civil rights guaranteed by the U.S. Constitution. The ACLU publishes and distributes policy statements, pamphlets, and the semiannual newsletter *Civil Liberties Alert.*

Amnesty International (AI)
322 Eighth Ave., New York, NY 10001
(212) 807-8400 • (800) AMNESTY (266-3789) • fax: (212) 627-1451
web address: http://www.amnesty-usa.org

Founded in 1961, AI is a grassroots activist organization that aims to free all nonviolent people who have been imprisoned because of their beliefs, ethnic origin, sex, color, or language. The *Amnesty International Report* is published annually, and other reports are available on-line and by mail.

Anti-Defamation League (ADL)
823 United Nations Plaza, New York, NY 10017
(212) 490-2525
web address: http://www.adl.org

ADL works to stop the defamation of Jews and to ensure fair treatment for all U.S. citizens. It publishes the periodic *ADL Law Report* and *Law Enforcement Bulletin* as well as other reports.

Cato Institute
1000 Massachusetts Ave. NW, Washington, DC 20001-5403
(202) 842-0200 • fax: (202) 842-3490
web address: http://www.cato.org

The Cato Institute is a libertarian public policy research foundation dedicated to limiting the role of government and protecting individual liberties. It researches claims of discrimination and opposes affirmative action. The institute publishes the quarterly magazine *Regulation,* the bimonthly *Cato Policy Report,* and numerous books.

Center for the Study of Popular Culture (CSPC)
9911 W. Pico Blvd., Suite 1290, Los Angeles, CA 90035
(310) 843-3699 • fax: (310) 843-3692
web address: http://www.cspc.org

CSPC is a conservative educational organization that addresses topics such as political correctness, cultural diversity, and discrimination. Its civil rights project promotes equal opportunity for all individuals and provides legal assistance to citizens challenging affirmative action. The center publishes four magazines: *Heterodoxy, Defender, Report Card,* and *COMINT.*

Citizens' Commission on Civil Rights (CCCR)
2000 M St. NW, Suite 400, Washington, DC 20036
(202) 659-5565 • fax: (202) 223-5302
e-mail: citizens@cccr.org • web address: http://www.cccr.org

CCCR monitors the federal government's enforcement of antidiscrimination laws and promotes equal opportunity for all. It publishes reports on affirmative action and desegregation as well as the book *One Nation Indivisible: The Civil Rights Challenge for the 1990s.*

Commission for Racial Justice (CRJ)
700 Prospect Ave., Cleveland, OH 44115-1110
(216) 736-2100 • fax: (216) 736-2171

CRJ was formed in 1963 by the United Church of Christ in response to racial tensions gripping the nation at that time. Its goal is a peaceful, dignified society where all men and women are equal. CRJ develops many programs for racial and ethnic United Church of Christ churches that help them meet the needs of their individual communities. CRJ also publishes various documents and books, such as *Racism and the Pursuit of Racial Justice* and *A National Symposium on Race and Housing in the United States: Challenges for the 21st Century.*

The Heritage Foundation
214 Massachusetts Ave. NE, Washington, DC 20002-4999
(202) 546-4400 • fax: (202) 546-0904

The foundation is a conservative public policy research institute dedicated to free-market principles, individual liberty, and limited government. It opposes affirmative action and believes that the private sector, not government, should be allowed to ease social problems and to improve the status of women and minorities. The foundation publishes the quarterly journal *Policy Review* and the bimonthly newsletter *Heritage Today* as well as numerous books and papers.

Hispanic Policy Development Project (HPDP)
1001 Connecticut Ave. NW, Suite 901, Washington, DC 20036
(202) 822-8414 • fax: (202) 822-9120

HPDP is a nonprofit organization that encourages analysis of public policies affecting Hispanic youth in the United States, especially in education, employment, and family issues. It publishes a number of books and pamphlets, including *Together Is Better: Building Strong Partnerships Between Schools and Hispanic Parents.*

National Association for the Advancement of Colored People (NAACP)
4805 Mt. Hope Dr., Baltimore, MD 21215-3297
(410) 358-8900 • fax: (410) 486-9257

The NAACP is the oldest and largest civil rights organization in the United States. Its principal objective is to ensure the political, educational, social, and economic equality of minorities. It publishes the magazine *Crisis* ten times a year as well as a variety of newsletters, books, and pamphlets.

National Urban League
120 Wall St., 8th Fl., New York, NY 10005
(212) 558-5300 • fax: (212) 344-5332
web address: http://www.nul.org

A community service agency, the National Urban League aims to eliminate institutional racism in the United States. It also provides services for minorities who experience discrimination in employment, housing, welfare, and other areas. It publishes the report *The Price: A Study of the Costs of Racism in America* and the annual *State of Black America.*

Poverty and Race Research Action Council (PRRAC)
1711 Connecticut Ave. NW, Suite 207, Washington, DC 20009
(202) 387-9887 • fax: (202) 387-0764
e-mail: prrac@aol.com

PRRAC is a national organization that promotes research and advocacy on behalf of poor minorities. It publishes the bimonthly newsletter *Poverty & Race.*

The Prejudice Institute
Stephens Hall Annex, TSU, Towson, MD 21204-7097
(410) 830-2435 • fax: (410) 830-2455

The Prejudice Institute is a national research center concerned with violence and intimidation motivated by prejudice. It conducts research, supplies information on model programs and legislation, and provides education and training to combat prejudicial violence. The Prejudice Institute publishes research reports, bibliographies, and the quarterly newsletter *Forum.*

United States Commission on Civil Rights
624 Ninth St. NW, Suite 500, Washington, DC 20425
(202) 376-7533 • publications: (202) 376-8128

A fact-finding body, the commission reports directly to Congress and the president on the effectiveness of equal opportunity laws and programs. A catalog of its numerous publications can be obtained from its Publication Management Division.

Index